DATE DUE

FEB 2 3 2014			

HIGHSMITH 45-220

FUNDING SCIENCE IN AMERICA

Since the 1950s, the federal government has relied on the peer review system for funding high-quality academic science. Yet, despite the success of American science, peer review is under attack for being a biased "good old boy" network that helps rich research universities get richer. As a remedy for these biases, university presidents and members of Congress have turned to the earmarking of science projects and facilities in the federal budget. Critics of earmarking call it little more than the pork barreling of research money, whereby political influence, not scientific merit, determines funding. *Funding Science in America* explores both the pros and cons of the academic earmarking issue. In his portrayal of both sides, Savage analyzes the earmarking decision of both university presidents and members of Congress, identifies those universities that have benefited most from earmarking, and examines the question of whether earmarking improves the ability of these universities to compete for research grants.

James D. Savage is associate professor in the Department of Government and Foreign Affairs at the University of Virginia. Dr. Savage is also the author of *Balanced Budgets and American Politics,* which received a *Choice Magazine* Outstanding Book Award, as well as the Harold D. Lasswell Prize from the American Political Science Association. He received his M.A.s in Economics and Public Policy and his Ph.D. in Political Science from the University of California, at Berkeley. Dr. Savage also received postdoctoral fellowships from Harvard University and the Council on Foreign Relations and a research grant for this book from the Dirksen Congressional Center.

FUNDING SCIENCE IN AMERICA

Congress, Universities, and the Politics
of the Academic Pork Barrel

JAMES D. SAVAGE

CAMBRIDGE
UNIVERSITY PRESS

PUBLISHED BY THE PRESS SYNDICATE OF THE UNIVERSITY OF CAMBRIDGE
The Pitt Building, Trumpington Street, Cambridge, United Kingdom

CAMBRIDGE UNIVERSITY PRESS
The Edinburgh Building, Cambridge CB2 2RU, UK http://www.cup.cam.ac.uk
40 West 20th Street, New York, NY 10011-4211, USA http://www.cup.org
10 Stamford Road, Oakleigh, Melbourne 3166, Australia

First published 1999

Printed in the United States of America

Typeface Sabon 10/12 pt.   *System* QuarkXPress 3.22[CS]

A catalog record for this book is available from the British Library.

Library of Congress Cataloging-in-Publication Data

Savage, James D., 1951–
Funding science in America: congress, universities, and the
politics of the academic porkbarrel / James D. Savage.
p. cm.
Includes bibliographical references and index.
ISBN 0-521-64315-5
1. Research – Government policy – United States. 2. Federal aid to
research – United States. 3. Peer review – Government policy – United
States. 4. Research – United States – Finance. 5. Universities and
colleges – Research – United States – Finance. I. Title.
Q180.U5S28 1999
338.97306 – dc21   98-11654
                                                                  CIP

ISBN 0 521 64315 5 hardback

For Lenore

Contents

Tables and Illustrations

Tables

Illustrations

Preface

The issue of academic earmarking, also known as "academic pork barreling," is personally a familiar one. During the 1980s, I served on the federal governmental relations staff of the President of the University of California system. Our president, David P. Gardner, was a leading opponent of earmarking, and it soon became one of my tasks to help represent the university's interests in the federal budget, to monitor the level of earmarking in the federal government's appropriations legislation, and in many cases to draft the president's correspondence and speeches on the topic. As a result, in 1989 the Office of the President released the first study of the distribution of academic earmarks, showing that a handful of states and institutions received the vast majority of earmarked projects. A number of university presidents and even the Association of American Universities, the organization leading the fight against earmarking, were none too pleased to see their institutions identified. To the University of California's credit, the Office of the President resisted efforts by several presidents who were engaged in earmarking and who attempted to persuade the university to halt the release of further analyses.

After I joined the University of Virginia, the Congressional Research Service (CRS) hired me in 1992 as a consultant to develop the same kind of report for the Science, Space, and Technology Committee of the U.S. House of Representatives. The committee's chair, George Brown (D-CA), used the resulting studies as the data base for his hearings on earmarking, which were held in 1993 and 1994. Like my University of California study, the CRS report indicated that a handful of schools, states, and congressional districts were the primary beneficiaries of earmarking. Rather than serving as a remedy for the biases of the peer review system, earmarking simply produced its own politically created biases. Members of Congress, specifically those serving on the appropriations committees, and universities that engaged in earmarking were displeased to see themselves identified, and they pressured CRS to withdraw the report. In its place, the same data were released in a subsequent CRS report showing total levels of earmarks, but without the analysis, particularly the identification, amount of earmarks, and ranking of recipient schools. The new report substituted for the term "earmark" the more neutral term "direct appropriations." Ironically, CRS's action made the original report something of a collector's item among the staffs of the members who opposed earmarking.

As a result of my work on earmarking, I was also employed as a consultant by the Office of Technology Assessment to analyze the various definitions of earmarking for its study, *Federally Funded Research: Decisions for a Decade.* In addition, I was employed by the General Accounting Office to review its 1994 evalution of the peer review process.

Chapter Summaries

Chapter 1 sets out the theoretical influences of this book, that the peer review process should be viewed as a "dominant policy regime," as suggested by Thomas Kuhn's notion of the dominant paradigm; that the problem of controlling earmarking is best understood as a collective action problem in controlling free riders; and that most fruitful way of analyzing the behavior of individual, high status decision makers is by drawing upon Donald Searing's theory of the motivational approach for evaluating leadership.

Chapters 2, 3, and 4 examine the politics of academic earmarking from the perspective of the leaders of higher education, particularly presidents of the nation's research universities.

Why do universities engage in earmarking? What are their incentives and justifications for doing so? Chapter 2 also reviews the creation of the peer review system after World War II and the results of numerous federal studies that have analyzed the equity of the process.

Chapter 3 traces the response of the academic science community to earmarking, an issue raised as a grave threat to the quality of American research. The various attempts made by the major higher education associations to control earmarking are evaluated. Chapter 4 reviews the efforts by opponents of earmarking to obtain federal facilities funds, which would be used largely as side payments, or what collective action theory calls "selective incentives," to earmarking universities to induce them to refrain from the practice.

Chapter 5 explores the role of the "go-betweens," the true entrepreneurs in the earmarking process – the lobbyists who solicit university clients while working the congressional appropriations process to secure earmarks for their clients. Lobbyists, according to political scientists, rather than simply acting as the representative of interests, are active in their own behalf as they encourage clients to pursue government benefits.

Chapter 6 examines the institutional incentives within Congress that encourage members to earmark and focuses on the appropriations process that funds these earmarks. This chapter also analyzes data showing that the distribution of academic earmarks is strongly related to committee power and member influence. Thus, academic earmarking, rather than providing a remedy to the perceived inequities of peer review, actually creates its own inequitable allocation system. These data also suggest that universities that receive large earmarks do not necessarily improve their ability to compete for competitive peer-reviewed awards.

Chapter 7 reviews the efforts of members of Congress who have opposed earmarking. Although members may be stereotyped as universally desiring pork barrel projects for their districts and states, and as avoiding contesting their colleagues' earmarks, neither of these assumptions is accurate in the case of academic earmarking. Members have employed a variety of procedural rules, hearings, and amendments to defeat earmarked academic projects. Chapter 8 concludes with some observations on the future of academic earmarking.

I am indebted to a number of people who assisted me during the years it took to complete this work. John Gilmour and Joe White read extensive sections of the manuscript and offered invaluable comments. Gerard Alexander, Martha Derthick, Paul Freedman, Anita Jones, Robert O'Neill, David Soherr-Hadwiger, and David Waldner all provided thoughtful advice on various chapters. Dennis Barnes, Susan Offutt, and Robert Park generously shared their thoughts and personal files on earmarking. Colleen Cordes not only offered her insights on earmarking, she singlehandedly held earmarking universities up to public scrutiny through her wonderful lists in the *Chronicle of Higher Education*. Alex Holzman is as supportive an editor as an author could hope to have. I wish also to thank Eugene B. Skolnikoff, who while serving as an anonymous reviewer for Cambridge offered many valuable suggestions for improving the final manuscript.

In addition, the University of Virginia and its Department of Government and Foreign Affairs provided me with timely and much appreciated support, including its Bankard Fund grants. I am particularly grateful in this regard to Ruhi Ramazani, former chair of the department, and to Gene Block, Vice Provost for Research. The Dirksen Congressional Center also supported this project through a grant to study the appropriations process.

Finally, this book is lovingly dedicated to my wife, Lenore, whose gracious, generous, and effervescent spirit made its writing so much easier.

1

The Politics of
Academic Earmarking

In 1983, Michael Sovern, president of Columbia University, and William Byron, president of the Catholic University of America, independently reached the same conclusion: to finance the construction of new research facilities on their campuses, they would use their institutions' political influence in Congress to obtain federal appropriations. At first glance, there appeared nothing unusual about university presidents seeking to expand their institutions' research capabilities or about the federal government's financing such facilities. Extensive federal facilities funding had, after all, taken place during the late 1960s. What mattered was that Sovern and Byron secured the $5 million for Columbia and the $5 million for Catholic by obtaining earmarks in federal legislation. By doing so, they created one of the most divisive issues to confront the higher education research community in the 1980s and 1990s: whether colleges and universities should seek earmarked – or pork barreled – federal funds for academic research and facilities projects.[1]

In response to Columbia and Catholic, many of the most powerful higher education lobbies and prestigious scientific societies passed resolutions denouncing academic earmarking. University presidents cajoled each other in public and private forums to refrain from this practice. Major scientific magazines, such as *Science*, *Physics Today*, and *Chemical and Engineering News*, began regular coverage of earmarking and published editorials attacking the practice. The *Chronicle of Higher Education* initiated its annual listing of earmarking schools. Watchdog groups such as Citizens Against Government Waste targeted academic earmarks in their newsletters and television programs. Stories critical of the academic pork barrel appeared on the front pages of the *Washington*

---

1. Kim McDonald, "Insulate Science from Politics, Presidents Urge," *Chronicle of Higher Education*, November 2, 1983, p. 1.

1

Post and the *New York Times*, as well as in such national news and public interest magazines as the *Wall Street Journal, U.S. News & World Report,* and *Common Cause.* Earmarking even gained coverage on network television news; NBC, in its series "The Fleecing of America," declared that earmarked academic projects wasted federal dollars.[2]

The debate over earmarking quickly spread to the source of funding for these projects, the federal government. Members of Congress decried their colleagues' earmarks on the floors of the House and Senate and attempted to defeat them in the appropriations committees. Other members countered that it was their constitutional right to aid their constituents through earmarking. During congressional hearings on the topic, university presidents and their lobbyists debated each other over the propriety of earmarking. In their State of the Union addresses, Presidents Ronald Reagan, George Bush, and Bill Clinton pronounced academic earmarking to be a cause of the federal deficit, pointing to examples of earmarked academic projects as justification for the line-item veto.

Despite more than fifteen years of controversy, however, the issue of academic earmarking has yet to be resolved and the practice continues. As shown in Table 1, between the federal fiscal years (FY) 1980 and 1996, no less than $5.1 billion, more likely $6 billion, was earmarked for universities in this fashion. In March 1997, the Office of Management and Budget identified dozens of academic earmarks for FY 1998 worth millions of dollars that President Bill Clinton might subject to his new line-item veto authority. During the same month, the *Chronicle of Higher Education* announced that the value of academic earmarks for FY 1997 reached $440 million, a 49 percent increase over FY 1996. Thus, the dollar value of identified academic earmarking has totaled at least $5.5 billion since FY 1980.[3]

---

2. For example, Florence Graves, "Hog Heaven," *Common Cause Magazine*, July–August 1986, pp. 17–23; Mary Jordan, "For Little College, a Big Helping Hand," *Washington Post*, June 24, 1992; Leslie Maitland Werner, "40 Unversities Agree to Reject Disputed Grants," *New York Times*, May 22, 1987; "Wastewatch Journal, Citizens against Government Waste," appeared on cable television in the fall of 1992; Thomas Toch and Ted Slafsky, "The Scientific Pork Barrel," *U.S. News & World Report*, March 1, 1993, pp. 58–9.

3. See letter from Franklin D. Raines, director, Office of Management and Budget, to Bob Livingston, chair, House Committee on Appropriations, March 10, 1997. Raines notes the absence of peer review in the selection of some of these earmarks. See also Stephen Barr, "OMB Releases Budget 'Hit List,'" *Washington Post*, March 14, 1997; Colleen Cordes, "Congressional Earmarks for Colleges Increased by 49% for Fiscal 1997," *Chronicle of Higher Education*, March 28, 1997, p. A36.

Table 1. *Apparent FY 1980–96 academic earmarks, by fiscal year*

Year	$ Amount	Number
1980	$16,537,000	21
1981	5,127,000	17
1982	17,477,999	46
1983	86,248,000	58
1984	129,958,000	53
1985	173,132,000	81
1986	182,418,000	96
1987	251,810,000	119
1988	330,538,000	152
1989	335,906,200	216
1990	245,060,333	253
1991	472,463,500	277
1992	708,439,000	496
1993	727,903,600	498
1994	586,333,000	438
1995	529,239,000	471
1996	327,808,000	417
Total	$5,126,398,632	3,709

The purpose of this book is to analyze the dynamics of academic earmarking and, in particular, to explain its rise and perpetuation by exploring the institutional and personal incentives that have encouraged university presidents and members of Congress to engage in or to oppose this activity. An examination of these competing incentive structures reveals why there has yet to be a solution to earmarking as a science policy problem. Efforts to curb earmarking by establishing federally funded facilities programs, passing voluntary moratoria against earmarking by universities, and creating procedural rules against earmarking in Congress are examples of such failed solutions. This study also analyzes the distribution of earmarked funds to determine if earmarking serves as a remedy for the perceived biases of the merit review process or simply acts as its own form of favoritism. The book also explores whether earmarks actually help universities improve the quality of their research, as measured by their ability to compete for research grants.

The issue of academic earmarking, therefore, is intimately connected to such topics as the legitimacy of the peer review process, the conduct of university presidents and their associations, the extent and obligation

of the federal government's funding for university research and infrastructure, the rise of university lobbyists in Washington, and the behavior of members of Congress who either engage in or oppose earmarking.
Moreover, the seemingly arcane subject of academic earmarking has
passed beyond the realm of internecine academic argument to become
grist for presidential State of the Union Addresses, justification for the
line-item veto, examples for media exposés decrying wasted government
spending, the activation of a Gramm–Rudman–Hollings sequester, and
accusations that academic pork is passed about to secure congressional
votes to pass such legislation as the 1994 Crime Bill and the North
American Free Trade Agreement.

In addition, for heuristic purposes, this study views the academic earmarking issue at three levels of analysis. At the macro level, the peer review process is regarded as a "dominant policy regime," a notion bor-
rowed from Thomas Kuhn's idea of scientific paradigms. The peer
review system is a long-standing, dominant policy arrangement that re-
sembles many of the conditions that Kuhn set for a dominant scientific
paradigm, including those situations in which a paradigm is challenged,
even by "small revolutions." At the level of academic and governmental
institutions, the dynamics of this challenge to peer review in the form of
earmarking and the efforts to constrain earmarking may be analyzed as
a variation of a collective action problem, with its concerns for free riders, side payments, rewards, and sanctions. To better understand the actions of the key decision makers in the debate over earmarking, the
study also turns to what is called the "motivational approach" to examine how their institutional roles and personal motivations influence the
positions they take on academic earmarking.

Academic Earmarking as a Science Policy Issue

What makes academic earmarking a significant science policy issue and
worthy of analysis is that it directly challenges the procedures employed
by the federal government to allocate the bulk of its funding for academic science. The term "science" refers to the creation and refinement
of new knowledge and specifically to basic, applied, and developmental
research. Science is often compared to "technology," which is commonly associated with the commercialization of research for the private
sector. Colleges and universities conduct almost half of all the nation's
basic research, "science for its own sake," which is associated with the
creation of fundamental knowledge, and nearly 20 percent of its applied

research, which begins to direct this fundamental knowledge toward more problem-oriented, purposeful ends. Sixty percent of academic research is funded by the federal government, with most of this amount consisting of contracts and grants in support of basic research.[4] Since the 1950s, the government has relied primarily upon the peer or merit review process for rationing these research dollars. In this process, the various research agencies select panels of "peer" experts to evaluate applications and award grants on the basis of scientific and other identified criteria. The purpose of the peer or merit review process is to support the best science in a way that maximizes and makes accountable the use of public resources through a process of competition and evaluation that insulates the allocation of research dollars from politics and political favoritism.

The justification for employing peer review has many sources.

The use of peer review may be traced as far back as 1665, when the Royal Society in England began employing peer review to evaluate journal articles submitted to the society's publication, *Philosophical Transactions*. In the United States, President Thomas Jefferson in 1804 requested that the American Philosophical Society evaluate the findings of the Lewis and Clark expedition before the results of the exploration were published. Later, in the 1840s, the Smithsonian Institution formed a commission of specialists to recommend which applicants should receive grants of federal research money. Vannevar Bush's *The Endless Frontier*, which broadly outlined the nation's science policy after the Second World War, advocated funding academic research through contracts and grants that require individual evaluation, as opposed to distributing research money through formula grants and institutional awards. The postwar legislation that created a variety of federal research and facilities programs called for peer review in these project funding decisions. Peer review, moreover, came to be regarded as a central factor in the American research university's almost astonishing ability to produce on a regular basis first-class, cutting-edge basic science. In this regard, peer review is often viewed as superior to the science-funding mechanisms employed by other nations. Thus, the peer or merit re-

---

4. For useful definitions of science and for data, see *Science and Engineering Indicators, 1996* (Washington, D.C.: National Science Foundation, 1996), pp. 5–8 and 5–9. For valuable examples of technology projects and a definition of technology, see Linda R. Cohen and Roger G. Noll, *The Technology Pork Barrel* (Washington, D.C.: Brookings Institution, 1991).

view process is rooted in history, doctrine, and law, as well as in its practical effectiveness in promoting academic science.[5]

This funding system is said to be compromised when universities bypass peer review by relying instead upon political influence and direct appropriations. These earmarked projects are rarely if ever screened for the quality of their science; their purpose may have little or nothing to do with the scientific programs and goals of the federal agency whose budget is being earmarked; and they are often funded from agency budgets that might otherwise support peer-reviewed research, thus limiting the availability of competitive support for all universities.

What Is an Academic Earmark?

An "earmark" is a legislative provision that designates special consideration, treatment, funding, or rules for federal agencies or beneficiaries. Members of Congress often employ earmarks to direct federal agencies to provide specified benefits for their constituents or friends, hence the sometimes negative interpretation of the term and its association with pork barrel politics. Success in obtaining an earmark for these purposes usually is a function of political influence and intervention. An academic earmark in particular is a provision inserted primarily in federal appropriations legislation that provides funding for specific university research projects or facilities. Buried in an appropriations subcommittee report, a typical earmark is stated in this fashion: "The Committee has included $1,000,000 for the Bioscience Center at the University of . . ." or "Included in these funds is $5,000,000 for conductor research at the University of . . . ." Sometimes these earmarks are more surreptitious and leave out the name of the university altogether. An example of ear-

---

5. Robert K. Merton with Harriet Zukerman, "Institutionalized Patterns of Evaluation in Science," in Robert K. Merton, *The Sociology of Science* (Chicago: University of Chicago Press, 1973), p. 463. On Jefferson, see Joseph P. Martino, *Science Funding: Politics and Porkbarrel* (New Brunswick: Transaction Publishers, 1992), p. 45. On the Smithsonian, see A. Hunter Dupree, *Science in the Federal Government* (Baltimore: Johns Hopkins University Press, 1986), p. 82. Vannevar Bush, *Science: The Endless Frontier* (Washington, D.C.: U.S. Government Printing Office, 1945), esp. Ch. 6. Also see Leonard L. Lederman, "Science and Technology Policies and Priorities: A Comparative Analysis," *Science*, September 4, 1987, pp. 1125–33. Georges Ferne, *Science and Technology in Scandinavia* (Essex, UK: Longman, 1989). In Finland, for example, state research funds are allocated to universities according to the number of students in an academic field. By comparison, see *Major Award Decisionmaking at the National Science Foundation* (Washington, D.C.: National Academy Press, 1994). Also see Bruce L. R. Smith, *American Science Since World War II* (Washington, D.C.: Brookings Institution, 1990), esp. Ch. 3.

marking is provided in Figure 1, a page from an FY 1992 appropriations subcommittee report. It earmarks $20 million for the University of Maryland's Christopher Columbus Center, $10 million for West Virginia University, $10 million for Utah State University, and $20 million for the University of Alaska's Poker Flat Range.

Defenders of earmarked funds such as these claim that peer review may seem like a good idea but that it is a flawed and biased system that leaves aggrieved institutions no other remedy than earmarking. Peer review panels are said to be inherently biased. They are composed of faculty and researchers from a handful of elite institutions, and they reward their colleagues with the booty of federal research funds. Peer review, it is claimed, is an old boys' network that helps the rich get richer. It rewards the same old schools, the same old scientists, and the same old science, and thereby denies funding for new and innovative research efforts for scientists other than the privileged few. To offset this inequity, earmarking provides necessary support for emerging institutions to become strong enough on their own to compete for peer-reviewed funds.

In addition to the issue of equity, earmarking is said to be a symptom of the federal government's breaching its understanding with academia to fund the full costs of research by supporting the upgrading and construction of the facilities necessary to conduct this research. Earmarking not only remedies the imbalance of funding produced through peer review, it also signals Congress and the executive branch that the lack of facilities funding is a significant problem that requires a federal solution.

Furthermore, members of Congress who defend academic earmarking assert that it is their prerogative and their responsibility to help their constituents. The Constitution empowers Congress to appropriate federal funds, even if these appropriations include academic earmarks. It is Congress that permits federal agencies to distribute peer-reviewed funds, and it is a congressional prerogative to earmark funds in agency budgets. Members of Congress, moreover, are elected to represent the interests of their district or state; it is their responsibility to assist their constituents when this is both reasonable and practical; and that assistance may include obtaining earmarks for constituent academic institutions. Many members contend that such projects strengthen their region's economy, just as research universities played a key role in the development of Silicon Valley in California, Route 128 in Massachusetts, North Carolina's Research Triangle, and the Silicon Gulch of Texas. Why, these members ask, should only those states and regions containing elite research universities funded through a biased peer re-

$13,500,000, and bill language, to construct, equip, and integrate facilities related to the National Technology Transfer Center.

$20,000,000 for construction of the Christopher Columbus Center of Marine Research and Exploration.*

$31,800,000 to continue long-term rehabilitation at NASA's field centers.

$10,000,000 for NASA to establish an independent verification and validation center in conjunction with West Virginia University. With the advent of major space initiatives, it is important for NASA to have a truly independent verification and validation capability for its computer software programs. The consolidation of proposed activities for these programs at a single site should result in programmatic efficiencies and significantly augment NASA's overall capability. A centralized NASA capability will facilitate independent review and test functions of multiprogram software verification and validation and will provide NASA programs with the assurance that program flight and ground software will function as required.*

$10,000,000 for construction and equipping a new space dynamics lab at Utah State University.*

The Committee is aware of the recent earthquake in Pasadena, CA, and will give expeditious consideration to any reprogramming for funds to deal with the rehabilitation of facilities at the Jet Propulsion Laboratory.

The Committee recommends that $20,000,000 be available to implement the improvement and modernization program at the Poker Flat Research Range located in Fairbanks, AK. The fiscal years 1990 and 1991 Department of Defense appropriations bills included funding to commence the upgrade of the Poker Flat rocket launch facility. In recent years, however, NASA has operated the Poker Flat facility to support U.S. Government and private research and sounding rocket launches.*

The Committee understands, based on the 2 years of program development and definition, that NASA, rather than the Air Force, is better situated to manage and execute this modernization effort. Currently, NASA funds the operation and maintenance of range facilities. For the past 2 years, NASA and the Air Force have been working with the Poker Flat Research Range to develop a comprehensive improvement and modernization program. The Committee expects NASA to utilize this relationship to conduct and execute the range improvement program. The Committee has reviewed the implementation plan submitted to the Air Force, and expects NASA to execute the upgrade program consistent with that plan. NASA shall evaluate the implementation plan submitted for the Poker Flat Research Range upgrade and report to the Committee its assessment of the plan along with a construction program outline not later than December 15, 1991.

RESEARCH AND PROGRAM MANAGEMENT

Appropriations, 1991 ....$2,211,900,000
Budget estimate, 1992...2,452,300,000
House allowance...2,211,900,000
Committee recommendation 2,342,300,000

*Denotes academic earmark. Note: Asterisks added to text.

Figure 1. Academic earmarks in the FY 1992 Senate report for the Veterans Affairs, Housing and Urban Development, and Independent Agencies Appropriations Bill (Report 102–7), p.146.

view system experience this sort of economic development? Finally, members recognize that if they are able to claim credit for building a new research lab at the local university and thereby aid the economy, they may be able to enhance their reelection opportunities.

Thus, academic earmarking, in its starkest terms, may be viewed either as the undermining of a system that rewards merit and quality in the funding of science or as a remedy for the inequities of a biased process that enables the rich to get richer.

Peer Review as a Dominant Policy Regime

In *The Structure of Scientific Revolutions*, Thomas Kuhn posits that a dominant paradigm, such as Copernican astronomy or Newtonian physics, provides the basic model for understanding the "rules and standards for scientific practice," from which scientists try to advance knowledge. Working within the confines of a paradigm, scientists engage in normal science, investigating, testing, and searching for facts while "articulating" the laws and theories provided by the paradigm. A crisis in the life of a paradigm occurs when the paradigm fails to account for findings generated by researchers testing its boundaries. The resulting "insecurity" among researchers is likely to produce a new paradigm, a scientific revolution, as the "failure of existing rules is the prelude to a search for new ones."[6]

In a somewhat similar fashion, the federal government's peer review system may be, for the moment, viewed as a "dominant policy regime." A dominant policy regime exists when, in a given area of public policy, the rules of the game, the cause-and-effect relations, and the rewards and sanctions are reasonably clear to all interested parties, and when the support of the winners and the level of acquiescence or simple weakness of the losers are politically sufficient to perpetuate the regime. Peer review is widely employed by the major federal research agencies; its guidelines and procedures are routinized and promulgated; the rewards of successful grant applications are professionally significant; and peer review has received sufficient political support to sustain its use for nearly fifty years.

An example of a dominant policy regime is the federal budgetary process of the 1950s and 1960s, described by Aaron Wildavsky and

6. Thomas S. Kuhn, *The Structure of Scientific Revolutions* (Chicago: University of Chicago Press, 1970), pp. 24, 68.

Richard Fenno.[7] The process was characterized by a generally agreed-upon norm of balancing the budget; all participants in the process, from member of Congress to agency heads, knew their respective roles; and spending grew in controlled, incremental levels above the previous year's budget base. The similarity between this period of budgeting and the dominant regime of peer review is that both placated most interested parties by way of sufficient, if not growing, resources to distribute adequate rewards that protected the policy regime from dissatisfied groups and individuals. Wildavsky called this conflict-minimizing aspect of the budgetary process distributing "fair shares." For the peer review process, that has meant awarding enough research funds to meritorious university science projects to maintain support for the system.

Maintenance of support for a policy regime depends upon more than distributing material rewards. It also requires a sense that the policy is achieving its goals. In the case of the budgetary process, Wildavsky noted that its purpose in part was to achieve a balanced federal budget. While that goal was realized, the institutional arrangement of the period remained intact. When the government began running concurrent deficits in the 1970s, members of Congress became, in Kuhn's word, "insecure," and the process was significantly altered in 1974. A paradigm shift, or at least a "small revolution," effectively occurred in the federal budgetary process.[8] Similarly, constraints in federal research funding, and in the financial conditions of many universities, have played a role in encouraging academic earmarking, a small revolution directed at peer review. "Many of the shortcomings of peer review," Daryl Chubin and Edward Hackett note in their study of the process, "result from intense competition for research resources. Several factors have made the competition more intense[, including] earmarking of funds for specific projects, which leaves a smaller pool from which to support proposals in open competition."[9]

Kuhn identified another critical aspect necessary for the preservation of a paradigm: it attracts "an enduring group of adherents" who would pass on an understanding of the paradigm to future generations of scientists. This is the purpose of a scientific education: that it provides a "professional initiation" into the rules of the paradigm, which become almost rote in nature to the young researcher in training:

7. Aaron Wildavsky, *The Politics of the Budgetary Process* (Boston: Little, Brown, 1964); Richard F. Fenno, Jr., *The Power of the Purse: Appropriations Politics in Congress* (Boston: Little, Brown, 1966).
8. Kuhn, p. 68.
9. Daryl E. Chubin and Edward J. Hackett, *Peerless Science: Peer Review and U.S. Science Policy* (Albany: State University of New York Press, 1990), p. 73.

One is at liberty to suppose that somewhere along the way the scientist has intuitively abstracted rules of the game for himself, but there is little reason to believe it. Though many scientists talk easily and well about the particular individual hypotheses that underlie a concrete piece of current research, they are little better than laymen at characterizing the established bases of their field, its legitimate problems and methods. If they have learned such abstractions at all, they show it mainly through their ability to do such research.

Allegiance to the paradigm, and to the rules it offers in guiding the researcher in choosing problems to investigate, binds that researcher to a "scientific group." In this way, the paradigm creates a cultural unit with its own norms and rules of behavior, so that those who fail to behave appropriately "are simply read out of the profession, which thereafter ignores their work," or they are forced to work in isolation or to form new groups and thus, by implication, new paradigms.[10]

The peer review process exhibits many of the cultural and normative characteristics of Kuhn's scientific group. For academicians, the peer review process is more than an external mechanism for allocating federal funds; it is deeply embedded in the norms of higher education. Peer review is the process by which faculty are promoted and evaluated, often on an annual basis. It is a fundamental element in the scientific method, by which scientific knowledge is developed and judged to be accurate. Peer review is the process by which scholarly books and articles are selected for publication. In some form, peer review is part of the daily life of the academy, and its violation is commonly regarded as a serious transgression. Thus, the academic and, more specifically, the scientific culture itself lends support to the use of peer review in decision making.

The normative role peer review plays in academic science is evident in Daniel Greenberg's description of "pure scientists":

> The xenophobia of scientists is intimately related to their reverence for the methodologies and formalities of science. Nature reveals its secrets grudgingly, and the presumption . . . is that these secrets are likely to be obtained only by those who have been formally initiated into the ranks of science and who employ the traditional techniques of science. . . . But how do the institutions of science function to advance truth, weed out error, honor the worthy, and reject the crackpots? The answer is that, over a period of three and one half centuries, science has evolved an intricate process of certification, no less labyrinthine than the western process of jurisprudence. . . . Who does this? Generally, [the researcher's] peers, other scientists who are familiar with his field of research.

10. Kuhn, pp. 10, 47, 19.

Greenberg went on to note that the peer review system was hardly infallible, that mistakes in judgment by peers had occurred, "but it is probably more immune from honest error, deceit, or partisanship than any other methodology for establishing truth."[11]

Robert Merton has also suggested that scientists operate by a set of norms and values that are legitimized through their institutionalization and reinforced by sanctions. One of these norms is that of disinterestedness. Why is fraud in science, Merton asks, a relatively rare experience? Not because scientists possess an unusual degree of honesty but because, "involving as it does the verifiability of results, scientific research is under the exacting scrutiny of fellow experts." So, even in cases when scientists are passionate, self-interested, and seeking, perhaps desperately, to surpass their rivals, the element of disinterestedness remains, as these scientists must necessarily submit their research findings to their peers for review in order to receive the rewards of their profession.[12]

If these observations are correct, if the federal government has institutionalized peer review to the extent that it may be characterized as the dominant policy regime for the allocation of federal academic science funds, such that it has been in place for nearly five decades, and if peer review serves as a powerful, institutionalized norm among scientists, then two important questions should be addressed: What are the conditions that have led to the small revolution, if not the policy regime shift, academic earmarking? How might we understand the failure of universities and concerned members of Congress to prohibit earmarking or to provide sufficient compensation to induce universities to abstain from this practice?

11. Daniel S. Greenberg, *The Politics of Pure Science* (New York: New American Library, 1967), pp. 39, 43, 46.
12. Robert K. Merton, op. cit., p. 276. On the idea that there are "counter norms" such as self-interest that play a positive role in science, see Ian I. Mitroff, "Norms and Counter-Norms in a Select Group of the Apollo Moon Scientists: A Case Study of the Ambivalence of Scientists," *American Sociological Review*, 39 (1974): 579–95. Also see Michael Mulkay, *Sociology of Science* (Bloomington: Indiana University Press, 1991). Mulkay looks to "bodies of knowledge, research practice and technique" rather than to norms to explain the sociology of science. Yet, he acknowledges that "social norms are to be regarded as institutionalized when they are positively linked to the distribution of rewards. Conformity to a given set of institutional norms is maintained fairly generally within a particular social grouping because it is regularly rewarded and/or because non-conformity is punished." Regardless of their research technique or body of knowledge, scientists submit their work to peer review to receive professional rewards (pp. 67, 65).

Academic Earmarking as a Collective Action Problem

An underlying argument of this book is that the politics of academic earmarking are best understood as what social scientists call a "collective action problem" and that earmarking will continue until the problem is resolved. A collective action problem exists when members of a group, acting in their own interest, undermine the group's ability to enjoy some shared benefit. Where the group would benefit most from mutual cooperation, to the point that the benefit would not exist in the absence of the group, the pursuit of individual benefits breaks down group solidarity, reducing its effectiveness and perhaps ultimately leading to the group's dissolution.

A classic source of collective action problems is found in "free riding." In free riding, a self-interested party refuses to bear his or her fair share of the burden or costs of group membership but continues to receive the benefits normally provided to group members. Over time, if enough group members free ride, the group will fail to achieve its collective goals and will likely dissolve. The essence of the collective action problem, therefore, is maintaining group cooperation and cohesion to prevent free riding. How can members be kept from ignoring their group responsibilities when they perceive that there are substantial benefits for doing so, at little or no immediate cost?

In the case of academic earmarking, the collective action problem is to prevent or limit the number of free riders, or defectors from the group's peer review resource allocation system. The group here consists primarily of research universities, but this study focuses particularly on the leading organization of these schools, the Association of American Universities. The free riders consist of those entrepreneurial university presidents who solicit earmarks from Congress while at the same time benefiting from competitive, peer-reviewed funding. They are, in effect, "double dippers" into the federal budget. Members of Congress insert academic earmarks in their legislation to benefit the schools in their states or districts as part of what political scientists describe as "distributive politics," primarily in order to enhance their reelection chances. In both cases, presidents and members respond to incentives that exist within their institutional settings, the university and Congress, to seek earmarks. Moreover, these earmarks are sometimes funded from peer-reviewed agency research budgets, thereby limiting the support available to those institutions that refrain from earmarking. Thus, there are often real costs to the group from this free riding.

In addition to these real and potential group costs, any scientific and economic costs stemming from academic earmarking may also be said to be an inefficiency borne by the nation as a whole. For basic science, the type produced by universities, is a truly unrestricted public good in that its benefits, such as the discoveries of biomedical research, potentially accrue to all members of society. To the extent that earmarking is a suboptimal allocation process suffering from its own biases and inefficiencies, it produces a net loss to the nation and its taxpayers from the allocation of scarce resources.

Resolving Collective Action Problems

Collective action theory offers several solutions to the free-rider problem. One solution, known as the "Folk Theorem," suggests that over a period of time members learn to cooperate, despite the rewards that may exist for a single instance of free riding. This cooperation ultimately depends on reciprocity between members of the group, enforced over time by way of a tit-for-tat strategy. Consider the hypothetical case of a two-member group. During the first opportunity for free riding, if the first member defects, the second member can also defect, which prevents the first member from receiving group benefits. During the second opportunity, the first member may then choose to cooperate, having learned that defection produces no reward. Then the second member will respond by also cooperating, and so on.[13]

Another solution for limiting or preventing group defections is to add to the group a third-party "Leviathan," to punish defectors. The third party's responsibilities include monitoring the group to identify defectors. Defectors are subsequently punished, where punishment can include permanent exclusion from the group. Defectors are not rewarded or bribed to keep them from defecting, as these practices would only act as incentives for members to threaten defection, even if they had no serious desire or intent to defect. The Leviathan solution depends upon the third party's ability to monitor the group's behavior and to administer punishment fairly and effectively.[14]

A third solution rests with group leaders who can encourage members to resist defection. In the "Leader-Follower" game, the leader allocates group benefits and inflicts meaningful punishment. What distinguishes

---

13. Robert Axelrod, *The Evolution of Cooperation* (New York: Basic Books, 1984); Axelrod, "The Emergence of Cooperation Among Egoists," *The American Political Science Review* 65 (1981): 306–18; Axelrod, "An Evolutionary Approach to Norms," *American Political Science Review* 80 (1986): 1095–1111.
14. Jonathan Bendor and Dilip Mookherjee, "Institutional Structure and the Logic of Ongoing Collective Action," *American Political Science Review* 81 (1987): 131–54.

the leader from the Leviathan in this game is that while both of them monitor behavior and inflict punishment, the leader possesses special skills in initiating and sustaining cooperation. These skills are idiosyncratic and are understood to be an aspect of the leader's reputation. The greater the leader's reputation and skill, the greater the group's cooperation.[15]

What characterizes each of these games is their dependence on real punishment and effective coercion. In each game, rules are established, criteria for good behavior are identified, and defectors are punished. Punishment may include permanent banishment from the group; the loss of potential group benefits, even those of a free rider, outweighs the benefits of defecting. Group cooperation is the result of the meaningful enforcement of rules on self-interested group members. As Dennis Mueller observed, "The idea that noncooperative (antisocial, immoral) behavior must be punished to bring about conformity with group mores is to be found in most, if not all, moral philosophies, and forms a direct linkage between this large literature and the modern theory."[16]

What quickly becomes apparent in the case of academic earmarking, however, is the absence of meaningful rules and sanctions to prevent self-interested defection. University presidents, for example, who engage in earmarking often receive praise rather than condemnation for providing new buildings for their campuses. Higher education associations that decry earmarking do little or nothing to punish members who earmark. Not a single university or college has been dismissed from an association for earmarking, and some earmarking schools have in fact been admitted to these associations. Moreover, despite protests by Presidents Reagan, Bush, and Clinton, and by some of their colleagues, members of Congress have every incentive to engage in earmarking to help universities and colleges in their districts and states. So, not only is punishment against earmarking weak and limited, significant incentives in the world of higher education and in Congress encourage the practice. Universities are free to double-dip from the federal budget by both earmarking funds and competing for peer-reviewed grants.

Yet constraints do exist against academic pork barreling. These constraints, in part, are rooted in norms rather than punishment and strictly

---

15. William T. Bianco and Robert H. Bates, "Cooperation by Design: Leadership, Structure, and Collective Dilemmas," *American Political Science Review* 84 (1990): 133–47.

16. Dennis C. Mueller, *Public Choice* (Cambridge: Cambridge University Press, 1979), p. 15. On the importance of group identity and the norm of exclusion, see Russell Hardin, *One for All: The Logic of Group Conflict* (Princeton: Princeton University Press, 1995), esp. Ch. 4.

self-interested behavior. "At the very least," as Jon Elster observed, "norms are soft constraints on action."[17] The norms of "quality science" and "good public policy" associated with peer review do serve to limit earmarking, though obviously not to prevent it. College and university presidents who can readily propose and obtain congressional earmarks with impunity have refused to do so or do so very reservedly. Powerful members of Congress who can easily earmark an appropriations bill with an academic project have abstained from doing so, and in several notable cases have actively opposed the projects of their colleagues. In collective action terms, where these academic and political leaders could have engaged in free riding, they preferred to cooperate.[18]

Other potential and real constraints on earmarking include the line-item veto and the availability of budgetary resources needed to continue playing the earmarking game. The president's ability to play the role of Leviathan, however, by employing a line-item veto against academic earmarks is currently under consideration by the federal court system.[19] Earmarking will continue as long as members of Congress have the resources to fund these projects, and given the projected surpluses for the federal budget, this constraint may therefore work in favor of additional earmarking.

17. Jon Elster, *The Cement of Society* (Cambridge: Cambridge University Press, 1989), p. 129.
18. Collective action theory often considers preferences to be exogenous to decision making. In other words, collective action theory takes preferences as a given and focuses on decision makers as they seek to maximize their preferences in various social and institutional settings. Nevertheless, institutional norms and preferences may be seen to be the result of a conscious imposition of values and organizational culture. This imposition occurs as institutional leaders ascertain that certain norms, and the behavior that stems from them, will lead to rewards for themselves and the institution. See both Elster, op. cit., and Hardin, op. cit. In addition to this collective action, rational-institutional model of culture and ideas, there is an extensive literature that views ideas and culture in themselves as important forces in policy making and decision making. See, for example, Paul Quirk, "In Defense of the Politics of Ideas," *Journal of Politics* 50 (1988): 31–41; Robert B. Reich (ed.), *The Power of Public Ideas* (Cambridge: Harvard University Press, 1988); Henry J. Aaron, Thomas E. Mann, and Timothy Taylor (eds.), *Values and Public Policy* (Washington, D.C.: Brookings Institution, 1994); Judith Goldstein and Robert O. Koehane (eds.), *Ideas and Foreign Policy: Beliefs, Institutions, and Political Change* (Ithaca: Cornell University Press, 1993); Peter A. Hall (ed.), *The Political Power of Economic Ideas* (Princeton: Princeton University Press, 1989).
19. Robert Pear, "U.S. Judge Rules Line Item Veto Act Unconstitutional," *New York Times*, February 13, 1998; "White House Seeks Overturn of Line-Item Veto Decision," *Washington Post*, February 21, 1998.

Leadership and the Motivational Approach

The major decision-making figures in the earmarking controversy are those who hold significant positions in their organizations, such as university presidents, chairs of congressional committees, research agency directors, and even lobbyists who run their own firms. Donald Searing recommends that political actors be analyzed by what he describes as a "motivational approach." Searing's framework takes into account not only institutional rules and rational preferences, which form the key elements of what is called the "new institutionalism," but also the roles individuals play in organizations that constitute the "dynamic interactions between rules and reasons, between institutional constraints and individual preferences." Roles are understood both by formal positions held within an organization and by personal motivations, which include "career goals and emotional incentives." Searing identifies two basic types of roles: position roles and preference roles. A "position role" reflects the formal structure and formal rules of the organization. A "preference role" reflects the individual motivations one brings to a formal position, and is "comparatively unconstrained by the institution and [is] therefore more easily shaped by the preferences of the role players." So, Searing writes, "a number of distinct types of roles can be tethered to these institutional positions." Examples of individual motivations are offered by Richard Fenno, who observed that members of Congress expressed a variety of goals, such as gaining reelection and being influential policy makers. The motivational model, therefore, integrates the economic formalism of the new institutionalism with the sociological understanding of roles.[20]

Leaders such as university presidents and committee chairs combine elements of position and preferential roles. Their positions and duties are formally defined, yet their rank, prestige, and power in their respective institutions are special, if not unique. As principal leaders, they set and control agendas, raise and articulate ideas, impose rules and sanctions, and manage and allocate resources. These role characteristics, therefore, grant them great latitude in influencing policy and organizational decisions. This is certainly true in the case of academic earmarking. As will be shown, university presidents are the primary actors in determining their schools' position on whether to seek earmarks.

---

20. Donald D. Searing, "Roles, Rules, and Rationality in the New Institutionalism," *American Political Science Review* 85 (1991): 1248, 1253. Also see James G. March and Johan P. Olsen, "The New Institutionalism: Organizational Factors in Political Life," *American Political Science Review* 78 (1984): 734–49.

Committee chairs, especially those serving on appropriations subcommittees, also play a central role in determining whether their subcommittees will fund earmarks and for whose benefit. These leaders, for example, often act as entrepreneurs for themselves and their organizations, and they make policy choices and determine sanctions, thereby shaping the norms and culture of their organizations. Consequently, as Searing suggests, this study will focus on institutional roles and motivations, as the policy decisions of individual actors who hold similar formal institutional positions but differ in their motivations explain much of the politics of academic earmarking.

2

The Incentives to Earmark

Why do some colleges and universities seek academic earmarks? What conditions and incentives lead an institution to violate the long-standing policy regime organized around the peer review system, which many educational leaders believe has contributed to the establishment of excellence in American academic science? The responses to these questions commonly revolve around the arguments that earmarking is justified because it serves as a remedy for the biases of peer review or that earmarking is a substitute for the federal government's failure to provide funding for academic research facilities. Yet, the incentives for a university to earmark are more varied and complex than simply the desire to rectify the flaws in the federal research grants allocation system. To understand the importance of these incentives in the institutional context of higher education, it is necessary to view the earmarking decision from the perspective of the university or college president, who, as the chief executive officer, possesses the authority to legitimize earmarking for that institution in ways that no other administrator or faculty member can.

The decision to seek an earmark is ultimately made by a president who is subject to a variety of incentives in making this often intensely personal choice. The contemporary university president faces the difficult goal of meeting rising institutional expectations with increasingly restrictive resources. Given these resource constraints, presidents may indeed be very receptive to obtaining a quick infusion of earmarked federal money at virtually no institutional or personal cost. Consequently, what is most surprising about academic earmarking is not that it exists, but that it does not occur more often.

Ambition

Earmarking takes place because universities are, in the best sense of the word, ambitious, and they seek the rewards that come from greater prestige and status. "All 2,400 non-'specialized' institutions of higher education in the United States aspire to higher things," Clark Kerr, former president of the University of California, observed. "These aspirations are particularly intense among the approximately 200 research and other doctorate-granting universities with 30 percent of all enrollment."[1] In a study of higher education finance, Duke University economist Charles Clotfelter described these aspirations as "unbounded," and he noted that organizational structure and culture contributed to these unbounded aspirations: "Featuring weak central control, a remarkable degree of freedom accorded to its faculty, and traditions of collegiality in governance, the university lacks any corporate goal other than the pursuit of excellence."[2] Within the university there are many sources for these ambitions and aspirations.

Universities are ambitious, first of all, because their presidents are ambitious. A president brings to the job a particular vision and a set of goals for improving an institution's performance, which may be measured by such considerations as entering student test scores, graduation rates, expansion in the institution's endowment, the number of professors admitted to prestigious academic societies, or the increase in the institution's rank as a recipient of federal research funding. Seeing one's efforts produce positive outcomes obviously creates its own reward, but presidents also desire to make improvements to enhance their reputations, their legacies, and their current and future job prospects. Improvement often brings with it the additional benefit of strengthening a school's resource base, so that greater prestige and perceived quality, for example, may convince parents and students to pay higher tuition.[3] These resources, in turn, assist presidents when they confront the various financial and other problems facing universities and colleges.

These personal ambitions are made explicit in the formal responsibilities commonly assumed by a president, who is ultimately the institution's chief fund-raiser and financial officer. Consequently, presidents spend much of their time raising money, often in massive fund drives, for endowment development, new buildings, scholarships, and chairs

1. Clark Kerr, "The New Race to Be Harvard or Berkeley or Stanford," *Change Magazine*, May–June 1991, p. 9.
2. Joye Mercer, "Expensive Ambitions," *Chronicle of Higher Education*, April 26, 1996, p. A33.
3. Barbara Vobejda, "Competition for College Feeds Elitism: Well-Off Applicants Flood Prestigious Schools as Tuitions Rise," *Washington Post*, May 4, 1989.

for faculty. In 1990, for example, Cornell University announced its plans for a $1.25 billion fund-raising drive, and Columbia University set its target at $1 billion. These efforts followed targets of $1 billion at Stanford University, $2.5 billion at Harvard, and $1 billion at the University of Pennsylvania. When Benno Schmidt, Jr., retired from his Yale presidency, he described his greatest achievement as the raising of $1.2 billion for new facilities. Even public universities that rely primarily on state appropriations for the financial support of their basic operations have significantly strengthened their endowment-raising and alumni development activities. At each of the University of California's nine campuses, for example, since the early 1980s, development officers have painstakingly searched out once-neglected alumni in order to add them to donor rolls. These efforts usually demand a significant time commitment on the part of the university president. "Fund raising has become the name of the game," Theodore M. Hesburgh, former president of Notre Dame, declared. "You can have the greatest vision in the world, but if you don't have money, you're up a creek." Moreover, whereas fund-raising campaigns once referred to a specified period of time in which money was raised, universities are increasingly running their drives one after the other, making fund-raising a perpetual institutional activity and the ongoing responsibility of their presidents.[4]

The pressure to enhance an institution's reputation and academic quality in an era of constrained resources has taken its toll on the nation's college and university presidents. The stress of serving as president, for example, is evident in the tremendous turnover in the position. During the late 1980s and early 1990s, the average term of office declined from seven or eight years to three or four in public four-year institutions.[5] Though no formal records are kept for private schools, according to the National Association of Independent Colleges and Universities, the decline for these schools roughly matched what has occurred in the public institutions. In just the two years 1990 and 1991, a third of the presidencies in the elite Association of American Universities, an organization of the nation's premier research schools, experi-

---

4. Mary Jordan, "Wanted: Presidents for U.S. Universities," *Washington Post*, June 15, 1992; Anthony Flint, "Cornell Citing Lean Years Ahead, Opens $1.25b Fund-Raiser," *Boston Globe*, October 21, 1990; Sara Rimer, "Columbia Sets a Fund Goal of $1 Billion," *New York Times*, October 26, 1990; and Julie L. Nicklin, "Perpetual Fund Raising," *Chronicle of Higher Education*, June 21, 1996, p. A26.

5. Clark Kerr and Marian L. Gade, *The Many Lives of Academic Presidents* (Washington, D.C.: Association of Governing Boards of Universities and Colleges, 1989), p. 21. Also see "Under the Glare of the Presidency," Education Life section special report, *New York Times*, November 5, 1995; Don Wycliff, "The Short, Unhappy Life of Academic Presidents," *New York Times*, July 25, 1990.

enced turnover. Part of the reason for this turnover is the great personal cost of serving as president, particularly the pressure to raise funds for one's university. In one highly publicized case, Harvard University hired Neil Rudenstine as president in 1991, but just four years later Rudenstine had to take a leave of absence, citing burnout and exhaustion as the cause. Citing his own fatigue, University of Virginia President John T. Casteen III declared, "I've realized that this is really taxing kind of work – it chews you up. It's a way of life that wears you down and from time to time you have to back away from it. . . . I spend roughly 80 percent of my time on fund raising."[6] Other presidents, including those at such schools as the universities of Arizona and Iowa, have identified their duties as the cause of divorce and illness. In 1992, out of 3,200 institutions of higher education in the United States, more than 300 conducted searches for vacant presidencies.[7]

In addition to fund-raising, a president is held accountable for an institution's governmental relations. The management of governmental and other forms of external relations differs significantly from a university's internal operations and decision making. Much of what goes on in university administration may be characterized by its internally directed standard operating procedures. There are numerous administrative and faculty committees that consider familiar, routine, and ongoing topics, such as the approval of courses, student affairs and conduct, admissions, and budget and planning. These committees often report to other committees, to the faculty senate, and to several administrators, all before a final, often consensus, decision is reached. Due process in this scenario is often more valued than speed in reaching a decision. This combination of administrative hierarchy and faculty collegiality has caused some researchers of organizational theory to label this process the "garbage can model" of decision making. However, although this may be true of the decision-making process for the internal operations of a university, the external, and particularly federal governmental, relations of most academic institutions operate far differently.[8]

In the case of governmental relations, a president, usually aided by a handful of senior advisors, commonly acts as the primary administrator and policy maker. The nature of governmental relations demands that decisions be made at the executive level because academic institutions

6. Ian Zack, "Casteen Will Remain at UVa, He and Dabney Say," *Daily-Progress*, May 24, 1995; "Casteen Keeps Pace with Challenges of the Job," *Inside UVA*, May 3, 1996.
7. Barbara Kantrowitz, "Wanted: Miracle Workers," *Newsweek*, April 8, 1991, p. 48; Jordan, op. cit.
8. Michael D. Cohen, James G. March, and Johan P. Olsen, "A Garbage Can Model of Organizational Choice," *Administrative Science Quarterly* 17 (1972): 1–25.

must speak to the outside political world with one coherent voice. It is not uncommon, for instance, for universities to require that faculty and other employees refrain from representing themselves as taking an official institutional position when they contact legislators on various political issues, even to the point of insisting that employees avoid using university stationary when writing to politicians.

Moreover, in terms of simple political effectiveness, presidents or their immediate advisors and representatives are the most appropriate coordinators of governmental relations. To be effective in governmental relations, an academic institution must be able to respond quickly to the decision-making processes of organizations over which it has no control, namely, legislatures and executive agencies. When Congress or a state legislature votes on a key bill with little prior notice, the university's decision-making process must enable the institution's representative or lobbyist to contact a key legislator or administrator literally within a few hours. The endless deliberation evident in internal policy making will not suffice for governmental relations. Furthermore, if a university or college is to use its full political influence in a critical moment, in many cases it is the president who must communicate the institution's position to the appropriate legislators and executive branch officials.

Thus, the central role of the university president in deciding whether the institution will pursue an earmark stems from the president's central and formal organizational task of setting governmental relations policy for the school.

University presidents, with their personal aspirations and administrative responsibilities, are not the only source of institutional ambition. Universities are also ambitious because their faculties are ambitious. Many faculty are themselves the recipients of advanced degrees from prestigious research universities, and they often aspire to be appointed at a similar institution or to transform their own school into such a place. Faculty know that these are the schools where research support is more generous, salaries are higher, students are smarter, teaching loads are lighter, and professional status shines brighter than at most teaching colleges. Faculty understand that the more resources their own institution possesses, the more likely it will be able to provide the support necessary for them to produce the research that will lead to tenure, promotion, and perhaps a position at a more prominent university.

Alumni, boards of trustees, and other members of the university community are also ambitious. Not only do they view their school with pride and seek to enhance its reputation, they take umbrage when outsiders consider their alma mater with less than proper respect. These concerns for ambition, pride, and status are intense, and in their own way they may be particular to higher education. Paul Fussell attributes them to America's "absence of a system of hereditary ranks and titles," so that "Americans have had to depend for the mechanisms of snobbery far more than other peoples on their college and university hierarchy. . . . You can drive all over Europe without once seeing a rear-window sticker reading CHRIST CHURCH or UNIVERSITE DE PARIS." For Fussell, school pride is intimately connected with self-esteem, achievement, and social status, and it provides another powerful source of pressure on a university president to boost the school's academic and public standing.[9]

Clearly, another important contributor to institutional ambition is the rise of college and university rankings. At one time, institutional prestige was simply marked by such formal and informal groupings as the "Ivy League," "The Seven Sisters," or the "Big Ten." After obvious references to Harvard, Yale, the rest of the Ivy League, and a handful of other institutions, the relative quality of colleges and universities was once best known to the general public by referring to a school's athletic prowess. Other than the sports pages, the public could rely upon only a small number of inferential indicators to assist them in evaluating the local college on a national basis. Between 1906 and 1982, for example, only seven major rankings were provided of the nation's graduate schools, all by different groups employing various survey techniques. During the 1970s, a few informal guides to colleges were published, such as the *Yale Guide to Colleges and Universities*, which remains in publication and continues to provide amusing anecdotal comparisons of institutions. Other, more formal guides, such as Barron's *Profile*, have been published, but they generally offer antiseptic and diplomatic institutional sketches that say little about comparative quality.

Since 1982, however, with the publication of Edward B. Fiske's *The New York Times Selective Guide to American Colleges, 1982–83*, and especially with the annual release of the *U.S. News & World Report*'s evaluation of colleges and universities, numerical rankings of virtually every significant institution have become available for all to see. "In a nation obsessed with being No. 1, and with quantifying the unquantifiable," *Time* magazine notes, "it was perhaps inevitable that someone would attempt to rate colleges as if they were cars." Commenting on the influence of the *U.S. News & World Report* rankings, University of Maryland law school dean Donald Gifford complained, "Thousands of prospective law students rush to the stand to purchase this issue believ-

9. Paul Fussell, "Schools for Snobbery: Universities and the Class System," *The New Republic*, October 4, 1992, p. 25.

ing it has something to do with quality of education."[10] Faculty, current and prospective students, administrators, alumni, and trustees are now keenly aware of where their institution ranks in comparison with others. The importance of these rankings should not be understated. Not only do they influence prospective students in their enrollment decisions, they also pose the ever-present questions to current students, faculty, administrators, and alumni: "Why did our ranking drop?" or "Why isn't our ranking going up?" These questions may be particularly embarrassing for a president when similar and readily comparable institutions experience an increase in rank. As a result, in some cases, school officials have been known to provide selective and institutionally beneficial data to the guidebooks' editors, such as altered graduation rates and student test scores, and to rely upon the opinion of guidebook editors in determining what changes need to be made at a school to improve its academic quality and presumably its rank. Meanwhile, the official publications of various disciplines publish articles when faculty have carefully subjected these rankings to more exacting statistical tests in order to validate or debunk the ordering of these ranks or, more precisely, to demonstrate that the ranking an institution or department received should have been higher. All the while, the faculty fear that cost-conscious administrators will employ these rankings as the basis for financially rewarding or punishing departments, depending upon how well they ranked.[11]

Perhaps the most important ranking for presidents of research universities is the least publicly known, the National Science Foundation's (NSF) ranking of the top 100 recipients of federal research support, based on an analysis of the 759 academic institutions receiving these funds. This is the ranking that has served as the focus for the discussion within higher education and Congress over the equity of the peer review system. To be ranked in the top 100 is considered very good among academics, but what truly counts is a ranking among the top 50 and, best yet, among the top 10. The goal of becoming a top 10 research university is indeed the pinnacle of ambition in the academic research community.

10. Elizabeth Gleick, "Playing the Numbers," *Time*, April 17, 1995, p. 52; Saundra Torry, "Law Schools Rated Out of Order; Magazine to Serve Corrections," *Washington Post*, March 7, 1997.
11. "Report Creates Close Scrutiny for College Rankings," *Daily-Progress*, April 18, 1995. For an example of a disciplinary journal analysis of rankings, see *PS: Political Science and Politics* 29(2) (June 1996): 144–67.

Facing the Fiscal Crunch

At the same time that universities aspire to higher status, presidents at even the most distinguished institutions face increasingly constrained financial resources. This period of constraint extends back to the inflation-plagued late 1970s, more recently to the recessions of the early 1980s and 1990s, and to an extended period of fiscal retrenchment throughout many of these years of both the federal and state governments. From 1974 to 1988, for example, total state appropriations for public universities remained relatively flat at about $35 billion. When inflation is accounted for, state funding for higher education actually shrank significantly in real terms. Funding for public institutions did experience a brief boom with the national economic recovery of the late 1980s, as state funding increased to nearly $43 billion in 1990. Yet, due to the recession of 1990–2, it fell to approximately $40 billion in 1993 and 1994.[12]

Faced with severe fiscal crises, state legislators cut deeply into higher education through the mid-1990s. Funding for public institutions in Massachusetts was cut by $221 million, a 29 percent reduction, from 1990 through 1995. Between 1990 and 1992, Virginia's higher education budget was trimmed by $300 million and Maryland's by $160 million; Ohio's was cut by $372 million between 1989 and 1992. State appropriations for the University of California system were cut by more than 25 percent – by $433 million, between 1990 and 1995. Higher education's share of the California state budget fell from 14 to 12.5 percent from 1990 to 1995, New York's from 9.8 to 8.5 percent, and Minnesota's from 13.8 to 11.3 percent. In many states, spending on prisons outpaces expenditures for higher education.[13]

Private institutions have also experienced difficult times. In response to the resource constraints of the five-year period 1989–94, 32 percent of presidents at private institutions imposed across-the-board budget cuts at their schools. For the 1993–4 fiscal year, 23 percent reported midyear budget reductions. A full third indicated that they had elimi-

---

12. William H. Honon, "State Universities Reshaped in the Era of Budget Cutting," *New York Times*, February 22, 1995; Brooke A. Masters, "Cuts in College Budgets Send Students Scrambling," *Washington Post*, January 29, 1992.
13. Larry Gordon, "Berkeley Battles the Blues," *Los Angeles Times*, June 13, 1993; Fox Butterfield, "New Prisons Cast Shadow Over Higher Education," *New York Times*, April 12, 1995; David W. Breneman, "The 'Privatization' of Public Universities: A Mistake or a Model for the Future?" *Chronicle of Higher Education*, March 7, 1997, p. B4.

nated academic programs, including such elite institutions as Yale, Columbia, and the University of Pennsylvania. At Columbia, to reduce a $50 million deficit in 1992–3, faculty positions were trimmed by 9 percent. In 1996, the Massachusetts Institute of Technology (MIT) announced plans to trim its $9.2 million operating deficit, and Stanford University and the University of Chicago also imposed budget cuts. During the period 1993–6, Stanford cut spending in its academic departments by $15 million. A very gloomy overall assessment of the financial health of higher education was reached by Wall Street's Standard & Poor's municipal finance department in 1992: "Private colleges and universities today are facing pressures unprecedented in their complexity and scope. Declining student populations, tuition constraints, and the possibility of sharp cutbacks in federal support are straining the finances of institutions of higher education."[14]

Trends in federal research funding have also added to higher education's financial worries. This assertion must be viewed in historical context, however, for despite deficit-plagued federal budgets, the government's agencies and accounts that support academic research have been among the most protected areas of federal spending. As shown in Table 2, between 1963 and 1994, federal spending on academic research usually experienced long-term growth in both nominal and real terms. The worst budgets for academic science in terms of inflation-adjusted, constant dollars came in the late 1960s and early 1970s, primarily due to shifts in funding to support the Vietnam War, and in the early 1980s, when nominal budget increases failed to meet the double-digit inflation experienced during the Carter presidency and because of the early reluctance of the Reagan administration to fund most types of academic science. More recently, analysis by the American Association for the Advancement of Science (AAAS) indicates that combined executive and congressional plans to balance the federal budget by the year 2002 could reduce funding for civilian research by 18 percent by the year 2000. President Bill Clinton's budget proposal for FY 1997, for example, while calling for short-term research agency budget increases, recommended long-term reductions of 11.7 percent in nondefense re-

14. *Chronicle of Higher Education Almanac*, August 25, 1993, p. 46; Anthony DePalma, "Short of Money, Columbia U. Weighs How Best to Change," *New York Times*, May 25, 1992; LynNell Hancock and John McCormick, "What to Chop?" *Newsweek*, April 29, 1996, pp. 59–67; Patrick Healy, Kit Lively, Joye Mercer, Julie Nicklin, and Peter Schmidt, "Private Colleges Fight for Financial Health; Public Institutions Find State Support Unreliable," *Chronicle of Higher Education*, June 14, 1996, p. A15.

search. Clinton's FY 1998 budget allowed only a 2 percent increase in research, which represented a real cut in inflation-adjusted dollars.[15]

Nevertheless, over the long run, Republicans and Democrats have generally agreed that support for basic research is vital to the nation's economic and social well-being. The longest period of uninterrupted, constant dollar growth in the last twenty years came in FY 1983–92. During the Reagan–Bush years the most favored agency budget was not the Department of Defense but NSF. Beginning in 1986 and throughout the Bush presidency, the Reagan and Bush budget proposals called for doubling over a five-year period the size of the budget of NSF, the only agency to receive such support from the White House. Although Congress failed to meet that target, until 1991 it provided NSF with annual increases of approximately 5 percent, even when most other domestic budgets were cut or frozen, or received minimal increases of 1, 2, or 3 percent. Meanwhile, though the Reagan and Bush administrations proved to be less supportive of biomedical and other forms of research, Congress generally protected and provided increases for the National Institutes of Health (NIH), the largest federal sponsor of academic research. Even efforts to balance the budget in 2002 by President Clinton's administration and the Republican-controlled Congress are relatively protective of basic research. The AAAS noted that federal agencies and programs that fund basic research "are likely to do reasonably well," given basic research's popularity with lawmakers.[16] Moreover, despite the ongoing worries expressed by the academic research community, the final FY 1997 appropriations approved by Congress and signed by President Clinton provided a 5.1 percent increase for NSF and a 6.7 percent increase for NIH. For FY 1998, NSF received a 6.1 percent increase, NIH received 7.1 percent, and total basic research grew by 4.6 percent over FY 1997.

In any case, despite short-term fluctuations and the federal government's long-term support for academic research, the rate of increase in funding has not and will not keep pace with higher education's demand for these funds. The simple fact is that the growth in academic science has outstripped the federal government's ability to provide complementary research funding.

15. James D. Savage, "Federal R&D Budget Policy in the Reagan Administration," *Public Budgeting & Finance*, Summer 1987, pp. 37–51; Colleen Cordes, "Report Predicts Cuts in Science Spending Under Clinton Budget Plan," *Chronicle of Higher Education*, April 26, 1996, p. A30; Ted Agres, "Conference Sees Cloudy Future for Federal Funding of R&D," *R&D Magazine*, July 1996, p. 10

16. Ibid., p. A30.

Table 2. *Federal obligations for academic research and development, FY 1963–94*
(Thousands of Dollars)

Fiscal year	Amount	Nominal percent change	Constant percent change
1963	$ 829,524	NA	NA
1964	975,597	17.6%	15.9%
1965	1,094,963	12.2	23.4
1966	1,252,146	14.4	−2.6
1967	1,301,242	3.9	.5
1968	1,398,305	7.5	3.7
1969	1,474,681	5.5	.3
1970	1,446,618	−1.9	−7.0
1971	1,551,391	7.2	2.2
1972	1,853,085	19.4	13.5
1973	1,870,690	.9	−4.1
1974	2,085,204	11.5	3.5
1975	2,246,182	7.2	−2.0
1976	2,430,970	8.2	.6
1977	2,803,017	15.3	6.6
1978	3,388,438	20.9	12.4
1979	3,874,384	14.3	5.3
1980	4,160,543	7.4	−1.6
1981	4,410,931	6.0	−3.8
1982	4,554,475	3.2	−3.9
1983	5,024,330	10.3	6.0
1984	5,448,821	8.4	3.8
1985	6,246,181	14.6	10.5
1986	6,456,743	3.4	.4
1987	7,241,001	12.1	8.9
1988	7,719,237	6.6	2.9
1989	8,523,190	10.4	5.7
1990	9,008,083	5.7	2.1
1991	10,031,058	11.4	6.9
1992	10,844,500	8.1	5.0
1993	10,923,070	.7	−1.6
1994	11,768,416	7.7	5.7

Source: Federal Support to Universities, Colleges, and Nonprofit Institutions, FY 1994
(Washington, D.C.: National Science Foundation, 1996), Table B-1.

Higher education has experienced rapid growth since World War II, the G.I. Bill, and the postwar baby boom. Prior to the G.I. Bill, particularly during the Great Depression, doctorates were limited to a privileged few, and true, research-oriented, Ph.D.-granting universities were relatively rare. As late as the early 1940s, one out of every eight Ph.D.s in the nation was awarded by one institution, Columbia University.[17] Since the war, to accommodate the returning servicemen and servicewomen, and then their baby-boom children, more than 1,000 colleges and universities have been established. Furthermore, despite current economic hardship, new campuses continue to be built in states like California and Florida to meet the demands of a growing population.[18]

Colleges and universities have hired approximately 700,000 faculty to staff these institutions, many of whom must conduct research and who rely upon federal support to advance in their careers. In addition to these regular line faculty, research universities depend heavily on research faculty such as postdoctoral fellows, whose primary if not sole source of support, known as "soft money," is competitive research grants most often funded by the federal government. Between 1981 and 1991, doctoral scientists at academic institutions who conducted research and development increased by 42 percent, twice the growth rate of the entire workforce of the United States. Altogether, nearly 58 percent of academic researchers received some funding in 1991 from the federal government, and 13 percent of all full-time graduate students served as research assistants as a result of federal support.[19]

These figures on personnel are indicative of the rise in the number of colleges and universities that regard themselves as capable of conducting serious research. Between 1971 and 1991, the number of academic institutions receiving federal research support grew by 34 percent, from 565 to 759. As institutions come to regard themselves as research oriented, the entire incentive system for faculty is influenced. Tenure, promotion, and continued employment increasingly become dependent upon obtaining research grants. Clearly, these expectations and sanctions contribute to institutional ambition.

As the pressure for federal research dollars has intensified within academia, this support has failed to match institutional ambitions to

17. Mary Jordan, "Wanted: Presidents for U.S. Universities," *Washington Post*, June 15, 1992.

18. Kerr and Gade, p. 680.

19. Boyce Rensberger, "More Scientists, Fewer Grants," *Washington Post*, December 25, 1994; Boyce Rensberger, "Vital Skill in Lab Is Grantsmanship," *Washington Post*, December 26, 1994; *Science & Engineering Indicators*, (Washington, D.C.: National Science Foundation, 1993), Tables 5–10, 5–14, 5–18, and 5–19.

achieve research university status and improve NSF rankings. While the number of academic researchers grew by 53 percent between 1981 and 1991, the total real growth in federal research expenditures at universities and colleges increased by only 49 percent. Over a longer time frame, the disparity in this relationship is even more pronounced. According to a report published by the AAAS in 1991:

> Since 1983, federal support for academic research in constant – that is, inflation-adjusted – dollars has grown by about 3 percent. . . . [T]his recent increase followed a long period of relatively flat funding which was itself preceded by a sharp drop between 1968 and 1974. Consequently, the amount of federal funding for basic plus applied research in universities in 1989 (expressed in constant dollars) is only 20 percent higher today than it was in 1968! At the same time . . . the number of doctoral scientists and engineers in colleges and universities has more than doubled. In other words, in 1990 there are over twice as many researchers competing for a pot of money not much bigger than it was in 1968.[20]

Thus, the dollar value of federal support per researcher has declined despite significant efforts by the federal government to increase support for academic research during the mid-1980s. Whereas once, for example, NIH could fund 40 percent of proposals evaluated as worthy of support, that figure dropped to 33 percent in 1988 and to about 25 percent in 1995.[21]

At the same time as the competition for federal research funding has intensified, sustained, programmatic federal support for academic research facilities has been essentially nonexistent. University presidents agree that the quality of academic research is heavily influenced by the availability of state-of-the-art research laboratories. Unfortunately, higher education suffers from an enormous research facilities deficit; billions of dollars are required to modernize obsolete infrastructure. Since the 1960s, however, federal funding for such facilities has dwindled. For example, the primary federal program to support academic facilities, administered by NSF, was budgeted at just $100 million in FY 1996; President Clinton's FY 1997 budget proposed that the program be zero funded.

Although all institutions are affected by this facilities deficit, the "emerging" or "have-not" research universities, as they are sometimes

---

20. Leon M. Lederman, "Science: The End of the Frontier?" (Washington, D.C.: American Association for the Advancement of Science, January 1991), p. 8. Also see Robert Finn, "Discouraged Job-Seekers Cite Crisis in Science Career Advice," *The Scientist*, May 29, 1995, p. 1.
21. Malcolm Gladwell, "Funding Squeeze Discourages New Medical Research," *Washington Post*, December 9, 1989.

called, feel particularly aggrieved by the absence of federal support. When funding was available, the established, elite research schools received the majority of facilities dollars. Meanwhile, the existing indirect cost system, whereby part of the dollar value of a research grant goes to the sponsoring institution to pay for the school's administrative support of the research grant, also benefits the elite universities. The larger a school's research base, the more money it receives from indirect costs. The federal government, in turn, requires that a portion of these indirect costs be used for research facilities modernization. As a result, the larger the research base, the more money that is available for new facilities. Thus, many presidents argue, the rich, elite research universities gain disproportionately from the dollars the federal government does spend on facilities.

Moreover, these presidents charge that the lack of money for new and renovated facilities, and the biased distribution of the funds that do exist, prevent their institutions from entering the ranks of the elite universities. Building new facilities, they contend, is the first step on the road to research excellence. "The existence of such facilities," Boston University President John Silber testified before Congress, "will inevitably attract groups of outstanding scientists. Those scientists, using the new and improved facilities and equipment, will compete for individual research grants through the traditional peer-review system, and will compete successfully."[22] To rectify this perceived injustice or simply to construct desperately needed laboratory space, over 100 schools engaged in academic earmarking, and many of these earmarks supported the construction of research facilities.

So, despite the federal government's efforts to fund academic research and research facilities during a period of extreme budgetary stringency, the growth, cost, and ambition of academic research institutions have exceeded these funds. Exacerbating the problem of scarce resources, however, is the perceived bias and inequity in the allocation of the federal funds that are distributed.

Equity and Peer Review

Even as they attempt to realize their personal and institutional aspirations at a time when resources are constrained, many presidents claim that the distribution of federal research funds is inherently biased in favor of a handful of elite research universities. This unequal, unfair allo-

22. "Testimony of Dr. John Silber, President of Boston University, Before the Committee on Science, Space and Technology, United States House of Representatives, June 25, 1987," pp. 6–7. For more on Silber, see Helen Epstein, "Crusader on the Charles," *New York Times Magazine*, April 23, 1989.

cation, they say, whereby the same schools time and again receive the bulk of research funding, is a direct result of the federal government's peer review system.

The Rise of Project Grants and Peer Review

Prior to World War II, the federal government only very reluctantly awarded research money to individual scientists who were not government employees, and when such money was forthcoming, it inevitably had to be justified on the grounds of national defense or commerce.[23] Moreover, on those rare occasions, experts sometimes were called upon to assist agency research directors in making decisions about which projects would receive funding. In the 1840s, Joseph Henry, director of the Smithsonian Institution, established an advisory commission to review and recommend grants for funding.[24] Elements of peer review may also be found in the creation of the Navy Consulting Board in 1915, chaired by Thomas Edison, whose twelve members were responsible for reviewing funding requests by civilian inventors.[25] A more enduring review process was established in 1937, by way of the National Advisory Cancer Council, which became the precursor of NIH's extensive peer review system.[26]

Nevertheless, before World War II, perhaps the most familiar federal funding mechanism for academic science consisted of institutional, rather than individual, formula-driven grants. The Hatch Act of 1887 and the Smith-Lever Act of 1914 supported agricultural research through cooperative research stations and the extension service. In the case of the Hatch Act, for example, state experiment stations attached to land-grant universities received funding based on a formula that estimated a state's agricultural product.[27]

During World War II, the federal government relied upon project grants to support academic and other types of research. "At the begin-

---

23. On the evolution of American science policy, see A. Hunter Dupree, *Science in the Federal Government* (Baltimore: Johns Hopkins University Press, 1986); Bruce L. R. Smith, *American Science Policy Since World War II* (Washington, D.C.: Brookings Institution, 1990); Harold Orlans (ed.), *Science Policy and the University* (Washington, D.C.: Brookings Institution, 1968); and James Penick, Jr., Carroll Pursell, Jr., Morgan Sherwood, and Donald Swain (eds.), *The Politics of American Science* (Cambridge: MIT Press, 1972).

24. Dupree, p. 82.

25. Smith, p. 29.

26. Congress of the United States, Office of Technology Assessment, *Federally Funded Research: Decisions for a Decade* (Washington, D.C.: U.S. Government Printing Office, May 1991), pp. 126–7.

27. Ibid., p. 129.

ning of our involvement in the war," observed Christian Arnold, "our military technology and machinery were almost hopelessly inadequate and obsolete. Therefore, the military agencies did what they had to do – they bought the information, engineering, and 'hardware' they needed by negotiating contracts with organizations and individuals that seemed most likely to do the best job for them." The awarding of individual project grants rather than formula-driven institutional grants, regardless of whether allocated by some sort of peer review or simply by the order of a research agency director, necessarily creates a hierarchy of results, as Arnold further describes:

> A major difficulty lies in the tendency of the project system to concentrate federal funds in a relatively small number of institutions. This tendency is inherent in the system. When research grants and contracts are awarded to the more competent scientists, the competence of their institutions is increased by their accumulation of additional scientists, better facilities, improved fiscal and supporting services, and the like. At the same time, the competence of the other institutions is relatively weakened by the loss of capable scientists and the lack of the newer, more sophisticated, and expensive facilities. At some point, the growing prestige of the grant-receiving institution and its improved facilities and services help the scientist to get grants . . . and the institution's competitive position in the scientific market place is even further strengthened. To the extent that proposals are in fact judged on the single basis of merit, this tendency to institutional concentration is inexorable.[28]

The debate over how the postwar federal research establishment would be organized focused, in part, on whether the distribution of federal money would be allocated as individual grants or through formulas.

In 1944, Senator Harley M. Kilgore (D-WVA) introduced legislation that would create a single federal agency to manage all federal research of all types, including the funding of basic research conducted in universities. Kilgore's plan, among other things, called for the agency director to be appointed directly by the president and for it to disperse research funds on a state-by-state formula basis. Kilgore was highly critical of what he considered an undue concentration of wartime contracts awarded to a few universities, particularly MIT, Columbia, and Harvard.[29] In response to Kilgore, Vannevar Bush, director of the Office

---

28. Christian K. Arnold, "The Government and University Science: Purchase or Investment?" in Harold Orlans (ed.), *Science Policy and the University* (Washington, D.C.: Brookings Institution, 1968), pp. 89–90, 91.

29. On the Bush report and the creation of NSF, see Nelson W. Polsby, *Political Innovation in America: The Politics of Policy Initiation* (New Haven: Yale University Press, 1984), pp. 35–54; Smith, op. cit., Ch. 3; Dupree, op. cit., Ch. 19; and Penick, op. cit., pp. 2–48, 120–137.

of Scientific Research and Development (OSRD), created by President Franklin D. Roosevelt, sent to the president his famous report, *Science: The Endless Frontier*. Bush proposed that there be a National Research Foundation (NRF), which would be the single major agency supporting basic research, comparable to the applied and developmental university research funded through the Department of Agriculture. The agency director would report to a board appointed by the president, and research funds would be allocated through individual project contracts and grants.

Bush's advocacy of project grants stemmed from his prewar experience at MIT, where he served as that institution's second-ranking administrator before being named president of the Carnegie Institution, then chairman of the National Defense Research Committee, and later chairman of OSRD. It was MIT that pioneered the use of research contracts with the private sector that became the model for defense contracting with universities. Bush was responsible for coordinating the nation's military research, but he was first and foremost an academic. Like many other leading academic scientists who served in the government during World War II, Bush grew leery of what might happen to the independence of university research if, after the war, the government directly managed the conduct of academic science. The creation of Bush's proposed NRF, which would fund only basic research, would counter the government's tendency to favor development and applied research, and the preservation of the project grant system would continue to provide some insulation between the government and what Bush called the "individual inventor." Moreover, Bush had little interest in Kilgore's formula funding, which he reasoned could only dilute the quality of the nation's research effort.[30]

Congressional hearings were held to consider what course the nation should pursue, that proposed by Kilgore or Bush. Supporters for both funding mechanisms offered their opinions. Among those defending the Kilgore formula was Edmund Day, president of Cornell University, who spoke for the Association of Land-Grant Colleges and Universities. The land-grant schools hoped to see their formula funding spread through the federal government, and Day defended this process as a "counterweight" to the resource-concentrating project grant process.[31] Speaking

---

30. On MIT and Bush's desire to protect academic research, see S. S. Schweber, "Big Science in Context: Cornell and MIT," and Allan A. Needell, "From Military Research to Big Science: Lloyd Berkner and Science-Statesmanship in the Postwar Era," both in Peter Galison and Bruce Hevly (eds.), *Big Science: The Growth of Large-Scale Research* (Stanford: Stanford University Press, 1992), Chs. 6 and 11. Also see Bush's testimony, in Penick, op. cit., p. 86.

31. Penick, Pursell, Sherwood, and Swain, op. cit., p. 19.

in favor of the Bush plan on this point was the director of the Bureau of the Budget, Harold Smith, who proclaimed:

> Only by specific contacts, rather than general purpose contracts, can [the science agency] make sure that it is supporting in each institution only the type of research which that institution is qualified to perform. . . . It would obviously be improper and ineffective to give funds to private institutions without some assurance of their ability to further the purpose of the program.[32]

This debate over the funding mechanism continued on during the next several years, though the focus of contention over the Kilgore and Bush plans touched on more volatile matters, such as whether patent rights on grants would be retained by the federal government.

President Harry S Truman supported Kilgore's bill and vetoed legislation advocating Bush's plan in 1947, largely because Truman objected to Bush's proposal that the agency chief be only indirectly appointed by the president through the NRF governing board. After the Republicans gained control of Congress in 1946, however, Kilgore's centralizing plan was also doomed, as the Republicans expressed little desire to create another large, New Deal–style bureaucracy. Meanwhile, other federal agencies, on an almost piecemeal basis, filled the policy void and provided their own funding support for academic science. These organizations included the Office of Naval Research, NIH, the Atomic Energy Commission, and the departments of Agriculture, Commerce, and the Interior. Then, in 1950, President Truman signed legislation creating the National Science Foundation (NSF). Later, additional agencies, such as the National Aeronautics and Space Administration (NASA), the Department of Health, Education, and Welfare (DHEW), and the Environmental Protection Agency (EPA) rounded out the list of federal agencies supporting academic research.

What emerged from the 1950s and 1960s is a relatively decentralized federal science establishment, although one dominated by national security interests, in which academic research support comes in the form of project grants awarded to individual university researchers. This system differs significantly from those of many other countries. In the United Kingdom, government research funds are distributed through university grants; in Germany by project grants of the Deutsche Forschungsgemeinschaft; in France through centralized block funds allocated by the Centre Nationale de Recherche Scientifique; and in Finland on a student enrollment basis at the country's several universities.[33]

32. Ibid., p. 19.
33. Smith, op. cit., p. 45, and Georges Ferne, *Science and Technology in Scandinavia* (Harlow, Essex, UK: Longman, 1989), p. 65.

The American reliance on a merit-based project grant allocation process means that in funding basic science, most major research agencies turned to some sort of applicant review method that incorporates a variation of peer review. NSF, NIH, and the Office of Energy Research of the Department of Energy adopted the most familiar brand of peer review with the expert advice of external peer review panels. Other agencies, particularly those funding defense research and NASA, employed peer reviews conducted largely by in-house agency experts.[34] Peer review thus benefited the various federal agencies sponsoring research by ensuring that quality would be maintained in the projects they funded, and it benefited academic researchers by assuring them that project grants would not be capriciously administered through some sort of patronage system managed by agency program directors. Indeed, for such key agencies as NIH and NSF, university researchers themselves would serve on peer review panels. For these reasons, the peer review system became the dominant policy regime for allocating federal funds for academic science.

The use of project grants, either external or in-house peer review, and the primary selection criterion of scientific merit, however, have led to both a concentration of federal research money at the nation's universities and a concern about the equity of funding.

Equity and Peer Review

This concern for equity and the biases of peer review is a familiar and much-studied topic in the long-standing debate over the distribution of federal research funds.[35] During the post–World War II years, for example, federal legislation directly addressed the subject of equity of funding. When NSF was created in 1950, its enacting legislation called upon

---

34. *Federally Funded Research: Decisions for a Decade*, pp. 126–7; William C. Boesman and Christine Matthews Rose, "Equity, Excellence, and the Distribution of Federal Research and Development Funds," U.S. Congressional Research Service, April 25, 1988, Report No. 88-422 SPR, pp. CRS-73-74.

35. The list of studies on peer review is voluminous, but a good place to start is Daryl E. Chubin and Edward J. Hackett, *Peerless Science: Peer Review and U.S. Science Policy* (Albany: State University of New York Press, 1990). Chubin and Hackett are critical of peer review, but note that their reforms are very limited and keep intact the basic elements of peer review. Marjorie Sun, "Peer Review Comes Under Peer Review," *Science* 244 May 26, 1989, pp. 910–12. For the view that peer review is a valuable evaluation process but a governmental control device over scientists, see Chandra Mukerji, *A Fragile Power: Scientists and the State* (Princeton: Princeton University Press, 1989), Chs. 4 and 5. For an anecdotal account of the misuse of peer review, see Robert Bell, *Impure Science: Fraud, Compromise and Political Influence in Scientific Research* (New York: John Wiley & Sons, 1992), Ch. 1.

the agency "to strengthen research and education . . . throughout the United States, and to avoid undue concentration." Similarly, the founding authorization for NASA stated, "It is in the national interest that consideration be given to geographical distribution of Federal research funds whenever possible." When the Department of Transportation was established, its enabling authorization declared that "to the maximum extent possible . . . contracts to carry out research and development under this Act shall be geographically distributed throughout the United States."[36] These laws reflected the congressional intent that the process allocating research funding include a serious consideration of geographic equity.

Congress has also been sensitive to the charge that the primary cause of any unwarranted concentration of research funds is the bias of the peer review system. Consequently, at least since the 1970s, various congressional committees, the research agencies themselves, and such watchdog advisory organizations as the General Accounting Office (GAO) and the Congressional Research Service (CRS) have conducted numerous evaluations of the process to determine if it is fundamentally fair and to order improvements in its operation.

With few exceptions, these evaluations have supported the basic idea of peer review. In 1975, for example, after examining NSF's system, the House Science, Research and Technology Subcommittee reported that "No method superior to peer review has been found for judging the scientific merit of basic research proposals and the scientific competence of proposers."[37] These analyses have also proposed a variety of recommendations to improve the fairness and the procedural process of peer review. In 1986, NSF's Advisory Committee on Merit Review, consisting of external consultants, stated that "by and large the system is functioning well" and suggested modifications in the process.[38] The committee also recommended that the term "merit review" be substituted for "peer review." This adopted name change reflected the explicit and legitimate consideration of nontechnical criteria in the decision-making process, such as making awards in part on the basis of geographical distribution

36. William C. Boesman and Christine Matthews Rose, "Equity, Excellence, and the Distribution of Federal Research and Development Funds" (Washington, D.C.: U.S. Congressional Research Service, April 25, 1988), Report No. 88-422 SPR, p. CRS-5 and pp. CRS-16-17.

37. Erich Bloch, "Peer Review and Special Interest Facilities Funding," prepared for the National Academy of Sciences Roundtable, November 19, 1984, p. 2.

38. *Final Report: NSF Advisory Committee on Peer Review* (Washington, D.C.: National Science Foundation, 1986), p. D1. On the issue of renaming peer review, see *Academic Research Facilities: Financing Strategies* (Washington, D.C.: National Academy Press, 1986), especially Part II.

and assistance to women and minorities. More recently, the GAO in 1994 conducted an evaluation of NSF, NIH, and the National Endowment for the Humanities and declared, "Overall, peer review processes appear to be working reasonably well and are generally supported by peer reviewers."[39] As in the NSF study, GAO noted that the peer reviewers included many who were not representative of the top ten, elite research universities. The biases that GAO did detect in the peer review panels worked less against have-not or emerging institutions than against women and minorities, regardless of their institutional affiliation. GAO recommended a number of procedural techniques to remedy these biases.

Although these studies found peer or merit review to be generally fair and procedurally sound, they noted the inherent conflict between scientific excellence and equity and the tensions these qualities created particularly in a democratic society. As stated in a 1988 CRS report:

> Whatever the merits of the peer/merit review system, and there are many, that system is intended to select best proposals for scientific research from among those available mainly on the basis of present scientific merit regardless of extraneous factors, including geographical considerations. Thus, the peer/merit review system is likely to reinforce the existing geographical distribution of R&D funding . . . as long as it correlates with the distribution of research excellence.[40]

The issue, as CRS indicated, was the weight assigned to the various criteria employed in the peer review process. In addition, as long as scientific quality was given the highest priority, a certain concentration of resources would necessarily result.

John Silber's Criticism of Peer Review

John Silber, the president of Boston University and an ardent critic of peer review, however, has rejected this supposed correlation between excellence and consequential concentration of funds. Many of the most

---

39. *Peer Review: Reforms Needed to Ensure Fairness in Federal Agency Grant Selection* (Washington, D.C.: U.S. General Accounting Office, 1994), Report GAO/PEMD-94-1, p. 2; David Brown, "Grant-Awarding System Gets Decent Score in GAO Report," *Washington Post*, July 28, 1994.
40. Boesman and Rose, op. cit., p. CRS-75. On the topic of equity and excellence in a democratic society, see "Expertise and Democratic Decisionmaking: A Reader; Science Policy Study Background Report No. 7; Report Prepared by the Congressional Research Service, Library of Congress, Transmitted to the Task Force on Science Policy, Committee on Science and Technology, U.S. House of Representatives, December 1986."

"dramatic breakthroughs" academic science has produced in the last twenty-five years, Silber testified before Congress in 1987, such as high-temperature superconductivity, have taken place at such schools as the University of Houston and the University of Alabama, not Harvard. Yet, despite these successes, the peer review system rewards entrenched scientific interests rather than promotes the potential of new and exciting research discoveries. "This narrow channelling of a huge percentage of federal research support to only a tiny handful of universities is relentlessly promoted by the schools that benefit from it," Silber charged. "They claim it is only in this way that the quality of American science can be preserved. This is demonstrably not true." Moreover, this concentration of funds actually harms the development of science. "I do not believe the national interest is being well served," Silber asserted, "when year after year the bulk of the nation's federal research funds are channelled to a handful of already wealthy research universities. Yet that is the current state of affairs, and this unfair concentration of resources hobbles the nation's overall research enterprise."[41] Silber went on to note that ten universities received more than a quarter of all federal academic research funding and nearly 30 percent of all funding provided by NSF, and that the top twenty schools received 40 percent of total federal and 44 percent of all NSF research funding.

The cause of this biased funding, Silber continued, was the federal government's peer review system. These panels of scientific experts supposedly steer research grants to their colleagues who teach at the same schools and who conduct similar research. Citing a report issued by GAO in 1987, Silber noted that at NSF, twenty universities supplied approximately 25 percent of the members of all peer review panels. These same institutions submitted 24 percent of all proposals received by NSF, and they obtained 44 percent of all the funds distributed by the agency. Furthermore:

> The existing peer review system of necessity mirrors the accepted orthodoxy within any scientific discipline, and tends to reward conventional research at the expense of unconventional, new or imaginative ideas. . . . [I]t is the unavoidable consequence of any process that relies . . . on a relatively small group of people who are engaged in the same work, who talk mostly to one another, and whose position in that small community depends upon the continued acceptance of the work they have done in the past.[42]

Thus, peer review not only biases the federal government's research allocation system, it stifles new and creative research.

---

41. Silber, op. cit., pp. 2 and 3.
42. Ibid., p. 5.

The GAO report also indicated, Silber noted, that these top twenty schools, as determined by their receipt of federal research funding, have for most years remained the same schools. Between FY 1967 and FY 1984, 4 institutions dropped out of the top 20, while of the top 100, 19 universities were new to the list. Moreover, of the $5.6 billion in research funds distributed in FY 1984, 86 percent went to the top 100 schools.[43] Thus, given this concentration of resources and power, Silber maintained, no matter what an institution might do to improve its academic standing, it would always be at a disadvantage when competing for federal research grants allocated by the old boy network of peer review. One remedy for this bias was for Congress to assist individual institutions through earmarking. The various technical fixes recommended by GAO and NSF to repair peer review were inadequate. The system itself was biased, and the only way to benefit from the funds distributed through the process was to be an elite school to begin with, to have an institution's faculty already regarded as members of the old boy network. To accomplish this, "Congressional initiatives [should] provide excellent facilities to universities outside the top twenty [to] enable those universities to attract teams of first-rate scientists who, once appointed, compete successfully for research funds through the traditional system of peer review."[44]

Silber's relentless critique added another dimension to the earmarking debate, in that his solution of earmarking and the measure of its success focused not on geographical equity in the allocation of research grants, but rather on institutional equity. The difference between the notion of institutional and other forms of equity is telling and has had a substantial influence on the debate over academic earmarking. To achieve geographic equity, members of Congress have often requested some consideration for the regional dispersion of research funds in agency funding decisions, and at least one congressional committee has recommended that "at least one major center of excellence in research and technology [be located] in each appropriate region of the Nation." An example of this type of allocation was NSF's Science Development Program, funded in the mid-1960s. Energized by President John F. Kennedy's declaration that each region of the nation should have an outstanding research university and be actively supported by Congress, the program funded thirteen grants in 1965 that totaled $47.3 million. Grants were deliberately

43. *University Funding: Patterns of Distribution of Federal Research Funds to Universities* (Washington, D.C.: U.S. General Accounting Office, February 1987), Report No. GAO/RCED-878-67BR; "Same Universities Sharing U.S. Funds," *New York Times*, February 28, 1987.

44. Silber, op. cit., p. 3.

awarded to have-not regions, and universities ranked in the top twenty were eliminated from consideration, so second-tier institutions were the program's primary beneficiaries. Applications were funded on the basis of merit and through an extensive review process. Thus, the federal government's traditional understanding of equitable distribution has focused on geographical equity.[45]

By defining equity in terms of institutions rather than regions, however, university presidents like Silber have greatly expanded the notion of what constitutes equity, and therefore they have expanded the scope of the remedy. With institutional equity as the goal, a region could theoretically have not just one, but two, three, four, or more institutions of excellence. This would be an acceptable, and even a preferred means of achieving institutional equity. Thus, for President Silber, that Harvard University and MIT are centers of excellence in a single city or state is insufficient. Boston University, directly across the Charles River from Harvard and MIT, should also potentially be a center of excellence, and any funding system, such as peer review, that limits this potential is presumably unfair and biased. This view of equity led Rep. Sherwood Boehlert (R-NY) to counter that "Boston, for example, is not a city lacking for federal research funds, and the federal government does not have a responsibility to ensure that an equal number of top scientists get off at each stop on the Boston subway."[46]

Institutional equity, in any case, is only one measure by which to evaluate the fairness of the federal government's allocation of its research funds. In fact, compared to equity based on a state, regional, or per capita state or regional basis, only the standard of institutional equity – whereby, for Silber, all the major research universities should receive relatively equal federal resources – in any way justifies Boston University's earmarking. By every other measure, Massachusetts and New England on a regional and per capita basis receive well above the average amount of federal academic research funds.[47] Furthermore, despite Silber's charge of bias, Boston University ranks among the top fifty academic recipients of federal research dollars. So, strictly speaking, even in the case of institutional equity, if the federal government were to employ

45. Boesman and Rose, op. cit., p. CRS-10. This is the recommendation of the Subcommittee on Science, Research, and Development of the House Committee on Science and Aeronautics in 1964. On the NSF Science Development Program, see Howard Page, "The Science Development Program," in Harold Orlans (ed.), *Science Policy and the University* (Washington, D.C.: Brookings Institution, 1968), pp. 101–23.
46. "Congressman Sherwood Boehlert (R-NY) Remarks for the National Association of Independent Colleges and Universities, February 4, 1988."
47. On the various measures of equity and on Massachusetts's ranking, see Boesman and Rose, op. cit., especially Sections IV and V.

a formula-based distribution process to achieve any of a variety of measures of equity, Boston University's allocation would be reduced substantially rather than increased.

Nevertheless, this broader notion of institutional equity reflects the growing aspirations of numerous universities and colleges, many of which have been established since World War II, to attain elite research university status. The presidents of these schools chafe at the limited availability of federal research dollars, which are necessary to reach elite status, and they deeply resent any perceived procedural biases that makes their personal and institutional ambitions more difficult to realize.

At the same time, these presidents are likely to remain frustrated, for the notion of true institutional funding equity runs counter to the primary missions of the federal government's research agencies, and it is nearly impossible for the federal government to achieve true equity as long as it utilizes the project grant, peer review system. In the effort to promote the best science and technology with scarce funds, while remaining accountable to Congress and the taxpayer for the efficient and appropriate use of those funds, these research agencies employ a granting system whose primary criteria reward scientific excellence and merit. Yet, any system that does so is inherently hierarchical unless these research dollars simply are awarded on a formula-driven, entitlement basis, and even President Silber has yet to reject the peer-reviewed project grant process in favor of such formulas. This hierarchy exists because academic institutions do not possess equivalent faculty, endowments, laboratory equipment, graduate fellowships, generous state governments, wise, judicious, and competent administrators, and organizational cultures that encourage research excellence. Moreover, the federal government simply lacks the resources to support fully the research aspirations of even the top 100 universities on an equal basis, let alone the more than 3,000 universities and colleges in the United States. Thus, the ambitions of many presidents and their institutions will be constrained by hierarchical allocation systems like peer review, and it is not surprising that they seek funding by academic earmarking to gain federal research dollars.

The Entrepreneurial Decision to Earmark

On April 1, 1992, the *New York Times* ran a half-page story entitled "Tufts President Helps His University Stand Tall Amid Giants of Academe." Headed by a quarter-page photo, the story trumpeted the accomplishments of Tufts's president, Jean Mayer. Mayer, who had just announced his retirement, was described as a visionary, a leader who had transformed his school from "a small liberal arts college . . . into a research university of renown," one that had emerged "from under the shadow of neighboring universities like Harvard and the Massachusetts Institute of Technology." Among Mayer's important accomplishments, the *Times* continued, "have been the creation of a graduate school of nutrition [and] the building of New England's only school of veterinary medicine."[48]

What the article failed to mention was that Mayer also was the father of academic earmarking. Long before his presidential peers, Mayer had hired lobbyists to obtain earmarks for Tufts to support both its nutrition and veterinary schools. In this sense, Mayer was an activist leader, a seeker, a path breaker, someone who political scientist R. Douglas Arnold would classify as an entrepreneur. More to the point, an "entrepreneur" is an active rather than a passive gatherer of resources, one who fits Arnold's description of an entrepreneurial member of Congress:

> The entrepreneur, on his own initiative, searches for ways to obtain funds for his district. If the funds require a formal application, he will find an appropriate . . . organization and encourage it to apply. If no formal application is required, he will suggest to the allocating agency that his district deserves a share. From the beginning to the end he is the prime mover.[49]

Tufts's earmarking began in the late 1970s and continued throughout Mayer's presidency; the lobbyists Mayer hired went on to become the premier earmarking lobbyists in Washington, D.C. In total, Tufts has received more than $57 million in earmarks for research facilities and grants. Mayer, perhaps more than any other university president, brilliantly employed these earmarked funds as part of a strategic effort to improve the quality of his institution, and his precedent-setting choice

---

48. Fox Butterfield, "Tufts President Helps His University Stand Tall Amid Giants of Academe," *New York Times*, April 1, 1992. For an example of Mayer's obituaries, see Myrna Oliver, "Jean Mayer; Tufts Chancellor, Adviser on U.S. Nutrition," *Los Angeles Times*, January 3, 1993.

49. R. Douglas Arnold, *Congress and the Bureaucracy: A Theory of Influence* (New Haven: Yale University Press, 1979), p. 32. Arnold was referring to members of Congress. He compared entrepreneurial members to local agent members, who respond passively to constituent demands, rather than those who actively seek out benefits for their constituents. Another analysis of the idea of the entrepreneur is presented by Norman Forhlich, Joe A. Oppenheimer, and Oran R. Young, *Political Leadership and Collective Goods* (Princeton: Princeton University Press, 1971), especially Ch. 2. In this interpretation entrepreneurs are also seen as suppliers of goods, but they are not portrayed as active seekers, as in Arnold. Also see the role of the "policy entrepreneur" in John Kingdon, *Agendas, Alternatives, and Public Policies* (New York: HarperCollins, 1995), especially pp. 122–31, 179–82, and 204.

began the process of legitimizing academic earmarking for other university presidents.

Equally significant, neither in the *Times* article nor in the obituaries that were written to commemorate Mayer's death in 1993 was Mayer taken to task for this earmarking. Instead, the realization of his aspirations, ambitions, and vision was heralded. What the press noted was Tufts's growing research capacity, not the methods by which Mayer encouraged that growth. Furthermore, no sanctions were ever imposed on Mayer by academe's various professional societies for earmarking, and his career as president was never placed in jeopardy because he obtained earmarked funds. Mayer was rewarded many times over for this earmarking, never punished. Upon his retirement from Tufts in 1992, Mayer was replaced by John DiBiaggio, president of Michigan State University, another major recipient of academic earmarks.

In 1989, another *New York Times* story proclaimed, "Rutgers' Prestige Growing with Corporate Aid and Emphasis on Research." The *Times* praised Rutgers's "carefully drawn plan to raise its image" and noted that the "architect of Rutgers' campaign to shed its second-class image was Dr. Edward J. Bloustein." Bloustein had just passed away, and the article noted that one of his last great accomplishments was Rutgers's admittance into the prestigious Association of American Universities (AAU). Again, what the story failed to mention was that Rutgers had obtained nearly $58 million in earmarked federal funds and that, paradoxically, the AAU was higher education's great opponent of academic earmarking.[50]

Like Jean Mayer and Edward Bloustein, other university presidents have many incentives to engage in academic earmarking. Presidents are rewarded personally and professionally for raising the standards and standing of their institutions, even as the resources for doing so are greatly constrained. To secure these resources and to remedy what some regard as a biased peer review system, many university presidents have followed Mayer's lead, have become entrepreneurs in their own right, and have turned to academic earmarking for relief.

---

50. Robert Hanley, "Rutgers' Prestige Grows with Corporate Aid and Emphasis on Research," *New York Times*, December 18, 1992.

3

AAU and the Fight against Earmarking

Despite the powerful personal and institutional incentives that encourage university presidents to engage in earmarking, most do not. Not only do the majority of presidents abstain from earmarking, significant numbers have actively opposed it. Consequently, the struggle over earmarking within higher education has proved to be highly divisive and sometimes quite personal. In particular, the debate within the AAU has reflected both this intensity and the range of issues associated with the earmarking of federal research and facilities funding.

There are three major interrelated reasons for the opposition to earmarking among many university presidents. First, despite their varied interests, academics, especially those in the sciences, share what might be called a general cultural and professional commitment to the scientific method and peer review. From the earliest days of their training, scientists are educated in such fundamental techniques of the scientific method as hypothesis testing, the use of experimental controls, and the replication of experimental findings. As part of the basic process of scientific inquiry, the review of research findings by peers is essential in determining the validity of scientific claims. Through peer review, the integrity of science is protected in the conduct of research. Through peer review, science is insulated from unwarranted political and social pressures that have little to do with the advancement of science. Academics are taught the necessity of peer review in virtually all aspects of the scientific discovery process. Peer review is not only the method used to allocate federal research grants, it is also the procedure employed to determine faculty promotion and tenure, and to select journal articles and books for scholarly publication.

Allegiance to this process has resulted in scientific progress and technological success. When, after World War II, the various federal agencies incorporated peer review into their decision-making process for distributing research money to universities and colleges, this process was recommended by academics to the government.[1] Peer review was a product of their own academic culture, and so consequently, when it was adopted by the government, academics could reasonably trust that the day-to-day allocation of research funds was made on a scientific rather than a political basis, with the results benefiting themselves and the nation. "In the last 40 years," declared Richard Atkinson, former director of NSF and later president of the University of California, "American science has dominated the international prize competition and has generated the technological revolution that touches every aspect of our lives. A key ingredient in the American system is peer review."[2]

Violating the application of peer review in higher education is commonly regarded as a scientific and ethical, if not legal, transgression, and the penalties can be publicly humiliating. In one case, University of Utah scientists B. Stanley Pons and Martin Fleischmann announced at a press conference in 1989 that they had discovered "cold fusion," a way of producing nuclear fusion energy from basically a tabletop experiment. Although they received worldwide coverage by the press, these researchers proclaimed their findings without submitting them to scholarly review. Efforts to replicate their results soon proved to be difficult, if not impossible, and both the scientists and the president of the University of Utah were subject to vehement criticism throughout the scientific community and even by other faculty at Utah. "If standard, accepted scientific procedure had been followed," observed Patricia Hanna, a professor of philosophy at Utah, "I think a lot of this [criticism] could have been avoided." Bypassing of the review process extended to an attempt by the president of the university, Chase Peterson, to obtain earmarked federal funds for cold fusion research at his campus. Peterson appealed directly to Congress for this funding, supposedly because of the urgent nature of the project. Speaking of his congressional testimony, Peterson noted, "We said the upside of this was so strong, we shouldn't dawdle." Although members of the Utah congressional delegation demanded that the Department of Energy redirect some of its research budget to Utah, Peterson failed to get federal funding, and in the

---

1. For example, Vannevar Bush's famous report, *Science: The Endless Frontier* (Washington, D.C.: U.S. Government Printing Office, 1945), which promotes the insulation of grant-making to universities from political pressure, was heavily influenced by academics. Virtually every advisory committee Bush consulted in writing the report was dominated by academics.
2. Richard C. Atkinson, "Science Gets Political: Congress' Pork-Barrel Grants Threaten Our Progress," *Los Angeles Times*, March 29, 1987. Also see Richard C. Atkinson and William A. Blanpied, "Peer Review and the Public Interest," *Issues in Science and Technology*, Summer 1985, pp. 101–14.

end, the University of Utah was publicly and professionally embarrassed. As Hugo Rossi, dean of science at Utah, concluded, Utah's problem was one of "trying to reconcile the traditional values of a university with financial necessities."[3]

The Utah experience highlights the "collision," as Peterson later described it, that may occur between an institution's respect for the scientific method and peer review, which are part of the culture of a research university, and the aspirations and financial needs of the school. In this sense, some important aspects of the organizational culture of academic science serve as a countervailing force or check on the personal and institutional incentives that promote earmarking.[4]

A second explanation for the unwillingness of some universities to pursue earmarking is the formal opposition to this process shown by virtually all major higher education associations and scholarly societies. This explanation is closely related to the first, for the policy statements issued by these associations both reflect and help shape the culture of academic science. Universities and their faculties belong to a host of professional associations and organizations, in which membership is both institutional and individual. These associations provide various benefits and services to encourage membership, and, in general, universities and faculty greatly value their participation and membership.[5]

In some instances, these associations may temper the positions their members take on group policy issues. This is certainly true in the case of academic earmarking. It was the AAU, not an individual institution, that identified earmarking as a high-level policy matter, one that required the attention of university presidents, Congress, and the White House. Moreover, the debate over earmarking has largely been conducted among association members. These members have been tested

3. Kim A. McDonald, "At U. of Utah, Cold-Fusion Controversy Offers Lessons for Scientists, Managers," *Chronicle of Higher Education*, November 14, 1990, p. A8.
4. On the role of organizational culture, see Edgar Schein, *Organizational Culture and Leadership* (San Francisco: Jossey-Bass, 1992); Joanne Martin, *Cultures in Organizations* (New York: Oxford University Press, 1992); Jon Elster, *The Cement of Society* (Cambridge: Cambridge University Press, 1989); and Jane J. Mansbridge (ed.), *Beyond Self-Interest* (Chicago: University of Chicago Press, 1990), especially Part III.
5. On the importance of rewards and group maintenance in organizations, see Terry Moe, *The Organization of Interests* (Chicago: University of Chicago Press, 1980); Jack L. Walker, "The Origins and Maintenance of Interest Groups in America," *American Political Science Review* 77 (1983): 390–406; David C. King and Jack L. Walker, "The Provision of Benefits by Interest Groups in the United States," *Journal of Politics* 54 (1992): 394–426.

concerning their willingness to abide by group decisions or to ignore what has been determined as the collective good in favor of self-interest.

A third reason some institutions refrain from earmarking is that the peer review system distributes significant institutionalized rewards in the form of federal contracts and grants. Many universities benefit greatly from the existing system, and they are loath to see it undermined and bypassed. Many, though certainly not all, of the presidents who denounce earmarking are likely to lead the more prominent and better-endowed universities. As a result, when some presidents debated whether to follow the admonitions of various higher education associations against earmarking or to pursue their individual interests, they found that their individual interests were consistent with those of the associations.

Higher education's organized response to academic earmarking has, therefore, been determined largely within the context of these associations, where the opposing interests of the separate institutions, the multiple and sometimes conflicting roles and identities of university presidents, the influence of scientific norms and culture, and the dynamics of group membership all have served to influence policy making on this issue.

The Emergence of Academic Earmarking as a Policy Issue

Although the earmarking controversy began in 1983, with the allocations to Columbia University and the Catholic University of America, the practice of academic earmarking dates at least to 1977. In that year, President Jean Mayer of Tufts University secured a $10 million earmark for a veterinary school. Despite the size of this precedent-setting project, the first of many for Tufts, for several reasons it failed to generate a great debate over earmarking.

One reason is that Tufts's funding came from agriculture appropriations. Most university presidents, especially those of the elite research universities, have at best a passing knowledge of or interest in agricultural research and how it is funded. To be kind, agricultural research simply lacks the prestige of other academic sciences at many universities. A number of elite universities – for example, all but Cornell in the Ivy League – do not include agricultural studies or research in their curriculum or in their research agenda. At those institutions where they do exist, agriculture research facilities may be physically separated from the central campus. Consequently, Tufts's earmark from an agriculture bill meant little to most of the elite schools, as the debate over earmarking would later demonstrate.

The Columbia and Catholic University earmarks, however, were funded from energy and water appropriations. This funding supported more prestigious research: basic research involving high-energy physics – expensive research that wins Nobel Prizes, research that university presidents comprehend and value. Furthermore, earmarking in this bill threatened the programs and budgets of the Office of Energy Research in the Department of Energy, one of the federal agencies that truly employed peer review in its allocation of research grants.

Regardless of the funding source, however, the principal reason the Tufts earmark went unchallenged or unnoticed, compared to those for Columbia and Catholic, was that these two universities were members of the AAU. "Columbia was different," recalled Robert Rosenzweig, former president of AAU, comparing Tufts's earmark to Columbia's. "Columbia was an elite institution, and their participation in this way of doing business was very different from anything that had happened before."[6] In addition, the money that went to Columbia came from Department of Energy funding intended for Yale University and the University of Washington, two other AAU schools. The Columbia and Catholic earmarks, consequently, quickly came to the attention of AAU, forcing an evaluation of earmarking by that organization. Moreover, in 1983, unlike in 1977, someone in a prominent position identified earmarking as a fundamental long-term threat to academic science and was willing to lead the fight against it even at the significant personal cost of antagonizing some of his employers – the earmarking presidents of AAU. For most of the next decade, Robert Rosenzweig served as the principal spokesperson for those institutions and higher education associations in the fight against academic earmarking.

For Rosenzweig, a former Stanford University vice president and a political scientist educated at Yale, earmarking was simply damaging to the research enterprise and bad science policy. "Science funding through primarily political processes," declared Rosenzweig, "and without regards to careful judgement of the scientific merits of the work to be done is a pernicious practice, destructive of high-quality science, wasteful of the public's money, and erosive of public confidence in the integrity of universities and the political process."[7] Compelled by

6. Interview with Robert Rosenzweig, December 10, 1991.
7. "Testimony of Robert M. Rosenzweig, Former President, Association of American Universities, United States House of Representatives Committee on Science, Space and Technology, June 16, 1993," p. 1.

this view, Rosenzweig placed the topic of earmarking on the agenda of the AAU.

The Association of American Universities

The United States Senate is often referred to as the nation's most exclusive club, yet certainly a contender for that title is AAU. Whereas the Senate consists of 100 members, the AAU during most of its existence admitted fewer than 50 university presidents. By 1997, AAU's membership expanded to a grand total of just 60. Founded in 1900, the AAU is the primary representative of the interests of the nation's elite research universities in Washington, D.C. Expressing these interests, AAU has acted as the primary opponent of earmarking within higher education's leadership and representative associations. AAU is only one higher education association and lobbying organization among dozens in Washington, but it is preeminent in research-related issues, particularly academic earmarking.[8] The National Association of State Universities and Land Grant Colleges (NASULGC), for example, with its 182 member institutions, has played a role in the earmarking debate, yet it generally defers to AAU leadership on the issue. Other umbrella organizations, such as the American Council on Education, the National Academy of Sciences, and the American Association for the Advancement of Science, have also generally followed AAU's position on earmarking. Yet, although collectively AAU formally opposes the practice, many of the association's members are among higher education's most egregious earmarking institutions.

If there is an organization that is perceived as an elitist "old boy's club," as one of its member presidents put it, the AAU is that association. With some exceptions, AAU's membership roster includes the nation's most prominent academic institutions. The universities that established AAU include Berkeley, Chicago, Columbia, Harvard, Michigan, Pennsylvania, Princeton, and Yale. Not surprisingly, therefore, AAU membership is generally regarded as a mark of distinction among college and university presidents. "AAU is besieged, literally besieged by folks who want to belong to it," observed Paul Gray, former president of MIT.

---

8. On the various higher education associations, see Stephen K. Bailey, *Education Interest Groups in the Nation's Capital* (Washington, D.C,: American Council on Education, 1975), and Lauriston R. King, *The Washington Lobbyists for Higher Education* (Lexington, MA: Lexington Books, 1975).

I mean I would get lobbied simply as an AAU president, even before I was a member of the executive committee. I would get lobbied by significant MIT alumni in states that had institutions, including New Jersey, which were trying to get into the AAU. I got lobbied by members of state legislatures, by governors, on behalf of their institutions. So there's a very constant, high pressure for new institutions to be brought into the AAU.[9]

To become a member of AAU, a school must be invited to apply for admission and undergo a review process that examines such factors as the size of the library, the number of graduate students and doctorates awarded, and, perhaps most important, the size of its research base, as measured in part by the dollar value of the federal grants it receives. The applicant must be approved by three-fourths of the general AAU membership.

AAU is a voluntary association of university chief executives. Only the presidents and chancellors of the member universities and the top AAU staff, for example, are allowed to attend the association's semi-annual general meetings. Presidents who are unable to attend the meetings may not send alternates in their place. Although the organization relies on a handful of committees to expedite business, decision making is highly collegial. The day-to-day activities of the association are conducted by a staff of eight, directed by AAU's president. The AAU presidency, in turn, is an appointed, full-time administrative position, which derives much of its influence from personal relationships with the member presidents, through the direction of the staff, and by setting the agendas for the various working committees and the biannual meetings.

AAU and the Moratorium on Earmarking

Higher education's first organized response to earmarking came in October 1983. At a general meeting of the AAU, Robert Rosenzweig raised the matter of the Columbia and Catholic earmarks. Rosenzweig brought a resolution he had drafted, which called upon universities and members of Congress "to refrain from actions that would make scientific decisions a test of political influence rather than a judgement on the quality of work to be done. . . . We believe that processes based on the informed peer judgements of other scientists need to be preserved and strengthened."[10] The resolution passed by a nearly unanimous vote, with three presidents abstaining, including those of Columbia and

9. Interview with Paul Gray, November 28, 1990.
10. "AAU Statement on Decision Making in Federal Funding for Research Facilites," AAU, October 25, 1983.

Catholic universities. The need for the resolution was obvious, Rosenzweig stated. "The absence of a statement of this group of universities would have left open the suggestion that it was now every man for himself, and that would have been unfortunate."[11]

At Rosenzweig's urging, NASULGC also soon adopted a statement on earmarking. Like the AAU resolution, the NASULGC version called upon the federal government to increase its support for academic research facilities and denounced the use of earmarks in the allocation of federal funding. "The outcome of such a process [of earmarking]," the NASULGC resolution stated, "could be an irrational system of distribution based solely on political influence." The AAU and NASULGC statements were quickly supported by similar resolutions offered by the National Academy of Sciences, the American Council on Education, the Council of Scientific Society Presidents, the American Association for the Advancement of Science, the National Science Board, the American Association of State Colleges and Universities, the American Physical Society, the Federation of American Societies for Experimental Biology, and the Council of Graduate Schools.[12]

In retrospect, that Rosenzweig obtained any type of resolution against earmarking was a remarkable success. For AAU, despite its elite status, was and is highly stratified in terms of its member institutions' research excellence and their relative financial resources. Earmarking, Rosenzweig observed,

> has been a difficult issue within this organization. It had generated some very, very tough discussions among the members. Feelings were hurt and divisions were generated. . . . There is within AAU a have and a have-not division. Everybody looks at AAU as sort of a homogeneous group of wealthy institutions. Far from it. We have a number of institutions that feel

11. Interview with Robert Rosenzweig, December 10, 1991.
12. "Statement on Federal Funding of Academic Facilities," National Association of State Universities and Land-Grant Colleges, November 14, 1983. Also see "Scientific Review of Federal Science Projects" by the Council of Scientific Society Presidents, August 1, 1985; "Resolution on Scientific Peer Review," American Association for the Advancement of Science, May 30, 1985; "Scientific Review of Research Facilities Funding," The American Physical Society, January 20, 1985; "Peer Review," Federation of American Societies for Experimental Biology, May 23, 1984; "Resolution in Decision Making in the Federal Funding for Research Facilities," The Council of Graduate Schools in the United States, December 1983; "Resolution 23," American Association of State Colleges and Universities, November 22, 1983; "Federal Funding for Research Facilities and Instrumentation," National Academy of Sciences, October 1983; and "National Science Board Statement on Bypassing Merit Revew in the Funding of Academic Research Facilities," undated. These are all association resolutions supporting peer review in opposition to earmarking.

themselves seriously disadvantaged in the competition for funds. . . . That's an issue that's never far below the surface in this organization, and it affected the way the debate was carried on among us.[13]

So, to the extent that the have-not schools were willing to support the idea of a resolution, a significant blow had been struck against earmarking. Enforcing such a resolution, however, was another matter.

Despite the AAU and NASULGC resolutions, it soon became clear that neither organization would punish any member university that violated them. Because these associations are voluntary, their penalties, ranging from public scolding to outright expulsion, were limited in scope and effectiveness. These options were never employed, as Rosenzweig recounted:

> What we didn't do, and never seriously considered doing, although it was proposed by at least one of our members, was sanctioning the institutions that had engaged in this practice. I ran into one former member yesterday in a meeting and he said, "you made a big mistake." He said that if we'd thrown them out then, it might have made a big difference. Well I don't know. I don't know whether it would have or not, but it simply wasn't in the cards. Nobody was prepared even to think in those terms.[14]

Rosenzweig's view on sanctions was supported by many of the AAU presidents, including those who, like Vanderbilt University President Joe B. Wyatt, opposed earmarking. Testifying before Congress, Wyatt remarked, "Some ask why organizations do not impose sanctions on members who engage in the practice. The answer is that these are voluntary organizations. They simply cannot control the behavior of their members or impose sanctions on them."[15] Nevertheless, by avoiding any effort to impose a sanction, whether expelling the worst earmarking offenders or identifying and criticizing them publicly, Rosenzweig and those presidents who opposed earmarking effectively destroyed their ability to apply the stick as well as offer the carrot in negotiating with earmarking institutions.

Moreover, by failing to take into account an institution's record on earmarking when it applied for membership, AAU actually provided an incentive for schools to earmark. As scrupulous as AAU's membership review process is, candidate institutions have never been evaluated on

13. Interview with Robert Rosenzweig, December 10, 1991.
14. Ibid.
15. "Testimony Presented Before the Committee on Armed Services, Presented by Chancellor Joe B. Wyatt, Vanderbilt University, On Behalf of Association of American Universities, Association of Graduate Schools, Council of Graduate Schools, National Association of State Universities and Land-Grant Colleges, June 20, 1989," p. 3.

the basis of whether they earmarked. Since the controversy began, AAU admitted several institutions, such as the University of Florida (1985), Rutgers University (1989), and the University of Arizona (1985), that have obtained millions of dollars in earmarks. Thus, Rosenzweig and those AAU presidents who opposed earmarking were left with little more than personal appeals, peer group suasion, concern for personal standing and reputation within the group of presidents, and voluntary moratoriums to induce their colleagues to refrain from earmarking. Yet, even the idea of "reputation" requires that some reward or punishment stem from one's behavior; for those presidents who decided to earmark, their colleagues could offer little in terms of a reward, and they refused to punish.[16]

During the next few years, from 1984 to 1987, Rosenzweig sought to control earmarking by publicizing its adverse consequences for academic science and by defeating individual projects as they came up for approval in the various appropriations and authorizations bills. This process involved supporting sympathetic members of Congress and educating as many others as possible on the issue.

Throughout the earmarking controversy, AAU turned to a few members who acted as opponents of earmarks. During the debate over the FY 1986 Urgent Supplemental Appropriations Bill, for example, Sen. John Danforth (R-MO) sponsored an amendment to delete ten projects worth $80.6 million from the bill. The Senate approved the amendment by a vote of 58 to 40, but nine of the projects were restored during the House–Senate conference. The conference deleted one project, a $25 million earmark for Arizona State University, because Sen. Barry Goldwater (R-AZ) voted with Danforth and opposed the earmark. Danforth's ultimate defeat greatly disheartened Rosenzweig, forcing him to reconsider AAU's strategy:

> That experience led directly to a change in AAU's approach to the issue. It seemed clear that it was difficult, if not impossible, to defeat an earmark once it had surfaced, had a sponsor, and was the subject of agreement inside the Appropriations Committees. In fact, it was often not possible to learn of projects until they had reached that point, and so the prospect of fighting them legislatively was not a happy one.[17]

16. Memorandum on "AAU Policy on Earmarking and Research Facility Funding" from Robert M. Rosenzweig to AAU presidents and chancellors, April 6, 1989, p. 2. On the idea of reputation, see Dennis Chong, *Collective Action and the Civil Rights Movement* (Chicago: University of Chicago Press, 1991), especially Ch. 3.
17. Interview with Robert Rosenzweig, December 19, 1991.

Furthermore, Rosenzweig and his allies within AAU noted with dismay that one AAU president after another ignored the 1983 resolution and pursued earmarks. In 1985 and 1986, such AAU universities as Brown, Indiana, Minnesota, North Carolina, Northwestern, Oregon, Purdue, and Tulane received earmarked funding.

To formulate a new plan of action, a special committee was formed to study the earmarking issue in the fall of 1986.[18] Chaired by Donald Langenberg, chancellor of the University of Illinois, Chicago Circle and a former deputy director of NSF, the committee's legitimacy was enhanced by its being cosponsored by NASULGC, the Council of Graduate Schools, and the American Council on Education. In March 1987, the Langenberg committee released its report, which attempted to answer the question of how a consideration for merit could be preserved in the face of congressional earmarking. The report offered three suggestions, which many university presidents felt would dramatically undermine the peer review process.

First, and most controversial, the report recommended that AAU and the other associations "reexamine their policy positions" and "explore arrangements that would make the congressional earmark process more reflective of both national needs and the concerns of the research community for merit."[19] Congress would be encouraged to incorporate some consideration for merit in its earmarking decisions, perhaps by employing agency evaluations in the appropriations process. The associations would "emphatically" continue to promote merit in allocating federal research funds. Yet, presumably the trade-off for Congress's employing some elements of merit in its earmarking decisions was that the associations would refrain from criticizing members of Congress and their earmarks.

The committee did provide one major exemption to this proposal. The associations would continue to oppose any earmark that came at

18. The committee's conclusions were heavily influenced by its charge: "The charge to the committee asks it to review the present dilemma and to suggest ways in which university and government leaders might be brought into agreement on how funding decisions on university science and engineering research facilities and projects can be based on informed judgements of intellectual quality while recognizing other legitimate interests." Those other interests implicitly included those raised to justify earmarking. "AAU Committee to Study Special Earmarking of University Research Facility Funds," AAU Press Release, October 1, 1986.

19. "Report of The Working Committee on Principles, Policies, and Procedures in the Award of Federal Funds for University Research Facilities and Research Projects," March 1987, p. 11.

the expense of peer-reviewed programs in the six major research agencies or the two National Endowments. Thus, if an earmark appeared in, say, the NSF budget, the associations would fight the project. Yet, if the earmark simply appeared somewhere in the Veterans Administration–Housing and Urban Development–Independent Agencies appropriations subcommittee bill, which provided funding for NSF, but did not specify NSF or any other of the six agencies as the funding source for the earmark, then the associations would refrain from criticizing that project if Congress considered merit when deciding to fund the earmark. Thus, to be consistent with the committee's recommendations, the higher education associations would be forced to make this assessment of every earmark and, perhaps more important, to demonstrate clearly to the scientific community and to the public why some earmarks were good and others bad, even when these projects appeared in the same piece of legislation.

Langenberg and his committee recognized how this proposal would be received by many opponents of earmarking: "It will be argued that any conceivable arrangement of the kind suggested here would have the effect of legitimizing an activity that many believe inherently destructive, without providing genuine assessments of scientific merit. That is not our intention."[20] Nevertheless, one committee member, Arthur Sussman, general counsel and vice president for administration of the University of Chicago, offered a dissenting opinion against Langenberg's "modification" of policy. "The higher education associations should continue their principled opposition to earmarking," Sussman declared. "Its elimination, not its modification, is in the long range interests of science and higher education."[21] Sussman argued that the Langenberg committee's proposal effectively terminated higher education's fight against earmarking. Congress would be given higher education's explicit approval to earmark if members agreed to include some undetermined degree of merit in their earmarking decisions.

Second, the report recommended that higher education encourage Congress to develop and fund a meaningful facilities program, thus reducing the incentive for universities to seek earmarks. Other forms of support for facilities, such as providing for more generous depreciation schedules in the calculation of indirect costs, were proposed, as was the repeal of provisions in the 1986 Tax Reform Act that limited the tax-

---

20. Ibid., p. 12.
21. "Addendum: Dissenting Statement by Arthur M. Sussman," p. 19.

exempt bonding authority for private universities. Third, the committee recommended that AAU strengthen its efforts to educate the public and members of Congress on the negative effects of earmarking.

The committee's report was debated at a general meeting of the AAU in April 1987 and was quickly subjected to intense criticism. David P. Gardner, president of the University of California system, declared that with the exception of the first recommendation, the others were essentially "irrelevant." The first recommendation, furthermore, was "an invitation to something that is inherently destructive." Virtually all earmarks contained some aspect that could be classified as meritorious, Gardner concluded. "What facility need is not meritorious?" Thus, just as Sussman argued, members of Congress would employ their own casual, weakened notions of merit in their earmarking process, thereby overriding the formal peer review process while gaining higher education's stamp of approval.[22]

More debate followed, with some presidents, including Howard Swearer of Brown University, Paul Olum of the University of Oregon, and William Gerberding of the University of Washington disagreeing with Gardner and calling for a broader interpretation of merit and support for the report. Other presidents, particularly Hanna Gray of the University of Chicago, Donald Kennedy of Stanford University, and Benno Schmidt of Yale University, argued that any embrace of earmarking would prove to be highly detrimental to academic science.

The members finally agreed to vote on a resolution to adopt the Langenberg report and to "discuss it further." Until the presidents concluded that discussion, however, AAU would operate under the proposition that earmarking harmed the interests of the nation and higher education. More important, the resolution stated that AAU would agree to a moratorium on earmarking even as it worked with Congress to establish new academic facilities programs.

The membership adopted the resolution by a 43 to 10 vote, with two abstentions. In a press release, Rosenzweig announced that AAU intended "to avoid expending the organization's energies in what are likely to be vain efforts to defeat earmarks once they have become visible in the Congress." AAU would continue to fight individual earmarks that funded research projects, compared to earmarks for facilities, and earmarks that were funded from the major peer-reviewed budgets such

22. AAU Meeting Minutes, "AAU Spring Meeting, Washington, D.C., April 6–7, 1987," pp. 1–6.

as NSF and NIH. Furthermore, he stated, sanctions would not be imposed on member institutions that violated the moratorium.[23]

The Effects of the Moratorium and the Pennsylvania Earmark

For the second time in five years, AAU's membership overwhelmingly adopted a resolution opposing earmarking and requesting its members to refrain voluntarily from seeking earmarks. Members who evaded the moratorium would not be punished, and to complicate further any attempts at enforcement, Rosenzweig opposed efforts by the press and other sources to publish lists of schools obtaining earmarks, including AAU institutions. Thus, if Rosenzweig had his way, potentially and actually offending schools would experience only personal persuasion and private reprimand.

The AAU moratorium was quickly put to the test. Between 1987, the year the moratorium was adopted, and 1989, at least seven additional AAU schools that had previously avoided earmarks obtained them: the universities of Arizona, Brandeis, Johns Hopkins, Michigan State, Nebraska, Washington, and Wisconsin. These schools had, for the most part, either voted against or abstained during the vote on the moratorium.

The most devastating defection from the moratorium, however, came in 1988, when President Sheldon Hackney of the University of Pennsylvania hired the lobbying firm of Cassidy and Associates to obtain a $10 million earmark. Hackney was the first president to vote for the moratorium and then reverse his position. When word of his decision reached his fellow presidents, Hackney immediately came under intense personal pressure from Paul Gray, president of MIT, and Derek Bok, president of Harvard, as well as a number of other Ivy League presidents, to change his mind.[24] As Hackney recalled, his decision forced him to choose between two loyalties: "The AAU seemed to be getting nowhere in its efforts to . . . get a facilities program authorized and appropriated. . . . During that time I certainly recognized my responsibility as a citizen and a university president to think and act in the public interest,

---

23. "AAU Votes to Observe Moratorium on Earmarking," AAU Press Release, May 14, 1987; Leslie Maitland Werner, "40 Universities Agree to Reject Disputed Grants," *New York Times*, May 22, 1987.

24. Interview with Paul Gray, November 28, 1990. According to Gray, "There was an enormous amount of pressure put on the president of Pennsylvania by his peers. I don't mean the fifty-eight AAU presidents, but most of the Ivy presidents and myself."

but I also have a responsibility to my institution to do what's best for it."[25] Hackney, who later became director of the National Endowment for the Humanities under President Bill Clinton, chose, in his own words, to earmark rather than stand by his own vote on the moratorium, as well as fulfill his duties as a citizen in behalf of the public interest. Bok called Hackney's action "a major defection" and "an unpleasant incident." When Boston University's John Silber learned of Hackney's decision, he proclaimed the AAU presidents "have lost the war," and that they were "selfish, hypocritical and arrogant in telling Congress not to do what it wants to do."[26]

Pennsylvania's decision caused Rosenzweig particular consternation. In a letter to five AAU presidents, he expressed his concern about the effect Hackney's new position would have on the fight against earmarking:

> Should Penn persist in its efforts, that fact, plus the visibility and prestige of the institution, will change the balance of forces in some way. Some Presidents will undoubtedly feel greater pressure from their faculties and deans, as well as from their congressional delegations. They and others may see no further reason to adhere to a policy that is eroding before their eyes.[27]

Rosenzweig's response, to booster the morale and purpose of AAU's struggle, centered on the passage of yet another nonbinding resolution against earmarking.

In April 1989, AAU Chairman Frank Rhodes, president of Cornell University, opened AAU's spring general meeting with the observation that earmarking was "probably the most divisive topic" ever considered by AAU, coupled with the plea that the presidents not make "moral judgments" about one another. The discussion then quickly turned to the issue of the moratorium. In preparation for the meeting, the Executive Committee drafted a new resolution that called for increased federal funding for facilities and denounced earmarking, but it failed to mention the moratorium. When asked why the draft made no mention of the

25. Interview with Sheldon Hackney, August 13, 1991.
26. Interview with Derek Bok, November 2, 1990. Said Bok, "I think he [Hackney] felt that he encountered a lot of disapproval by people whose good opinion he valued." Stanley Meisler, "Halls of Ivy Research the Pork Barrel," *Los Angeles Times*, April 15, 1988.
27. "AAU Memorandum to Richard Atkinson, James Duderstadt, William Gerberdin, Eamon Kelly, and Harold Shapiro, from Robert M. Rosenzweig, Subject: Earmarking, February 14, 1989."

moratorium, Rhodes replied that "it is difficult for us to go on making statements we do not intend to keep." Rhodes and Rosenzweig added that the old statement was still in force, but that "compliance was a matter of individual choice." Some members announced that the absence of explicit language supporting the moratorium would be publicly misunderstood and regarded as a retreat by AAU. Several other presidents declared that the moratorium was infeasible and unequitable, as federal research funds were too concentrated in their geographic distribution.[28] Despite their differences, however, the members soon agreed upon the first proposal, the "AAU Statement on Research Facilities," which called for new facilities money in programs that would be administered by NSF and NIH.

The resolution also expressed support for NSF's Experimental Program to Stimulate Competitive Research (EPSCOR) program. Authorized by Congress in 1978, EPSCOR was established in response to members' concern about the geographical concentration of NSF's research grant. By FY 1994, six other agencies had established EPSCOR programs, awarding a total of $65.7 million to academic institutions.[29] EPSCOR was created as a type of affirmative action program designed to aid less successful states and their universities in their competition for federal research funds. As of 1997, eighteen states became eligible for merit-reviewed EPSCOR grants funded through NSF. Because these grants were allocated through a competitive review process, they were consistent with AAU's policy that merit may include decision-making criteria other than purely scientific achievement. Thus, AAU could endorse NSF programs targeted at women and minority researchers as long as these programs employed competition and external review in the distribution of awards.

By a mail ballot, the presidents also approved the second proposal, the "1989 AAU Resolution on Facilities Funding," which dealt with the moratorium. The resolution asked that AAU institutions and members of Congress refrain from earmarking, "at least" in the five major federal research agencies: NSF, NIH, NASA, and the departments of Defense and Energy. The resolution defined earmarking as "appropriations that

---

28. For the debate over earmarking at the spring 1989 meeting, see the minutes of the meeting: "AAU Spring Membership Meeting, April 16–18, 1989," especially pages 3–6 and 8–12.

29. On EPSCOR, see NSF's annual program solicitation guidelines for the program and the executive summary handout. Also see *Science & Engineering Indicators, 1996* (Washington, D.C.: National Science Foundation, 1996), pp. 4–33.

designate funding . . . without prior designation either from the agency concerned or from a competitive process in which proposals . . . are evaluated first in an open, competitive review of their merit."[30]

Defining an Earmark and the Problem of Funding Facilities

Although AAU's presidents approved the resolution, its wording raised the critical issue of defining an earmark. A precise definition was needed in order to outline the scope of the problem to friends and foes alike.[31] Clarity was needed in defining an unwanted earmark because in fact the federal government supported a variety of higher education programs through earmarking, or specifically designating funds for a particular recipient in appropriations legislation and reports. Acceptable earmarks, in other words, had to be distinguished from unacceptable ones so that criticism could be directed at the types of projects that AAU considered to be a true threat to peer review. Moreover, a number of publications had begun to publish lists of earmarks, and if AAU did not define a earmark in the context of this controversy, the press and other interested parties would do so.

One category of earmarks that neither side of the debate associated with the issue were the direct line-item appropriations the government provided for a number of Historically Black Colleges and Universities (HBCU), Gallaudet College in Washington, D.C. for the hearing impaired, and several Native American schools. The government's relationship with some of these institutions dates back to the post–Civil War era. Howard University's base budget of hundreds of millions of dollars is funded by the District of Columbia Appropriations Subcommittee and has never been accused of being improperly supported. Nevertheless, when a group of historically black medical schools banded together

---

30. "AAU Spring Membership Meeting, April 16–18," Attachment 2, "1989 AAU Resolution on Facilities Funding."
31. On the role of the various definitions of earmarking, see James D. Savage, "Where's the Pork? To Root It Out, We Must Begin with a Strict Definition of What Is Unacceptable," *Issues in Science and Technology*, Spring 1993, pp. 21–4. On problem definition in policy analysis, see, for example, David Dery, *Problem Definition in Policy Analysis* (Lawrence: University Press of Kansas, 1984); Duncan MacRae, Jr., and James A. Wilde, *Policy Analysis for Public Decisions* (Belmont, Calif.: University Press of America, 1985), Ch. 2; and David A. Rochefort and Roger W. Cobb, "Problem Definition, Agenda Access, and Policy Choice," *Policy Studies Journal* 21 (1993): 56–71.

to obtain funding for specific research projects through earmarking, these projects were generally considered to be academic earmarks because they were not part of the regular base budgets for these institutions and because the HBCUs could have competed for these funds in Department of Health and Human Services research programs.[32]

Another set of earmarks the associations excluded from the earmarking debate were those supporting the university-managed Federally Funded Research and Development Centers (FFRDCs) and University Affiliated Research Centers (UARCs). Nineteen FFRDCs and seven UARCs either receive their appropriations through designated earmarks, or their management contracts have historically been awarded without the benefit of competition. Most of these contracts, such as those for the Applied Physics Laboratory at Johns Hopkins University, the Stanford Linear Accelerator, the Lawrence Livermore and Los Alamos laboratories managed by the University of California, and the Lincoln Laboratory at MIT, stemmed from federal funding during World War II and the Cold War, with their contracts awarded and renewed on a sole-source basis.

In 1989, Sen. Sam Nunn (D-GA), an opponent of academic earmarking, added a provision to a defense authorizations bill requiring the Department of Defense to award its funds for academic institutions through competition. AAU, NASULGC, and the Association of Graduate Schools, in turn, requested that these contracts be exempted from the new requirements on the grounds that while FFRDCs and UARCs were managed by universities, their activities differed significantly from the conduct of basic academic research. Although a few defenders of earmarking, such as President Jean Mayer of Tufts University, claimed that the associations advocated a double standard to protect the funding for these major university-managed research units, AAU and its allies effectively excluded the FFRDCs and UARCs from the earmarking debate. They pointed to the unique historical origins of these projects as the basis for the exemptions, noted that FFRDCs and UARCs supported development rather than basic or applied science, and stated that much of the research activity at these sites was classified, whereas university research is predominantly unclassified. Defense funding for its FFRDCs and UARCs effectively continues to be sole-source, as the Department of Defense generally regards its contracts with these units to be simple

32. Colleen Cordes and Katherine McCarron, "Academe Gets $763 Million in Year from Congressional Pork Barrel," *Chronicle of Higher Education*, June 16, 1993, p. A21.

renewals, with the agency's internal peer review process, known as the "comprehensive review," evaluating the performance of the contracts.[33]

Although AAU offered compelling and successful arguments to dismiss HBCUs, FFRDCs, and UARCs from the debate over academic earmarking, other categories of research, particularly research funded by the Department of Agriculture, proved to be more troubling for AAU. William Gerberding, president of the University of Washington, raised the issue of how earmarks should be defined when he abstained on the AAU moratorium vote because of his decision to seek an earmark for his College of Ocean and Fishery Sciences. In his letter to the AAU executive committee explaining his decision, Gerberding stated that "I'm not sure that I understand – or, if I understand, whether I agree with – the definition of 'earmarking.' For example, I do not favor exempting Department of Agriculture–funded facilities from the definition."[34] The AAU resolution had denounced earmarking only if it affected the funding of the five major federal research agencies, despite the fact that by 1989, a quarter of all earmarks that had been identified at that time by the press and other sources originated in the agriculture appropriations bill. A strict reading of the resolution clearly indicated that if a school obtained an earmark from the Department of Agriculture, even if the project itself involved the construction of, say, a biomedical facility rather than an agricultural facility, that project was above AAU's reproach. Nevertheless, by splitting definitional hairs to obtain dollar amounts that for some institutions were trivial given the size of their research base, and even embarrassing when the earmarks became public knowledge, these universities helped to undermine the principle of peer and merit review and aided in the legitimization of earmarking.

Rosenzweig and AAU were motivated for several reasons to exempt agriculture from the definition of earmarking. Many of the AAU schools had received earmarks from the agriculture bill, and criticizing these

33. Jean Mayer, "Earmarking: A Question of Fairness," *Forum for Applied Research and Public Policy*, Fall 1992, pp. 84–8. Colleen Cordes, "Critics of 'Earmarked' Funds for Specific Universities Now Seek to Weaken Law They Backed," *Chronicle of Higher Education*, September 13, 1989, p. A31. On the implementation of the Nunn rule, see *Defense Research and Development: Mandated Reports on Noncompetitive Awards to Colleges and Universities* (Washington, D.C.: U.S. General Accounting Office, December 1994), Report GAO/NSIAD-95-72. Also see communication with Anita K. Jones, professor of engineering, University of Virginia, and former director of defense research and engineering, Department of Defense, during the first term of the Clinton administration.
34. "Letter to AAU Executive Committee from William P. Gerberding, Subject, Proposed AAU Resolution on Facilities Funding, May 9, 1989."

projects only antagonized more AAU presidents. Moreover, the powerful chair of the House Appropriations Committee, Jamie Whitten (D-MS), also chaired the agriculture appropriations subcommittee. Irritating Whitten, who favored earmarking, would do little to strengthen AAU's political standing with Congress. Furthermore, in March 1989, the University of California's Office of the President released an analysis of earmarking, which showed that nearly 30 percent of the earmarked dollars that could be identified for the preceding nine years had benefited AAU schools.[35] These data embarrassed AAU because, for the first time, the earmarking AAU institutions were named. Many of these universities received earmarks from the agriculture bill, and Rosenzweig charged that they should not have been included in the analysis. Agriculture funding, he argued, "traditionally" had been earmarked, and the federal government had a long-established "special relationship" with land-grant colleges.[36] In fact, an internal Department of Agriculture study revealed that earmarking was relatively limited in the late 1970s and that institutional formula funds provided the bulk of agricultural academic research support. Also, a significant number of agricultural researchers favored an expansion of Agriculture's limited competitive grants program in opposition to the growing number of earmarked projects.[37]

Other AAU presidents soon criticized the exclusion of agriculture from the association's definition of earmarking. Vanderbilt University President Joe Wyatt, for instance, asked his fellow presidents, "Is AAU's stated position in opposition to earmarks undercut by tolerance for Agriculture earmarks?"[38] Within a few years, Rosenzweig conceded that the AAU moratorium should have included the Department of Agriculture. The lack of clarity and precision in AAU's resolution, however, enabled numerous institutions, including AAU's most elite universities, to redefine what constituted an earmark so that they could solicit federal

35. James D. Savage, "The Distribution of Academic Earmarks in the Federal Government's Appropriations Bills, FY 1980–89," University of California, Berkeley Institute of Governmental Studies Working Paper 89-5, 1989.
36. Colleen Cordes, "Congressional Practice of Earmarking Research Grants Does Not Broaden Allocation of Funds, Study Finds," *Chronicle of Higher Education*, March 1, 1989, p. 22.
37. Dale L. Stansbury, "An Inventory and Analysis of Congressional Earmarking of Agricultural Research: Trends and Inflections Between Fiscal Year 1978 and Fiscal Year 1989," prepared for Science and Education, U.S. Department of Agriculture, December 1988.
38. Letter to Members of AAU from Joe B. Wyatt, September 25, 1991.

funds without AAU's criticism that they were engaging in pork barrel science.

The variations and strict readings of the definitions were readily apparent to the university presidents. At the University of California's Office of the President, for example, Vice President for Budget and University Relations William B. Baker worried that the AAU resolution might indeed include Department of Agriculture funding when, at that very time, Baker was planning how the university might secure for itself an earmarked trade center from the agriculture appropriations bill. Writing to President David Gardner regarding the resolution, Baker warned:

> My primary concern here is whether this statement is intended to apply to all budget functions including agriculture. . . . Our efforts seeking funding for a trade center may be criticized if this new definition explicitly includes earmarking from all sources. . . . Our position of seeking ag [agriculture] funds is therefore somewhat Pollyannish.[39]

The AAU resolution excluded agriculture funds from its definition of earmarking, however, thus allowing Baker and the university to justify seeking the trade center by invoking the resolution's tolerance for such projects. Charles E. Hess, dean of the College of Agriculture at the University of California at Davis, explained the university's position:

> The dilemma was as follows. President Gardner has said, no way should we be involved in pork activities, and I agreed with that, and as I said I went with his noble cause in trying to find an alternative. . . . And that didn't work, and I saw what Iowa State was doing, and other universities, and it really became a situation where we were being noble, but in the meantime losing ground in terms of possible facilities we felt could do good research that would benefit not only California, but certainly the nation.[40]

Although the university failed to obtain the center referred to in Baker's letter, during the next several years it sought earmarks funded from the agricultural appropriations bill for its Davis and Riverside campuses, which by 1996 totaled $22.9 million for Davis and $9 million for Riverside. Not surprisingly, these efforts to obtain earmarks by a leading institutional critic of the practice became public, received prominent coverage in *The Chronicle of Higher Education*, dismayed opponents of earmarking, and openly encouraged its practitioners. Baker later wrote

---

39. Letter from William B. Baker to President David P. Gardner, April 25, 1989, p. 2.
40. Interview with Charles E. Hess, March 23, 1993.

a letter to the editor of the *Chronicle*, declaring the university's commitment to peer review despite its pursuit of the agriculture projects.[41]

Another example of redefining an earmark was Harvard University's involvement with a consortium called the National Institute for Global and Environmental Change. The institute, denounced as "pure lard" by the American Physical Society, began as an earmark in the FY 1990 Energy and Water appropriations bill. As *The Wall Street Journal* observed, the "pork" project was "fashioned with an eye for votes from appropriators. . . . The University of California at Davis – in the home district of the institute's chief sponsor, Rep. Vic Fazio (D-CA) – would manage the project. Regional partners included Harvard, Indiana, and Tulane universities."[42] The votes referred to by the *Journal* were the sponsoring votes of a few key appropriations subcommittee chairs and senior members. The sponsors of the project included Fazio, chair of the House Legislative Branch Appropriations Subcommittee and member of the Energy and Water Appropriations Subcommittee; Rep. John T. Myers (R-IND), ranking member of the House Energy and Water Appropriations Subcommittee; and Sen. J. Bennett Johnston (D-LA), chair of the Senate Energy and Water Appropriations Subcommittee. Not surprisingly, the earmark was funded by the Energy and Water Subcommittee.

Harvard justified its participation in the institute by claiming that it won the center through a regional peer review and was thereby declared the subcontractor. In a letter from Harvard's president, Derek Bok, to the institute's director at Harvard, Richard Wilson, Bok described why he allowed Harvard to participate in the project:

> I believe that Harvard should not try to avoid the regular peer review procedure for evaluating the merits of scientific proposals. Hence, I would be very concerned if representatives of the University solicited members of Congress to earmark funds for us as line-item appropriations. On the other

41. See Collen Cordes, "Senate Committee Opens Debate on Earmarking Funds; U. of Cal., a Foe of 'Pork-Barrel' Projects, Seeks One," *Chronicle of Higher Education,* June 28, 1989, p. A14. The article quotes Roy Meyers, communications director of Cassidy and Associates: "It is significant that the University of California has finally agreed that in many cases a direct Congressional appropriation is the only way that some universities can obtain federal aid for vitally needed projects." On the other side of the earmarking debate, Robert L. Park of the American Physical Society, opponent of earmarking, declared, "I'm very disheartened – not by what they're doing, but by the rationalization" (p. A19).
42. Deborah Blum, "UCD Scientists in Pork-Barrel Feast, Critics Declare," *Sacramento Bee,* September 3, 1990; David Rogers, "House and Senate, Recognizing a Pork Barrel When They See One, Warm to the Environment," *Wall Street Journal,* August 16, 1989.

hand, if money is given to another university which wants us to collaborate in a worthy scientific or research enterprise, I would have no objection.[43]

Thus, if the other institutions engaged in politics, bypassed merit review, and secured the earmark, Harvard would willingly share the subcontracted funds as a member of the consortium. By lending its name and reputation to the institute, particularly in the early stages before the regional reviews took place, Harvard no doubt added to congressional willingness to fund this earmark.

In another case of redefinition, the University of Rochester claimed that even though it bypassed peer review, the project that was funded was not an earmark because it had been authorized and had undergone an after-the-fact evaluation by the Department of Energy (DOE). Although the AAU resolution denounced earmarked appropriations, it neglected to say anything about an authorization for an earmark. Though the difference appears trivial, it is very important, as it involves different committees in Congress. The loophole in the definition is that, for AAU, if a project is funded through specified appropriations subcommittee bills, excluding agriculture, it is an earmark, but if it is funded through an authorizations committee bill, it is not an earmark.

For more than a decade, the University of Rochester received no less than $73 million in earmarked money for its Omega laser program. Rochester declared that although its project never went through competitive peer review, whereby other institutions could compete for the same funds, the money was not earmarked because it had been authorized and subject to agency evaluation after the project was funded. The authorization for the project was sponsored by Rep. Sam Stratton (D-NY), who served as chairman of the House Procurement and Military Nuclear Systems Subcommittee of the House Armed Services Committee, which had jurisdiction over all defense nuclear weapons programs and DOE laboratories. Stratton, whose district included the university, had also graduated from Rochester and was later named a "Life Regent" of the university. Rochester was the only university permitted to participate in the DOE Inertial Fusion program. Although the laser's scientific contribution was evaluated after it was funded, the review team consisted of researchers who used the laser. The University of Rochester never had to submit a proposal to DOE for peer-reviewed competition

43. Letter from Derek Bok to Richard Wilson, Lyman Lab 231, April 3, 1989. In an interview, Bok reiterated his position: "I suppose if another university received a lot of money and the question was who they subcontracted to, and if the subcontracting were done in some principled way to assess the scientific merits, we would feel that's fine." Interview with Derek Bok, November 2, 1990.

against other universities, a number of which had higher-ranked physics departments.

Between 1980 and 1996, AAU institutions received approximately $1.467 billion in academic earmarks, 28.6 percent of the total distributed to all schools, as shown in Table 3. Some of these funds were obtained by the truly elite schools, which, no matter how small the amount involved, compromised the principled nature of AAU's fight against earmarking. In any case, the earmarks obtained by the most prestigious institutions amount to only a tiny fraction of the earmarked dollars.

More important, if these prestigious schools, including Harvard and the University of California, had truly flexed their political muscles, they could have increased their share of earmarked dollars and projects many times over. The latent threat of the major universities becoming serious earmarkers was continually raised by the presidents of these institutions. "At some point," noted MIT President Paul Gray, "the institutions that think of themselves as principled in their opposition to earmarking are going to begin to think of themselves as patsies. If that happens, it's going to be Katie-bar-the-door. If a place like MIT or Stanford or the University of California wanted to play an earmarking game, they could do pretty well at the expense of other high-quality institutions and ultimately at the expense of the research system." In fact, in 1987 and 1988, the University of California had begun to outline plans for obtaining earmarks for its nine campuses in response to the rapid growth in the number of earmarks benefiting other schools and the uncertain effectiveness of the AAU moratorium. President Gardner ultimately rejected the idea because of the harm it might inflict on the peer review process.[44] Ultimately, of course, the success of a university in receiving an earmark depends on whether its representatives in Congress sit on the powerful appropriations committees, not on its academic reputation.

Meanwhile, at least through FY 1996, seven AAU schools apparently refrained from academic earmarking: the California Institute of Technology, Case Western University, Princeton University, Rice University, the University of California at Berkeley, Vanderbilt University, and Yale University.

44. Interview with Paul Gray, November 28, 1990. On the University of California's initial plans, see letter from James D. Savage to Special Assistant Shaw, August 27, 1987, and memorandum from Paul Sweet to Vice President William Baker, "Meeting of August 27 – Alternative Means of Funding U.C. Capital Projects," August 31, 1987. Discussions on the topic were held at the presidential and chancellorial levels in 1988. Letter to the Editor from William B. Baker, Vice-President, Budget and University Relations, University of California, *Chronicle of Higher Education*, July 12, 1989, p. B3.

Table 3. *Apparent academic earmarks for AAU institutions, FY 1980–96*

Institution	Amount
Brandeis University	$ 9,000,000
Brown University	13,436,000
Carnegie Mellon University	32,610,000
Catholic University	14,200,000
Clark University	279,000
Columbia University	36,500,000
Cornell University	21,634,333
Duke University	100,000
Emory University	360,000
Harvard University	6,860,000
Indiana University	51,338,800
Iowa State University	142,941,300
Johns Hopkins University	17,050,000
Massachusetts Institute of Technology	5,165,000
Michigan State University	77,506,334
New York University	10,100,000
Northwestern University	33,700,000
Ohio State University	15,956,500
Pennsylvania State University	81,107,000
Purdue University	15,319,000
Rutgers University	60,448,000
Stanford University	1,540,000
State University of New York, Buffalo	380,000
Syracuse University	12,380,000
Tulane University	34,610,000
University of Arizona	25,813,000
University of California, Los Angeles	30,000
University of California, San Diego	2,100,000
University of California, Santa Barbara	6,060,000
University of Chicago	317,000
University of Colorado	7,929,000
University of Florida	87,323,500
University of Illinois	47,738,000
University of Iowa	7,097,000
University of Kansas	3,624,000
University of Maryland, College Park	67,601,000
University of Michigan	18,010,000
University of Minnesota	22,028,000
University of Missouri	21,358,000
University of Nebraska	67,035,300
University of North Carolina	9,875,000
University of Oregon	46,156,000
University of Pennsylvania	19,708,000
University of Pittsburg	151,720,000
University of Rochester	73,527,000

(*Continued*)

Table 3. *(cont.)*

Institution	Amount
University of Southern California	30,000
University of Texas, Austin	16,318,000
University of Virginia	490,000
University of Washington	26,773,600
University of Wisconsin	43,932,000
Washington University	277,000
Total	$1,467,341,667[a]

[a]This total accounts for 28.6 percent of all academic earmarks.

To this extent, therefore, the AAU moratorium can be described as having some, though limited, influence on the growth of academic earmarking among its members. For a brief time, perhaps two years, a number of schools abstained from earmarking, and others restrained their earmarking efforts for a longer period. President Frank Rhodes of Cornell, for example, rejected a $5 million earmark that Congress was willing to provide. In another case, Purdue University employed the moratorium to counter the efforts of the Indiana delegation to bring projects to the school. As Robert O'Neil, then president of the University of Virginia, recounted, "I know [President] Steve Baring of Purdue has made this comment: he said my congressional delegation comes to me . . . and says I can get you one of these buildings . . . I know it was helpful to Steve to be able to pull out the policy and say I voted for this, we believe this . . . and if you do this for us, the next thing you know you're going to have a delegation from Ball State, from Indiana State, from the University of Evansville, from Marion College, they'll all be in here [looking for an earmark]. And you won't be able to say, 'Oh, but Purdue is a very distinguished research university.' And I think there's been some force to that."[45] So, for some institutions, the moratorium provided political cover to avoid earmarking. For others, adhering to it remains a matter of principle, and not simple self-interest, as the formal penalties within AAU for violating the moratorium are nonexistent, and the informal penalties are limited to isolated instances of peer pressure and some negative coverage of academic earmarking on the part of the media.

Meanwhile, other AAU universities have pursued earmarks unabashedly. Such institutions as the universities of Pittsburgh, Florida,

45. Interview with Robert O'Neil, May 15, 1990.

Michigan State, Pennsylvania State, Iowa State, Maryland, Rutgers, Rochester, and Indiana have all benefited substantially from a few powerful members of Congress, who championed earmarks for the home school. During FYs 1980–96, each of these schools received more than $50 million in earmarked funds.

The Demise of the Earmarking Fight at AAU

By the time Robert Rosenzweig left the AAU presidency in 1993, the association's active opposition to earmarking had virtually collapsed. In particular, the proliferation of earmarking universities had made the AAU staff extremely reluctant to speak out or campaign against earmarking. Cornelius J. Pings, who replaced Rosenzweig as president, confirmed the staff's passivity in the face of so many earmarking presidents. "I think it absolutely restricts our ability to express ourselves on behalf of the organization. Bob was cautious, and I certainly am about running around with a flag that's labeled AAU policy on earmarking. Does that inhibit speaking up on it? I think somewhat. I feel I have to be very cautious when I'm espousing that."[46] To a great extent, the leadership in the fight against in earmarking within AAU shifted from the organization's president to individual member presidents, especially Joe Wyatt of Vanderbilt University. Wyatt, rather than Pings, has testified before Congress on behalf of AAU in opposition to earmarking.

In addition to having a cautious staff, AAU remains unwilling to sanction its members for earmarking. So many AAU institutions have engaged in earmarking that any meaningful sanctions would dissolve the association. So AAU is seriously limited in its ability to influence or control its member presidents, let alone the presidents of unaffiliated institutions. Consequently, university presidents continue to make individual choices either to pursue their self-interest and aspirations or to abide by the stated principles and interests nominally agreed to by the majority of the organization.

What is surprising, given the lack of collective pressure and influence, is that some AAU schools have refrained from earmarking altogether, and others have exercised significant self-control in the cost and size of the earmarks they have pursued. Perhaps, as Cornelius Pings suggested, they have done so out of a concern for good science and good science policy: "It may be a shocking concept, but I think it is a matter of principle. There are those that believe this is bad science policy . . . and we could see in certain agencies almost all the money going out by earmark.

46. Interview with Cornelius J. Pings, June 9, 1993.

Science by politics, science by political clout, rather than science dictating science. I think it's altruism, an attempt to hold the line."[47]

What AAU has succeeded in accomplishing is raising the topic of academic earmarking from isolated instances of political favoritism to a major policy issue within the academic science community and, perhaps more important, to an issue of ethical judgment for university presidents who have sought earmarks. Clearly, for some presidents, such as John Silber, the decision to seek an earmark has been an easy one, based on the belief that earmarking benefits both the institution and academic science. Yet for others who have obtained earmarks, including Sheldon Hackney, the decision has been more difficult because the potential harm for science is thought to be greater. For those presidents who denounce earmarking but then proceed to solicit projects on the side, their behavior may very well raise troubling questions about personal integrity and principled institutional leadership. What Robert Rosenzweig and his allies achieved was to transform the decision to earmark from what could have been a simple and easy one – as just one more way to raise funds, such as soliciting alumni for donations – to one that apparently has required more thought and consideration of principle and public policy.

Finally, just as AAU proved unable to punish earmarking members, it failed to supply the positive incentive that universities would receive in trade for abstaining from earmarking, namely, a large-scale federal facilities program. If the absence of adequate federal facilities money created the problem that earmarking was to remedy, new money funding a new program was required to end the earmarking contagion. Yet, just as the 1989 resolutions created controversy over the definition of earmarking, they also pointed to another set of divisions among member institutions. Although university presidents could agree in principle that the federal government should provide such a facilities program, agreeing upon which institutions should benefit from the program and how it would be funded were altogether different matters.

---

47. Ibid.

4

The Struggle to Fund
Academic Research Facilities

When Columbia University pursued its $5 million earmark for a chemistry building in 1983, its efforts were not intended as an attack on the peer review system. Columbia, after all, was a major benefactor of peer review. In FY 1982 and FY 1983, it ranked seventh in the nation in terms of federal research funds awarded to academic institutions, so Columbia could hardly claim that the system was biased against it.

Instead, what precipitated Columbia's actions was the university's seriously deteriorating fiscal condition and a recognition that it had to increase faculty-generated revenues. To accomplish this task, Columbia sought to accommodate the facility requirements of its faculty, especially faculty in the hard sciences who were successful in obtaining large federal grants. Without drawing down further on its increasingly overused endowment, Columbia's president, Michael Sovern, looked to another funding source to finance some of its facilities, namely, the federal government. What Columbia realized, however, was that the government's programs for such support had either been greatly reduced in size or terminated altogether. "Federal funds to help sustain the costs of running educational institutions," noted one senior Columbia official as early as 1975, "have vanished from the federal budget."[1] Unable to apply to an agency for a facilities grant, Columbia, with the assistance of Rep. Charles Rangle (D-NY), obtained its funding by way of an earmark.

1. James S. Young, "Endangered Species: The Research University," *Columbia Today*, September 1975, p. 5. Also see "Academic Planning: Perspectives, Priorities, Strategies," by James S. Young, Deputy Vice President for Academic Planning and Deputy Provost, Columbia University, 1975. Stated Young, "The University's fiscal experts have already shown that staying where we are now will eat up endowment at a rate that may drastically shorten Columbia's life expectancy.... Strategies for enlarging revenue will now have to focus on income generated by our academic programs ... which has its source in the work the faculty does."

The controversy that Columbia helped to precipitate in organizations such as the AAU stemmed not from its search for federal facilities money but from the perception that it was stepping outside the peer review process to do so. President Sovern replied to his critics that Columbia had not violated peer review, as the federal government's peer-reviewed facilities programs had ceased to exist. Consequently, earmarking was the only way to obtain federal funding. Regardless of whether one accepted Sovern's explanation, all parties to the debate over earmarking agreed with him on the need for a significantly funded federal academic research facilities program.

The Federal Government's Early Facilities Programs

The federal government has supported the construction and maintenance of research facilities in two ways: through institutional grants specifically awarded for that purpose and by the reimbursement of "indirect costs" or the "overhead" on research grants awarded to individual faculty. Efforts to curb earmarking have focused more on reinvigorating facilities programs because the grants they provide could perhaps serve as the incentive needed to induce have-not or developing universities to limit their earmarking, while indirect costs primarily reward those institutions already receiving significant research funds.

Federal facilities funding dates from the end of World War II. In 1948, Congress authorized the National Cancer Institute to make "grants-in-aid" to various state and nonprofit institutions, including colleges and universities, for the "erection of buildings."[2] This was the first such authority for federal support for academic facilities since the end of World War II.[3] Another important precedent for federal funding was set by the National Science Foundation Act of 1950, which established NSF. Although the act did not explicitly provide for facilities grants, its broad statutory authority for the "promotion of basic research and education in the sciences" enabled the agency to initiate its own facilities program.[4]

Another significant piece of legislation was the Higher Education Facilities Act of 1963. Whereas other legislation mentioned academic facil-

2. *United States Statutes at Large*, V. 62, Part 1, 1948, p. 401.
3. See "Brick and Mortar: A Summary and Analysis of Proposals to Meet Research Facilities Needs on College Campuses, Report Prepared by the Congressional Research Service, Library of Congress, for the Subcommittee on Science, Research and Technology," September 1987, p. 19.
4. *United States Statutes at Large*, V. 64, Part 1, 1950, p. 149.

ities in passing or by inference, the act's "findings and declaration of policy" stated that the "security and the welfare of the United States" required the federal government's commitment in assisting academic institutions to finance their facilities.[5] Such financing could take the form of either direct grants or loans. The purpose of the act clearly was to assist in providing the facilities needed to serve the incoming baby-boom generation of students. Research facilities were cited as a necessary ingredient in training the future faculty, who would, in turn, teach the boomers. The costs of construction would be shared, with a third paid for by the federal government; this fraction would later be increased to half in 1968.

Congress inevitably tried to find a happy compromise in setting the broad criteria used for awarding construction grants. In the National Science Foundation Act, NSF was called upon to "strengthen basic research . . . in the United States." To fulfill this mission, NSF would fund research that was performed by those "qualified by training and experience to achieve the results desired." So the need for merit was the initial consideration in funding decisions. At the same time, however, the act stated that the agency should take care "to avoid undue concentration of such research." Similarly, the act's reauthorization in 1959 provided for the funding of graduate fellowships, where "such selections shall be made solely on the basis of ability." However, in choosing among applicants of equal merit, fellowships should be allocated "in such manner as will tend to result in a wide distribution . . . among the States. . . ."[6]

In the Higher Education Facilities Act, Congress sought the same balance between merit and equity. In undergraduate facilities funding, money would be distributed by simple formulas dependent upon student populations within the various states. Graduate and research facilities grants would be allocated in a manner that would "contribute to achieving the objectives of this title," which included the provision that these grants should "assist in the establishment of graduate schools and cooperative graduate centers of excellence." Nevertheless, consideration would also be given to distributing resources in a manner that would "aid in attaining a wider distribution throughout the United States of graduate schools and cooperative graduate centers."[7]

Each of these three pieces of legislation provided for some form of oversight and expertise in the management and allocation of resources, which in effect constituted early versions of peer review. The National

5. *United States Statutes at Large*, V. 77, Part 1, 1963, p. 363.
6. *United States Statutes at Large*, V. 64, Part 1, 1950, p. 150; ibid., V. 73, Part 1, 1959, p. 468.
7. *United States Statutes at Large*, V. 77, Part 1, 1963, p. 371.

Cancer Institute Act of 1948 relied upon the "recommendations of the National Advisory Cancer Council." In NSF, the National Science Board would oversee NSF's administrative network of divisions, committees, and special commissions. The board, in turn, would consist of members selected "solely on the basis of established service" who were "eminent in the fields of the basic sciences." Last, the awarding of facilities grants in the Department of Education would also be directed by an Advisory Committee, consisting of various "leading authorities in the field of education," plus representatives from NSF and the Office of Science and Technology Policy in the White House.[8]

The effect of these and other laws was that during the 1960s the federal government provided higher education with an important though relatively small number of facilities grants. As shown in Table 4, between 1963 and 1968, for example, the federal government awarded $655.5 million for facilities. These have often been referred to as the "golden years" of federal support for higher education. Beginning in 1969, however, facilities funds were cut nearly in half, and then dwindled throughout the 1970s and early 1980s, until earmarking began increasing the totals in the mid-1980s. What caused this decline was a shift in funding during President Nixon's administration away from institutional grants to support for individual students, principally in the form of financial aid. This trend was accelerated due to the federal government's reluctance to award institutional grants to private religious colleges. Moreover, "the inability of the higher education community to agree on an equitable geographical distribution of institutional grants" encouraged Congress to shift from supporting facilities to focusing on student aid and research.[9]

Even in the golden years and throughout the period of the federal government's support of academic facilities, federal funding constituted only a minority share of higher education's expenditures for facilities. In 1968, the peak year for facilities expenditures, federal dollars accounted for about 30 percent of the total. Other, more common and traditional sources of funding included state appropriations for public universities, private donations, endowments, and borrowing. In 1992–3, federal support accounted for 17 percent of facilities funding at private institutions and 16 percent at public schools, including earmarked dollars. Meanwhile, other sources became the dominant providers for these institutions; tax-exempt bonds contributed 29 percent of the total at private schools, and state appropriations accounted for 46 percent at

8. *United States Statutes at Large*, V. 62, Part 1, 1948, p. 401; ibid., V. 64, Part 1, 1950, p. 150; ibid., V. 77, Part 1, 1963, pp. 371–2.
9. "Brick and Mortar," p. 28.

Table 4. *Federal obligations for academic research facilities,*
FY 1963–94

Fiscal year	Amount	Percent change
1963	$105,896,000	NA
1964	100,837,000	−4.8%
1965	126,196,000	25.1
1966	114,767,000	−9.1
1967	111,309,000	−3.0
1968	96,148,000	−13.6
1969	54,516,000	−43.3
1970	44,778,000	−17.9
1971	29,942,000	−33.1
1972	36,917,000	23.3
1973	43,338,000	17.4
1974	29,009,000	−33.1
1975	44,787,000	54.4
1976	23,899,000	−46.6
1977	36,471,000	52.6
1978	34,328,000	−5.9
1979	32,068,000	−6.6
1980	37,780,000	17.8
1981	27,694,000	−26.7
1982	31,200,000	12.7
1983	37,547,000	20.3
1984	49,764,000	32.5
1985	113,932,000	128.9
1986	105,827,000	−7.1
1987	229,875,000	117.2
1988	202,907,000	−11.7
1989	237,010,000	−16.8
1990	124,841,000	−47.3
1991	151,808,000	21.7
1992	204,722,000	34.9
1993	259,421,000	26.7
1994	214,385,000	−17.4

Source: Federal Support to Universities, Colleges, and
Nonprofit Institutions, Fiscal Year 1994 (Washington, D.C.:
National Science Foundation, 1996), Table B-1.

public institutions.[10] In any case, regardless of whether the source was public or private, total facilities support declined rapidly after 1968, reaching a low point in 1979, just a few years before Columbia obtained its earmark.

Federal Facilities Legislation in the 1980s and 1990s

What earmarking accomplished was to bring the facilities problem to the forefront of higher education's agenda with Congress. Universities had bemoaned the condition of their facilities for years prior to 1983, when Columbia and Catholic University obtained their earmarks. Yet, the primary policy concern of higher education lobbying organizations like AAU, the American Council on Education (ACE), and NASULGC was to maximize federal dollars for research and student financial aid. To defend the peer review system and the research budgets against a potential onslaught of earmarks, however, the higher education associations pressed Congress to reinvigorate federal facilities funding. During the next decade, members of Congress did respond with numerous bills that authorized facilities programs, but these bills, with one notable exception, failed either to become law or to receive meaningful appropriations.

Immediate congressional response to higher education's pleas came in the form of S. 1537, the University Research Capacity Restoration Act of 1983. The bill was introduced by Sen. John C. Danforth (R-MO), who had a special interest in earmarking. The senator's brother, William Danforth, was chancellor of Washington University and a firm opponent of earmarking. Encouraged by his brother, Danforth proved to be one of earmarking's steadfast critics in the Senate. This bipartisan bill proposed that six agencies would allocate $980 million for facilities renovation and construction during a four-year period beginning in FY 1984. The legislation died in committee.

In 1985, Don Fuqua (D-FL), chairman of the House Committee on Science and Technology, introduced H.R. 2823, The University Research Facilities Revitalization Act of 1985. This bill served as the precursor for the legislation that established NSF's facilities program. Fuqua's bill provided a ten-year, $5 billion authorization for academic facilities, to be matched by an additional $5 billion in nonfederal sup-

10. *Scientific and Engineering Research Facilities at Universities and Colleges,* 1994 (Washington, D.C.: National Science Foundation, 1994), Report 94-315, pp. 4–7 and 4–8.

port. Like Danforth's bill, the act would employ six agencies to distribute the money through a peer review process. Significantly, however, 15 percent of the total funding would be set aside for institutions that were not ranked among the top 100 colleges and universities receiving federal research funds. These schools could choose to compete in either or both categories of the program to maximize their funding opportunities. In addition, the bill included a formula that attempted to set a minimum annual percentage of approximately 10 percent of agency budgets for facilities. Finally, the bill called upon NSF to conduct biennial surveys to identify and assess higher education's research facilities needs.

Higher education welcomed Fuqua's bill, but the legislation raised several issues that haunted the entire facilities debate. In 1985, when the bill was introduced, federal support for university-based research had finally become a national priority, primarily due to the idea that science and technology played a critical role in the nation's economic competitiveness. Academic researchers, who had experienced either cuts in funding or deep losses in purchasing power due to inflation during the late 1970s and early 1980s, were loath to surrender research money to fund facilities. This opposition by faculty to trading research money for facilities was especially pronounced in the nation's elite research institutions. That, however, was the choice posed by Fuqua's bill and the federal government's overall budgetary constraints. Higher education could have its facilities, but there would be no new money. Facilities would be funded from research budgets.

In the first year alone, H.R. 2823 authorized $470 million for facilities, which was to be taken from research. Within the AAU, the diversion of funds raised concerns among a number of university presidents. One assessment of the feeling of AAU presidents indicated that

> Presidents Paul Olum and [C. Peter] McGrath [of the Universities of Oregon and Minnesota, respectively] also support for the intent of the bill [sic], but they oppose any funding of facilities at the expense of research programs, a view echoed by representatives of faculty and agency program managers. . . . President Hanna Gray [of the University of Chicago] opposes the ten percent reserve feature of the bill on the philosophical grounds cited above.[11]

The AAU's own advisory Space Science Working Group also objected to the bill, declaring that "It is our view that if NASA is to begin to re-

11. Memo from AAU Staff to the Committee on Science and Research, AAU, October 21, 1985, p. 2. Also see Memo from Jack Crowley and AAU Staff to AAU Ad Hoc Committee on Research Facilities, August 1, 1985, which outlines AAU's proposed revisions in the bill.

place equipment and renovate laboratories, it must be done with new funds and not with a set-aside of existing funds."[12] This concern was expressed openly to Fuqua by Frank Press, president of the National Academy of Sciences. "Our concern is with the implicit tithing of agency R&D budgets," Press stated in testimony before the House Subcommittee on Science, Research and Technology.

> I know that the hope is to have facilities funding be an add-on rather than a set-aside. . . . Of course, given the millstone of the federal deficit, any attempt to write in an add-on would almost certainly doom the bill.[13]

Despite his concern, however, even Press recognized the impossibility of securing new money to support facilities.

The bill's 15 percent set-aside for smaller schools also troubled the elite universities. Gregory Fusco, vice president of Columbia University, for example, declared that the language in the bill concerning eligible universities should be strengthened. Fusco argued that given the 15 percent set-aside, the remaining funds might best be reserved for the "top level performers." "With the set-aside for smaller schools," Fusco wrote, "no one can effectively argue that federal facility money should go to those who do not carry out major work for the respective agencies. We must be very firm about this principle, or we will end up with a 'post office' funding pattern with one small grant in each congressional district."[14] An assessment of the bill in the Office of the President of the University of California concluded, "this will provoke a vigorous protest from the faculty, for there is little constituency for this set-aside."[15]

What the facilities bill brought to the fore was the matter of setting priorities, a task that higher education and the academic science community approached with great distaste. "We must set priorities," Bernadine Healy, deputy director of the White House Office of Science and Technology Policy, pointed out in her testimony before the House Subcommittee on Science, Research and Technology. "The choice is rela-

---

12. Letter from Space Science Working Group to Robert M. Rosenzweig, President, AAU, p. 1.

13. "Testimony by Frank Press, President, The National Academy of Sciences on The University Research Revitalization Act of 1985, before the Subcommittee on Science, Research, and Technology, Committee on Science and Technology, U.S. House of Representatives, July 30, 1985," pp. 7–8.

14. Letter from Gregory Fusco, Vice President, Columbia University, to Jack Crowley, Vice President, AAU, June 10, 1985.

15. Memo from Calvin C. Moore, Associate Vice President for Academic Affairs, to William Frazer, Senior Vice President for Academic Affairs, July 31, 1985, p. 1.

tively simple: shall the nation use the resources we now have to address and solve the facilities problem, or shall we allow the imbalance in distribution of research dollars to persist with the risk to our long term research capability?"[16]

Healy's interpretation of priority setting, however, did not fully reflect the choice facing the elite research universities. In general, for the presidents of the elite academic recipients of federal research funds, the continued imbalance in funding obviously worked to their benefit and, from their perspective, did not present a risk to the nation's "long term research capability." Moreover, to them the imbalance in funding, as determined through peer review, reflected the true hierarchy of merit, talent, and scientific capability as it existed throughout the academic science community. The problem confronting the presidents was to determine how much of the federal research budget should be transferred into facilities programs to satisfy earmarking institutions, so that they would refrain from the practice. The optimal amount would be just enough to please the earmarkers without irritating research faculty at the major schools who might feel the pinch of reduced research funds. The optimal facilities program would also be structured in a way that would allow maximum participation by the elite institutions. Finally, the program had to preserve the concept of merit by subjecting all applications to peer review.

The difficult matter of setting priorities and balancing interests would be postponed, however. H.R. 2823 proved to be too complex and unworkable. The bill's funding formula, which was intended to provide a minimum level of facilities funding, for example, had been tested by committee staff only on the basis of one year of appropriations, not for all five years of the authorization. When the five-year period was tested, the funding scenario potentially could run counter to Fuqua's intent. The postponement would be brief, for a revised version of H.R. 2823 was offered in the next session of Congress.

The third major legislative attempt to support facilities, H.R. 1905, The University Facilities Revitalization Act of 1987, was sponsored by Fuqua's successor as committee chair, Robert Roe (D-NJ). Roe's bill also called for a ten-year authorization that required a 50 percent match from nonfederal funds. However, given the increasing budgetary constraints and the concern that too much research money would be shifted to facilities, the authorization was cut from $5 billion in federal money to $1 billion. Another change was that instead of relying upon the cum-

---

16. "Proposed Testimony of Dr. Bernadine Healy, Deputy Director, Office of Science and Technology Policy, Executive Office of the President, before the House Subcommittee on Science, Research and Technology, July 30, 1985," p. 8.

bersome six-agency model proposed in both the Danforth and Fuqua bills, NSF alone would manage the facilities program and distribute funds through merit review. The 15 percent set-aside would be maintained, but it would go to institutions that had received less than $10 million in federal research funds in each of the two preceding years. Finally, in response to the Reagan administration's concern that the Fuqua bill "restricts the flexibility of executive agencies to make priority choices in support of R&D," the funding formula in H.R. 2823 was dropped.[17]

In the Senate, companion legislation to the Roe bill was introduced by Sen. Christopher J. Dodd (D-CT), partially to promote the nation's economic competitiveness. "I don't think there's any doubt that the competitiveness issue in Congress has accelerated congressional concern about the facilities problem," noted one of the senator's senior aides.[18] Dodd's amendment to NSF's 1988 reauthorization act would have limited the program to five years, providing $1 million for FY 1988 for planning purposes, $142 million for the following two years, and "such sums as may be necessary" for the two years after that. In addition, the 15 percent set-aside was modified, so that 10 percent of these funds would be further reserved for institutions that served substantial numbers of minority and disadvantaged students.

As with the Fuqua bill, the initial reaction of higher education to H.R. 1905 was positive. In testimony before Roe's Committee on Science, Space and Technology, President Steven Muller of The Johns Hopkins University presented the basic AAU position: the academic research community strongly supported the bill; higher education's research facilities were increasingly dated and falling into disrepair; and the federal government had an obligation to help rebuild these facilities. Moreover, the nation's economic competitiveness depended upon academic basic research. "The position of sheer dominance in the world economy that we once enjoyed is gone," said Muller. "We have seen our competitive edge in one technology after another either lost or seriously jeopardized."[19] For AAU, the bill was "assigned a top priority" and a "reason to feel encouraged."[20]

17. Ibid., p. 9.
18. Barbara Vobejda, "Renewing the College 'Infrastructure,'" *Washington Post*, July 7, 1987.
19. "Statement for the Record on H.R. 1905, 'University Research Facilities Revitalization Act of 1987,' by Dr. Steven Muller, President, The Johns Hopkins University, before the Committee on Science, Space and Technology, U.S. House of Representatives, June 25, 1987," p. 3.
20. Memorandum from Robert M. Rosenzweig to AAU Presidents and Chancellors, Council on Federal Relations, July 17, 1987, p. 1.

Nevertheless, further reaction to Roe's bill and the Dodd amendment pointed to divisions within higher education more prevalent and potentially more disruptive than those of elite versus emerging research institutions. Also testifying before Roe was President John Silber of Boston University, an avid defender of academic earmarking. Silber too supported the bill, found it "sound," and restated Muller's concerns over deteriorating facilities. Silber continued on, however, to decry the concentrated distribution of federal research funds to "a handful of already wealthy" institutions. The schools, in turn, became wealthy because "peer reviewers award the largest grants to their own or similar institutions." As a result of the conservative old boy network of peer review, the nation was being deprived of great scientific discoveries. "I am president of a university located on the banks of the Charles River," declared Silber, "but I am not so parochial as to think that the scientific genius of America is confined to the banks of the Charles."[21]

To help remedy the abuses of peer review, Silber offered several suggestions for improving Roe's bill. The set-aside for institutions receiving less than $10 million in federal research funds would be increased from 15 to 25 percent. Another set-aside of 50 percent of the total would be reserved for undergraduate colleges. Similar to a provision in the Dodd amendment, 10 percent would be set aside for Historically Black Colleges and Universities (HBCU). A cap of $3 million would be placed on individual institutional awards to spread the money as widely as possible. Last, only 15 percent of the total would be designated for open competition.[22]

Silber's concerns about undergraduate facilities were echoed by Glenn Stevens, executive director for the Presidents' Council, State Colleges and Universities. Supportive of the bill, including its peer review provisions, Stevens proposed adding a further title to H.R. 1905 that would fund undergraduate instructional as well as graduate, research-oriented facilities. "We do not believe that the federal government can meet its responsibility for strengthening universities," Stevens declared, "by simply supporting the primary contractors – or even by encouraging the development of new competitors for federal contracts. In our opinion, the federal responsibility necessarily extends to strengthening undergradu-

21. "Testimony of Dr. John Silber, President of Boston University, Before the Committee on Science, Space and Technology, United States House of Representatives, June 25, 1987," p. 3.

22. Letter from John Silber, President of Boston University, to Representative Manuel Lujan, Jr., Ranking Member, Committee on Science, Space and Technology, June 30, 1987.

ate science."[23] If the universities were to get new research facilities, the undergraduate colleges asserted that they should get new instructional facilities.

What the elite research universities and their lobbyists promoted as a specific solution to the earmarking problem had become an example of "Christmas tree" legislation, in which a little bit of something went to everybody. Although elite and emerging research universities were initially intended to benefit from the bill, lobbying organizations principally representing undergraduate institutions or interests, such as the ACE, soon announced their intent to seek funding for instructional facilities. Moreover, as shown in the Dodd amendment, HBCUs would get their own set-aside. Under President Silber's proposal, the elite research schools essentially were shut out altogether from the facilities bill.

To keep the undergraduate schools as allies rather than force them to become opponents, AAU reluctantly agreed to push for the ACE amendment to Roe's bill. As AAU President Robert Rosenzweig indicated to his member presidents, "In response to objections to the proposed distribution of funds under these proposals [H.R. 1905 and the Dodd amendment], the legislative process may take a troubling turn. . . . Unless we are now prepared to see the initiative fail . . . we urge you to lend your support to the associations' recent but promising efforts to establish a companion program for undergraduate instructional facilities."[24]

Confronted by the growing size and potential cost of H.R. 1905 and by the Reagan administration's opposition to a new undergraduate instructional facilities program, Roe dropped the bill. Instead, he employed the National Science Foundation Authorization Act of 1988 to pass a leaner version of the plan. The NSF authorization was a more comprehensive and popular piece of legislation than the stand-alone facilities bill, and it was on a fast track to become law. The act, for example, accommodated President Reagan's proposal for doubling the size of NSF in five years, which ensured that it would gain Republican support. So by incorporating provisions for the "Academic Research Facilities Modernization Program" into the act, Roe gained approval for the basic components of his old bill. As passed, the act included these major provisions: $2.5 billion was authorized for the five-year period FY 1989 through FY 1993; funding would be used only to support research facilities; merit review was required in the allocation process; individual in-

23. "Statement for the Record on H.R. 1905, University Research Facilities Revitalization Act of 1987, by Dr. Glenn Stevens, Executive Director, Presidents' Council, State Colleges and Universities," June 25, 1987, p. 7.
24. Memorandum from Robert M. Rosenzweig, op. cit., p. 1.

stitutions could receive no more than $7 million in facilities grants over the five-year life of the program; different categories of institutions were established on the basis of federal research funds received, which would improve the opportunity of small schools to obtain funding; and 12 percent of the funding would be set aside for minority institutions.

Despite their success in passing the bill, neither Roe nor Doug Walgren (D-PA), the chair of the Subcommittee on Research, believed that the new facilities program would control earmarking, nor should it. "This facilities program should not be seen as limiting the important prerogative of Congress to provide funds directly to deserving colleges or universities when the circumstances merit it," observed Walgren. "Such initiatives," said Roe, "can assist institutions that aspire to greatness."[25]

The passage of NSF's facilities program proved to be the high point of congressional support for academic research facilities. Several other efforts were made to pass similar legislation that would be administered by other federal agencies, but they failed either to become law or to gain appropriations. Two of these efforts, however, do justify some mention.

In 1989 and 1990, Sen. Edward Kennedy (D-MA) introduced three bills – S. 1392, S 1863, and S. 2222 – authorizing facilities as part of the NIH reauthorization legislation. Kennedy's bills failed to pass the Senate. Yet what is significant about them is that they once again emphasized the split among elite universities over whether new facilities should be paid for with existing research funds. By the time Kennedy introduced his bills, the federal budget's spending constraints were clear. There would be no new money for facilities; it would all come at the expense of NIH's research accounts.

On July 13, 1990, President Donald Kennedy of Stanford University indicated the position Stanford would take on Senator Kennedy's latest bill, S. 1863, with the AAU's Executive Committee. "I know that on my own campus this issue has caused much discussion," Kennedy's stated, "and some division between faculty investigators concerned about program support and administrators concerned about providing necessary infrastructure." Nevertheless, Kennedy declared his support for the bill, for "we must return to a policy of long-term investment in basic research. That entails more than just supporting on-going programs."[26] Kennedy then asked his colleagues for comment.

25. Phil Kuntz, "House Agrees to Double Funding for National Science Foundation," *Congressional Quarterly Weekly Report*, October 1, 1988, p. 2726.
26. Letter from Don Kennedy, President, Stanford University, to AAU Executive Committee and AAU California Members, July 13, 1990, and "NIH Funds for Facilities, Statement to Stanford University Faculty from Donald Kennedy, President, Stanford University," p. 3.

Some university presidents disagreed with Kennedy's position. In his response to Kennedy, David P. Gardner, president of the University of California system, recommended an alternative course of action:

> The current fiscal condition at the federal level has created a situation in which NIH, NSF and other research support agencies operate in a zero-sum environment, and policymakers must choose among competing priorities for scarce funds. We are not persuaded that we should support the trade-off . . . because it would indicate our acceptance of the zero-sum approach for our research budget. . . . We must, instead, push hard for new sources of federal funding.[27]

Gardner's opposition to facilities at the expense of research effectively meant that the bill would die. Key members of the California congressional delegation, like Henry Waxman (D-CA), chairman of the House Subcommittee on Health and the Environment, would not respond favorably to the bill without the University of California's firm endorsement. AAU's support for the bill subsequently proved to be lukewarm, and the legislation ultimately failed.[28]

Another significant piece of facilities legislation, S. 1150, the Reauthorization of the Higher Education Act of 1965, was considered in 1991 by the Senate Committee on Labor and Human Resources. The bill extended and revised Title VII of the act, which included the facilities program created by the Higher Education Facilities Act of 1963. The new title provided a seven-year, $400 million authorization for graduate and research facilities, with funds to be allocated on a formula basis to the states.

More important, the revised Title VII contained an interesting example of a penalty that could be imposed by Congress on earmarking schools. A provision in Title VII required that a given state's allocation be reduced by the amount received for "a direct, noncompetitive award" by an institution in that state. Thus, all the other colleges and universities in the state would suffer if one of their number engaged in earmarking. The product of Sen. Claiborne Pell (D-RI), chair of the Sub-

---

27. Letter from David P. Gardner, President, University of California, to President Donald Kennedy, Stanford University, July 23, 1990.
28. Letter from Robert M. Rosenzweig, President, Association of American Universities, to David P. Gardner, President, University of California, August 2, 1990. On Rosenzweig's view of the University of California's influence, "AAU has not taken a position specifically on the Kennedy bill, S. 1863. It was discussed during our last Executive Committee conference call, but largely in terms of the need to engage the Universities of California and Illinois as active proponents because of key roles of Henry Waxman and Edward Madigan and whether it was worth going forward without that involvement."

committee on Education, Arts and Humanities, the penalty was one of the most creative and insightful efforts to limit earmarking. At minimal political cost to individual members of Congress, the bill would have forced state governments and the universities and colleges within the states to police themselves and impose real costs for failing do so. Needless to say, this was a clause that universities and colleges bitterly disliked. They did not want to be placed in an enforcement role, nor did they want to lose potential funding due to another school's behavior.

An ironic footnote to the legislation is that while it contained this sanction against earmarking, it also included separate earmarks of $2 million for Eastern Michigan University, $550,000 for Shaw University in North Carolina, $1.8 million for the Rochester Institute of Technology, $1.2 million for the University of Connecticut, and $300,000 for Senator Pell's home state school, the University of Rhode Island.[29]

After a decade of encouraging Congress to establish facilities legislation in the 1980s and 1990s, higher education could point to just one new, meaningful program: NSF's Academic Research Facilities Modernization Program. Despite its annual authorization of $250 million, however, the program's outlays, the actual dollars spent on facilities, consisted of $103,000 in FY 1990, $1.1 million in FY 1991, $13.1 million in FY 1992, $17.1 million in FY 1993, $30.9 million in FY 1994, $61 million in FY 1995, and an estimated $105 million in FY 1996, for a total of $228.3 million spread over seven years. For FY 1997, Congress approved President Clinton's budget request that the program be zero-funded.[30]

During those same years Congress also approved more than $3.6 billion in academic earmarks. Consequently, the strategy of pacifying earmarking institutions with some form of peer-reviewed facilities money had basically failed. As Columbia University's Gregory Fusco observed, "The entire annual appropriation, while it's great to have a program like that, isn't enough to build one major science building at one institution."[31] Earmarking proved far more rewarding for universities and colleges than participating in the federal government's meagerly funded facilities program.

29. "Reauthorization of the Higher Education Act of 1965, Report of the Committee on Labor and Human Resources, United States Senate, to Accompany S. 1150," Report 102-204, November 12, 1991, pp. 452-71.
30. Budget outlay numbers are drawn from the Appendix sections of the *Budget of the United States Government* for FYs 1991-7. Outlays are not to be confused with appropriations or obligations; outlays refers to actual expenditures.
31. Interview with Gregory Fusco, August 8, 1991.

In addition, rather than presenting Congress with a united front and an agreed-upon legislative solution to its problems, higher education exposed its divisions, personal animosities, and conflicts in a sometimes openly hostile fashion. Members of Congress on the key science committees were left to themselves to craft legislation that would satisfy the various segments of higher education. As one key staffer on the House Committee on Space, Science and Technology put it, "The academic research community speaks with many voices. They want facilities, but they also want research money. They want to build research facilities, but they also want undergraduate instructional facilities. With our budget deficit, they simply can't have it all."

The NSF Facilities Surveys

Part of the difficulty supportive members of Congress, university presidents, and the higher education associations experienced in drafting and gaining approval of facilities legislation was that for some time the scope of the facilities problem remained unclear and undefined. In the mid-1980s, the size of the facilities deficiency, the cost of modernization, which institutions were suffering, and to what degree essentially were matters of speculation.

Early cost estimates for facilities modernization varied widely, ranging from as much as $10 to $20 billion, a staggering sum, to as little as $1 billion. In 1981, respondents to an AAU study estimated their facilities construction and modernization expenses at $765 million spread over a three-year period. In 1983, a National Academy of Sciences report found the facilities deficit to range from $1 to $4 billion. At just the nine campuses of the University of California, a 1983 study estimated the expense of bringing its facilities up to state-of-the-art quality at $4 billion. A survey prepared for the American Cancer Society in 1985 stated that the facilities deficiency in academic biomedical science required $2 billion spread over a five-year period. In 1986, the Government-University-Industry Research Roundtable estimated the ten- to twenty-year price tag for facilities to be anywhere from $5 billion to $20 billion. Meanwhile, a General Accounting Office survey of twenty-eight universities released in 1986 found the increase in the average cost of research facility construction and renovation from 1983 to 1984 to be $5.5 million.[32]

32. These early studies include "National Survey of Laboratory Animal Facilities and Resources," National Academy of Sciences, Washington, D.C., 1978; "The Nation's Deteriorating University Research Facilities," AAU, Washington, D.C., 1981; "Strengthening the Government–University Partnership in Science: Report of the Relationships

Perhaps the most important statement on facilities costs during the early 1980s came from the White House Science Council's Panel on the Health of U.S. Colleges and Universities. President Ronald Reagan ordered the panel to study the relationship between the federal government and universities, particularly how this relationship affected "the U.S. ability . . . to conduct the research needed to sustain America's leadership in industry and defense."[33] David Packard, chairman of the board of Hewlett-Packard, served as the panel's chair, and D. Allen Bromley, the Henry Ford II professor of physics at Yale University, served as vice-chair. The study issued by the panel in February 1986, often called the "Packard–Bromley report," fully supported the Fuqua bill, H.R. 2823, with its $5 billion authorization for new facilities, to be matched by an additional $5 billion from nonfederal sources. "Additional support is urgently needed to reverse the decay in physical plant and obsolescence in research equipment that has occurred in the past decade," the report urged. Furthermore, the panel determined, "quite independently of the Fuqua initiative," that the facilities problem would cost $10 billion to remedy, just the amount in H.R. 2823.

In addition to supporting Fuqua, the Packard–Bromley report proposed that universities receive more generous depreciation and indirect cost recovery rates for academic facilities.[34] A federal grant for academic research is commonly divided into direct and indirect cost components. The direct costs are those items incurred by the researcher for such items as equipment, salaries, and research assistants. These expenses are generally managed by the researcher, in accordance with relevant federal and university guidelines, and are usually itemized as part of a grant application. An indirect cost is that portion of the grant that the university controls, and can apply to the administrative and institutional expenses of supporting the scientist who conducts the research. The degree of

in Support of Science of the National Academy Complex," National Academy of Sciences, National Academy of Engineering, and the Institute of Medicine, Washington, D.C., 1983; "University of California Report to the Governor's Task Force for Infrastructure Review," University of California, Office of the President, November 1983; "Survey of Cancer Research Facilities Needs," American Cancer Society, Washington, D.C., 1985; "Academic Research Facilities Financing," Government–University–Industry Research Roundtable, Washington, D.C., 1986; and *University Finances: Research Revenues and Expenditures* (Washington, D.C.: U.S. Government Accounting Office, 1986), Report No. GAO/RCED-86-162BR.

33. "Report of the White House Science Council: Panel on the Health of U.S. Colleges and Universities," Executive Office of the President, Washington, D.C., February 1986, pp. 14–15.

34. Letter from G. A. Keyworth, Science Advisor to the President, to Dr. Solomon J. Buchsbaum, Chairman, White House Science Council, May 3, 1984. This letter authorized the creation of the panel and its report.

control varies among institutions and is generally greater for private compared to public universities because the indirect costs reimbursements of some public institutions are turned over to the state. As part of the calculation of an indirect cost, universities are permitted to recover 2 percent of the nonfederal acquisition cost of their research facilities. They have the option of converting to depreciation rates but are charged a penalty for doing so. When the various elements that constitute a university's indirect costs are determined according to federal rules, an indirect cost rate is set.

In 1958, the Bureau of the Budget issued its famous rules for calculating costs, Circular A-21. Following World War II, the indirect cost rate was set at 8 percent; throughout the early 1960s, it grew to 15 and then to 20 percent. In 1968, at the urging of universities as the funding of regular facilities programs began to decline, the cap was lifted, and each school's rate was determined individually in accordance with A-21, which has been updated numerous times. If, for example, an institution's rate is 50 percent, then for a $150,000 grant, $50,000 would be kept by the institution as its overhead recovery, and a portion of that would in principle be applied to reimburse the institution's costs for maintaining its research facilities. By the early 1990s, the average modified direct cost for universities was 54 percent, with private universities generally running higher rates than public universities, as public schools often receive significant facilities funds from their states that are not included in the indirect cost calculation.[35]

Simply increasing the indirect cost and depreciation rates, as the Packard–Bromley report recommended, however, remains at best a partial solution to the problems of facilities and earmarking. In order to benefit from these rates, an institution must first have been awarded a research grant. Thus, only major research universities with a high vol-

35. On the history of indirect costs, see Peter Likins and Albert H. Teich, "Indirect Costs and the Government–University Partnership," in David H. Guston and Kenneth Keniston (eds.), *The Fragile Contract: University Science and the Federal Government* (Cambridge: MIT Press, 1994), pp. 177–93; Kenneth T. Brown, "Indirect Costs of Federally Supported Research," *Science* 212(24), April 1981, pp. 411–18; Stephen E. Selby, "Indirect Cost Rate Composition and Myths," *Journal of the Society of Research Administrators* 15 (Winter 1984): 29–37; "Indirect Costs at the University of California," *Contracts and Grants*, UCLA Office of Contract and Grant Administration, February 1981; *University Research: Effect of Indirect Cost Revisions and Options for Future Changes* (Washington, D.C.: U.S. General Accounting Office, March 1995), Report GAO/RCED-95-74; Genevieve J. Knezo, *Indirect Costs at Academic Institutions: Background and Controversy* (Washington, D.C.: Congressional Research Service, November 10, 1991), Report IB91095; and Ray Spangenburg and Diane Moser, "Rising Indirect Cost Threaten Research," *The Scientist*, May 30, 1988, p. 4.

ume and dollar value of grants would accumulate sufficient reimbursement through indirect costs to build large, expensive research facilities. The distribution of indirect costs matches the distribution of direct costs because both are determined by the peer review system. Moreover, because of federal action to cap and restrict certain indirect cost rates – for example, the administrative elements of the rate are capped at 26 percent – the level of reimbursements to universities has stabilized and even fallen for some major agencies during the 1990s.[36] So universities that only recently emphasized their research activities would not receive the same level of support that academic research institutions benefited from in the 1970s and 1980s. Consequently, regardless of what these rates might be, have-not schools with relatively little research activity would still be left with the incentive to earmark.

Finally, although discussions about indirect costs presume that overhead reimbursement provides universities with an important source of facilities funding, the federal government has never determined exactly how much of the total reimbursement to universities is due to the facilities elements of the indirect cost, though estimates range as high as 47 percent for Department of Health and Human Services grants. More important, the federal government has never collected data on how much universities have actually applied from their reimbursements to facilities construction and maintenance.[37]

In any case, beset by college and university officials bemoaning the condition of their facilities, Chairman Fuqua and the House Committee

36. See, in particular, *University Research: Effect of Indirect Cost Revisions and Options for Future Changes*, op. cit., and Knezo, op. cit.
37. An indirect cost consists of eight "cost pools," one of which reflects the building use allowance. Other cost pools reflect such expenses as libraries, equipment use, and departmental administration. On the capping of the administration cost pool, see Spyros Andreopolous, "David Packard Calls OMB-Proposed Cuts a 'Serious Mistake,'" *Campus Report*, Stanford University, April 2, 1986, p. 1. On the federal government's calculation of the facilities cost pool, according to Ann T. Lanier, senior sciences research analyst at NSF, the federal government has never determined what the total building use allowance cost pool has been in any given year. What data do exist are "not in a useable format." Moreover, universities have not been asked to account for how they use their reimbursement, that is, whether it has been reapplied to cover facility maintenance and construction cost. John Jankowski, the director of NSF's Research and Development Statistics Program, states, "One major drawback is that there is not a hard and fast rule on whether they [the institution] must/should use these funds, plus, until just recently, institutions did not have to keep separate records." E-mail correspondence, February 25, 1998. Under urging from OMB, for the FY 1998 NSF facilities survey, universities will for the first time be asked this question. Lanier is the coordinator of the NSF survey of the condition and financing of academic research facilities. Interview, February 24, 1998.

on Science and Technology decided that a response by Congress first required a more systematic and authoritative analysis of the true extent of the problem than was provided in these various estimates. Consequently, in the National Science Foundation Reauthorization Act of 1986, Congress directed NSF to collect and permanently maintain a data base on the status of academic research facilities and to issue every two years a report assessing the condition of these facilities.

NSF complied and undertook a large-scale survey, the results of which were immediately denounced by higher education. The survey was the largest of its kind. The survey sample consisted of all 165 universities designated as doctorate-granting institutions by the Department of Education. NSF's report, however, tended to focus on the top fifty academic recipients of federal research funding, which possessed more than half of all facility space and which conducted more than half of all academic research in the United States.

The report indicated that the majority of these top fifty schools classified their facilities as in good or excellent condition. To modernize and improve their facilities further, these institutions were planning and constructing new facilities. "When completed," the report stated, "new construction currently in progress will increase research space at all doctorate-granting institutions by as much as 7 percent. New construction planned between 1986 and 1991 will increase existing space by as much as 19 percent."[38] These universities, moreover, were financing this construction with minimal federal support, about 10 percent of the total funding. At the next tier of research universities, the following fifty institutions, the majority ranked their facilities in fair or poor condition, but even some of these schools were in the process of constructing or planning new facilities. Altogether, the cost of current construction in 1985–6 was $1.7 billion, and costs during the next five years were estimated at $5.8 billion.

Thus, NSF's picture of the academic facilities problem was that real needs existed, particularly among lesser-ranked institutions. Yet, at the elite research universities that conducted the bulk of the nation's basic research, the facilities were in reasonably good condition, with additional facilities being constructed or planned. All this was taking place without significant federal participation or cost.

NSF's report elicited an intensely hostile response from the higher education community. "Virtually everyone we have discussed the report with," a joint higher education association rebuttal proclaimed, "says

38. *Science and Engineering Research Facilities at Doctorate Granting Institutions* (Washington, D.C.: National Science Foundation, 1986), p. xiii.

that the message it conveys, especially in its executive summary, is that universities do not face critical problems with research facilities."[39] The associations argued that the report severely underplayed the concerns of researchers and university officials, who believed that the lack of adequate facilities limited the quality and production of research. The survey's focus on the top fifty schools greatly underestimated facilities needs throughout higher education. Furthermore, although federal money did constitute only about 10 percent of the direct funding involved in ongoing facilities construction, the use of federally tax-exempt bonds and special federal tax incentives for private donations and endowments accounted for another 33 to 53 percent of the financing of this construction. Even this form of federal contribution would be reduced, as the Tax Reform Act of 1986 capped the amount of tax-exempt bonds private colleges and universities could use for this purpose at $150 million per institution. Not until the passage of the Taxpayer Relief Act of 1997 would this cap be repealed.[40]

Higher education's reaction was to be expected. Any official report of this significance, identified even by the higher education associations as a "landmark work," which portrayed the facilities problem as less than dire in its consequences for academic research and the nation, could seriously undermine all the efforts undertaken to create a federal facilities program. Many higher education lobbyists in Washington, moreover, had long suspected that the White House and NSF were trying to downplay the facilities issue. By minimizing or even denying the existence of the facilities problem, the White House could justifiably refuse to spend the billions of dollars that would be required to remedy the problem. In 1985, for example, NASULGC's political office, led by Jerry Roschwalb, issued its assessment of the facilities situation, and of the White House Office of Management and Budget's (OMB) opposition to any facilities survey:

> Those very bright folks [at OMB] recognized that any survey or study conducted would lead to a conclusion that substantial funds be committed that

39. "The Research Facilities Needs of Universities: A Critique of the NSF Report, 'Science and Engineering Research Facilities at Doctorate-Granting Institutions, September 1986,'" American Association of State Colleges and Universities, American Council on Education, American Society for Engineering Education, Association of American Universities, Council of Graduate Schools in the United States, Council on Governmental Relations, National Association of Independent Colleges and Universities, and National Association of State Universities and Land-Grant Colleges, Washington, D.C., March 1987, p. 3.

40. On the possible effects of the lifting of the cap, see Kim Stronsnider, "Lifting of Cap on Tax-Exempt Bonds Gives Private Colleges New Options," *Chronicle of Higher Education*, September 19, 1997, p. A41.

the Administration would rather not have to spend. . . . The point is that any studies conducted are desirable as they lend both statistical and anecdotal evidence for the need. However, as noted, the need is so enormous and the probabilities of funding levels even at the most reasonable expectations are so small, a percentage of the need hardly seems worth a major debate.[41]

Just getting Congress to require the NSF to conduct the survey was a victory, but the report's findings tarnished the victory.

The report simply reinforced the position taken by NSF's director, Erich Bloch, that facilities funding should be the federal government's lowest priority in supporting university research. Bloch acknowledged that NSF conducted the survey in haste and that it "was not as thorough as it could have been." Nevertheless,

> [t]he issue, the outcome of all these studies is that A, there is a facilities problem, no doubt about it; B: it was not as bad as people said it was, because there were other forces at work, not the federal government. Yes, the federal government didn't spend anything, but we knew that before we went into it. There was a lot of state money going into [facilities]. There was a lot of private money going into [facilities]. So it was not as bad as people thought it was. That convinced me that, you know, in a tight environment, facilities are not my first priority, and I said so.

Bloch's priorities were funding research grants and graduate fellowships; people came before bricks and mortar. If the federal budget provided additional money for new facilities, that might be acceptable, but higher education wanted new money for both research and facilities in an era of budget constraints. "[The higher education associations] always have been after me," Bloch complained. "'Why don't you fund facilities?' I told them: tell me where I should take the money from. If you tell me I should put it in facilities, tell me where I should take it out. Well that's it, that wasn't acceptable. They wanted new money, additional money. Well, yes, so do I. That's not the real world for heaven's sake." Besides, Bloch believed that facilities funding would never solve the earmarking problem anyway, as he testified on numerous occasions before the House and Senate appropriations subcommittees that funded NSF. "I don't care how much money you put in there," he said. There would always be the university president "who lost," who failed to obtain facilities money through an established program and who would seek an earmark.[42]

41. Jerry Roschwalb, National Association of State Universities and Land-Grant Colleges, June 28, 1985, p. 2.
42. Interview with Erich Bloch, January 16, 1992.

During the 1980s, Bloch served as the earliest and most influential spokesperson for the Reagan and later the Bush White House on the earmarking issue. Despite the enthusiastic support offered for a new facilities program in the Packard–Bromley report, it was Bloch, in cooperation with OMB, who set the tone for the Reagan administration's position on facilities. For Bloch, facilities just did not rank high on NSF's list of priorities. The federal government, Bloch said, never had and never would have the obligation to fund academic facilities:

> The obligation is not to fix the roof of a university, that's not an obligation. . . . I just don't believe that people have a right to expect that the federal government does everything. It doesn't have that obligation. Never did. Never will.[43]

The White House Science Council might have an impressive title, but it was Bloch who managed a real federal agency with a real budget, and he rejected using that budget to fund facilities. When Bloch defended his FY 1990 budget proposal before the relevant House appropriations subcommittee, he declared that the problem of earmarking for bricks and mortar was one that could not be solved by an NSF facilities program. Subcommittee Chair Robert Traxler (D-MI) then observed, "this is indeed a utopian view, and has as much relevance to the real world as Alice in Wonderland," to which Bloch readily agreed.[44] Meanwhile, the administration expressed no interest in obligating the federal government to solve a $10 to $20 billion facilities problem. When Ronald Reagan sent his warm letter of thanks to David Packard for the panel's report, no endorsement was offered for the Fuqua bill or for academic facilities funding.[45]

There would be more surveys, studies, and proposals to come, each in some way characterizing nearly half of academic research facilities as being in a state of disrepair and decay. In response to higher education's repeated and justifiable claim that the 1986 facilities report was flawed, NSF expanded its later surveys to encompass more institutions. In the 1988 survey 247 schools were included in the sample. As the samples grew, so did the scope of the problem. In both the 1988 and 1990 sur-

---

43. Ibid.

44. Interview with Raymond E. Bye, director, NSF Office of Legislative and Public Affairs, June 15, 1995. Bye pointed out this significant difference between Eric Bloch's position as the leader of a line agency and an advisory group with no budget. On the exchange between Bloch and Traxler, see author's notes of the testimony of Eric Bloch before the House Veterans Administration–Housing and Urban Affairs–Independent Agencies Appropriations Subcommittee, March 16, 1989.

45. Letter from President Ronald Reagan, The White House, to The Honorable David Packard, Chairman, Panel on the Health of U.S. Universities, May 16, 1986.

veys, approximately 25 percent of facilities were suitable for state-of-the-art research; about 33 percent were designated as effective for most uses; and some 40 percent required repair or renovation. Facilities tended to be in better condition at the top 100 research universities and less so in other research and nondoctorate-granting schools. The cost of ongoing and planned construction numbered in the billions of dollars, with the federal government providing only a tiny fraction, less than 10 percent, of the total.[46]

Higher Education, Facilities, and the Fight against Earmarking

During the 1980s, the higher education community sought unsuccessfully to encourage the federal government to fund a large-scale academic facilities program. Although the condition of the nation's research facilities had been, and remains, a topic of concern for the leaders of academic science, the practice of earmarking facility funds forced the higher education associations to make the enactment of federal facilities legislation one of their major initiatives. Despite the support of influential congressional allies, higher education failed in this effort, with the notable exception of the facilities program located in NSF. Even this program, however, has received minimal appropriations, an amount that pales in comparison to the need and demand for funds.

Congressional support for new facilities programs continued into the early 1990s in the guise of the Higher Education Colloquium on Science Facilities, a group chaired by Sen. Terry Sanford (D-NC) and cochaired by Sen. John Danforth (R-MO) and Rep. George Brown (D-CA). The group unsuccessfully petitioned President Bush to create a plan for in-

---

46. See, for example, *Scientific and Engineering Research Facilities at Universities and Colleges: 1988* (Washington, D.C.: National Science Foundation, September 1988), NSF Report No. 88-320; *Scientific and Engineering Research Facilities at Universities: 1990* (Washington, D.C.: National Science Foundation, September 1990), NSF Report No. 90-318; and *Scientific and Engineering Research Facilities at Universities and Colleges: 1994* (Washington, D.C.: National Science Foundation, 1994), Report 94-315. Also see "University Research Facilities: A National Problem Requiring a National Response," The Ad Hoc Committee on Academic Research Facilities, Association of American Universities and National Association of State Universities and Land-Grant Colleges, June 1989; "Perspectives on Financing Academic Research Facilities: A Resource for Policy Formulation," Government–University–Industry Research Roundtable, National Academy Press, Washington, D.C., October 1989; and "Research Facility Financing: Near-Term Options," Government–University–Industry Research Roundtable, Washington, D.C., February 1991.

vesting in academic facilities. It disbanded after Sanford lost his reelection bid and Danforth retired from the Senate.[47]

As higher education discovered in the 1980s and 1990s, the federal budget's overall constraints prevented the government from appropriating sufficient money even to meet the authorized levels for the programs that do exist, let alone solving the facilities problem.[48] Furthermore, with tight budgets, funding research has proved to be a higher priority for the elite institutions than supporting bricks and mortar to appease earmarking schools. The elite schools would receive some federal funding anyway, through indirect cost recovery; the politics of facilities construction clearly indicated that these institutional grants would come at the expense of research funding. Summarizing higher education's dilemma, Richard Atkinson, chancellor of the University of California at San Diego and former director of NSF, concluded: "I just think there are too few dollars. I mean you've got to have mammoth dollars flowing into facilities to make any difference. And I just don't think there's any likelihood of that kind of funding being available. I mean I'd love to have a facilities program too, but not at the expense of the dollars that exist now for funding research in the universities, because they're already sparse."[49] Without a large-scale facilities program, however, the elite research schools have little to offer to induce the earmarking institutions to change their ways.

47. Letter from Sanford and twenty-six other members to President Bush, July 26, 1990, and a "dear colleague" letter from Sanford asking members to write to Bush on facilities, August 13, 1990. In an interview Sanford stated, "If we are going to allocate scarce resources and keep a strong science base in the country we ought to do it through an orderly process. . . . I wasn't too disturbed about [earmarking] until some of the major research universities that had been well advantaged under the peer review system began to come down here seeking funds." Interview with Sen. Terry Sanford, September 6, 1991.

48. On higher education lobbying: "Given the squeeze on dollars for this year's appropriations, the research institution associations have testified in favor of no funds for FY 90 to be accompanied by a major effort to convince the Administration to put funding into the NSF budget for FY 91. . . . Regrettably, there is no unanimity in the higher education community on this subject and the lines are drawn as was predicted decades ago, not between public and private but between large and small. . . . It began as the Roe bill, one aimed almost entirely at research intensive institutions with additional attention to minority schools," in "Memorandum, to the NASULGC Federal Relations Network and Interested Parties, from Jerry Roschwalb, Subject: A Mid-Year Conversation Updating Major Issues in Higher Education Federal Relations," National Association of State Universities and Land-Grant Colleges, Washington, D.C., July 10, 1989, p. 9.

49. Interview with Richard Atkinson, March 12, 1992. Also see Richard C. Atkinson and William A. Blanpied, "Peer Review and the Public Interest," *Issues in Science and Technology*, Summer 1985, pp. 101–14.

5

Lobbyists, Lobbying, and the Pursuit of Academic Earmarks

Lobbyists have played a critical role in the spread of academic earmarking. Not only do they perform their traditional function as intermediaries between legislators and special interests, they actively recruit universities as clients and encourage them to engage in earmarking. Behaving as what John Tierney calls true "policy entrepreneurs," often on a fee-for-earmark basis, with few if any sanctions imposed on their actions, lobbyists have greatly expanded the number of institutions willing to engage in earmarking, as well as the dollar value of their earmarks.[1] These lobbyists make it possible for busy university presidents inexperienced in the ways of the federal government to obtain earmarked funds through an increasingly fiscally constrained federal budgetary process.

The Rise of Academic Lobbying in the 1980s

Prior to the early 1980s, universities and colleges relied primarily upon the various higher education associations to represent their interests in Washington. A few schools had opened their own governmental relations offices in the capital (the University of California system did so as early as 1966), but the total number was relatively small. By 1981, only twenty-seven schools had registered in *Washington Representatives* for

---

1. John T. Tierney, "Organized Interests and the Nation's Capitol," in Mark P. Petracca (ed.), *The Politics of Interests* (Boulder: Westview Press, 1992), p. 211. On the traditional function of lobbyists, see Jeffrey M. Berry, *Lobbying for the People: The Political Behavior of Public Interest Groups* (Princeton: Princeton University Press, 1977); Lester W. Milbrath, *The Washington Lobbyists* (Chicago: Rand McNally, 1963); Norman J. Ornstein and Shirley Elder, *Interest Groups, Lobbying, and Policy Making* (Washington, D.C.: Congressional Quarterly Press, 1978); and Robert H. Salisbury, "An Exchange Theory of Interest Groups," *Midwest Journal of Political Science* 13 (1969): 1–32.

either locating their own in-house lobbyist in Washington or hiring a D.C. consultant. By 1988 the number had grown to 73 and by 1993 to more than 120.[2] What stimulated this growth were the real and perceived effects of President Ronald Reagan's "revolution" and the rise of academic earmarking.

Reagan's initial budget requests contained significant cuts in federally supported domestic research. Actual obligations for domestic research fell from $15.3 billion in FY 1981 to $14.3 billion in FY 1982 and then to $13.9 billion in FY 1983. In the area of basic research, the source of funding for academic science, many domestic agency budgets suffered either nominal or real reductions when inflation is taken into account.[3] These cuts, proposed by the president and approved by Congress, sent shock waves throughout the academic science community. At the University of California system, for example, not only did the dollar value of federal contracts and grants fall, but so did the number of faculty proposals for such awards, suggesting that faculty had at least momentarily lost faith in the government's willingness to support their research.[4] As a consequence of the budget cuts and the view that there were issues of particular concern to the university that were not being addressed adequately by the higher education associations, the university expanded its Washington staff and spent $1 million on a new building to enhance its presence and represent its interests more effectively. The University of California was not alone in this effort. Other institutions, whether to protect their own research funding or to secure academic earmarks, built buildings or rented office space, expanded their faculty and student programs in Washington to gain visibility, added to or established their own lobbying staffs, or hired contract lobbyists.

When it comes to federal government relations, universities usually hire one of three types of lobbyists, often more than one, and occasionally all three simultaneously.[5] The first type of lobbyist is the trade asso-

2. For the number of lobbyists in 1993, see *Washington Representatives* (New York: Columbia Books, Inc., 1993). For 1981 and 1988, see Grace Tsuang, "'Pork Barrel Science': Implications for University Research Efforts and Interest Group Theory," unpublished manuscript, Yale University Law School, May 18, 1989.
3. James D. Savage, "Federal R&D Budget Policy in the Reagan Administration," *Public Budgeting and Finance*, Summer 1987, pp. 37–51.
4. For the consequence of the Reagan budget on the University of California, see "President Saxon's Statement on the Effects of the Federal Budget on the University of California," February Regents' Meeting, February 19, 1982, and "Report on Federal Funding for the University of California, Report to the Regents' Committee on Finance," February 4, 1983.
5. For this classification, see Clive S. Thomas and Ronald J. Hrenbenar, "Changing Patterns of Interest Group Activity: A Regional Perspective," in Petracca, op. cit., p. 156.

ciation, in the form of the various higher education associations located in Washington. Universities that are members of these organizations pay dues and share a common lobbying staff. Some institutions that do not want to invest personnel in federal government relations may rely solely on these associations to represent their interests. Institutional membership in these organizations may be very restrictive, or it may be very broad and resemble a form of entitlement, with all institutions of a certain classification expecting access. In either case, academic trade associations, particularly the more prestigious and long-established ones, rarely employ their resources to recruit new members. Because of their status and the collective benefits they provide, individual institutions approach them for membership. The policy scope of these organizations may be very broad, such that they address, for example, all research issues, or all undergraduate issues, or all matters regarding land-grant institutions. Or their focus may be narrow and represent just academic disciplines, such as the social sciences, or they may be even narrower and represent fields within disciplines, such as physics. Regardless of scope, the services provided by trade association lobbyists are generally diffuse and benefit all member clients rather than particular institutions.

The second type of federal relations specialist is the in-house lobbyist, who is a regular, salaried university employee. The in-house lobbyist usually directs or is assigned to a university public affairs or federal government relations office. The nature of federal relations activities may require a rapid, even same-day decision, such as when presidential action is required to respond to changes in federal legislation. Consequently, the chain of command linking a university president to the lobbyist is rarely very long, perhaps involving one or two individuals, such as a vice president for university relations. Moreover, universities often rely upon a very small number of federal relations lobbyists. Whereas a public university may employ a staff of five or more to lobby the state on its budget, that same university will often hire a single lobbyist to manage federal relations.[6] The in-house federal lobbyist, therefore,

---

6. Chris Snowbeck, "Lobbyists Help Push UVA Bill," *Daily Progress*, March 3, 1996. To lobby on its state budget, for example, the University of Virginia relied upon in-house lobbyists; numerous high-ranking administrators, including the president; and a private firm. At the same time, only one in-house administrator was employed to monitor federal legislation – a vice provost for research, who had numerous other responsibilities. Otherwise, the university depended primarily on the various higher education associations for monitoring federal actions. The University of Virginia ranked fortieth in the receipt of federal research funds in 1993. Also see Scott Ellis Ferrin, "Logrolling for Alma Mater: An Investigation of the In-House Lobbyist in American Colleges and Universities," unpublished doctoral dissertation, Harvard University, 1996.

serves as the direct agent of a university president, although the level of oversight over the lobbyist varies among institutions.

The third type of lobbyist, and the most entrepreneurial, is the independent contractor or consultant. Although the independent contractor may have many clients, like the trade association lobbyist, the services and benefits offered by the independent contractor resemble those provided by the in-house lobbyist, as they are very specific for each client institution. One university may seek a $10 million earmark for a polymer laboratory; another university may desire half that amount for a biomedical facility. Because lobbyists of this variety depend on their client list for financial survival, they actively recruit their fee-for-earmark university clients, unlike either in-house or trade association lobbyists, both of whom receive salaries rather than commissions. Typically, to entice prospective clients, the independent lobbyist offers a university the opportunity to obtain an earmarked project worth several times the lobbyist's fee. Moreover, independent contractors – and their clients – have sought to justify academic earmarking in congressional testimony, speeches, and editorial statements.

Schlossberg and Cassidy, and Cassidy and Associates

Kenneth Schlossberg and Gerald Cassidy are the most important independent contractor lobbyists. It was the firm of Schlossberg and Cassidy, and later that of Cassidy and Associates, that perfected the art of academic earmarking, as they located the money for earmarking in the remotest and most obscure accounts in the federal budget. All the while, they have aggressively encouraged the expansion of earmarking by promising universities, some of them eager, others reluctant, the scarce dollars needed for their most desired research facilities and projects.

Schlossberg and Cassidy served together as staff director and chief counsel of the Senate Select Committee on Nutrition and Human Needs, chaired by Sen. George McGovern (D-SD) from 1969 to 1975. They then left the committee and formed their own lobbying firm. Soon they were approached by Tufts University President Jean Mayer to help secure funding for Mayer's planned nutrition and aging center. Mayer, a prominent nutritionist, had come to know Schlossberg and Cassidy during McGovern's hearings on hunger in America. Working their network of political friends, Schlossberg and Cassidy obtained their first great success in academic earmarking: a $32 million project for Tufts. In addition to this earmark, due to their efforts, Tufts received $10 million for a veterinary school and $7.5 million for an intercultural center.

In the early 1980s, Schlossberg and Cassidy's client list also included Columbia and Catholic universities. To help Columbia get $5 million for its chemistry building, the team urged the university to justify its project to members of Congress by playing up the need to strengthen the nation's research in chemistry and chemicals in the face of the "threat" posed by Japanese research. With this argument, Columbia then asked for help from Rep. Charles Rangel (D-NY) to sponsor legislation for the project.

To help Catholic University, the school's religious affiliation became an important means of access to the political process. The president of Catholic, William J. Byron, had served at Loyola University in New Orleans, where he had come to know Sen. J. Bennett Johnston (D-LA), the ranking member of both the Senate Energy and Natural Resources Committee and the Energy Appropriations Subcommittee, and Rep. Lindy Boggs (D-LA), the ranking member of the House Energy Appropriations Subcommittee. With their aid, that of the Archbishop of New Orleans, Philip Hanna, a former auxiliary bishop at Catholic, and Humberto Cardinal Medeiros of Boston, who served on Catholic University's board of trustees, Byron approached another noteworthy Catholic, House Speaker Thomas P. O'Neill (D-MA), for assistance in obtaining that university's earmark. O'Neill used his clout to pass the floor amendments that authorized the two projects. Through these contacts, Schlossberg and Cassidy took on another Catholic school as a client – O'Neill's alma mater, Boston College – and another New England institution, Boston University.

Schlossberg and Cassidy justified their earmarking efforts in several ways. They claimed that federal research funds were disproportionately allocated. In particular, they argued that federal research funds were unfairly being sent by the Reagan administration to a DOE national laboratory managed by the University of California and that earmarking was needed to offset the regional bias. As Schlossberg observed, "We could argue how unfair it would be if the West Coast got everything and the East Coast got nothing."[7]

They also tried to legitimize their lobbying by claiming that their earmarks had funded "brick and mortar" facilities projects, and not actual

---

7. Burt Schorr, "Breaking Tradition, More Colleges Go Directly to Congress for Funds," *Wall Street Journal*, March 5, 1984. Also see Daniel S. Greenberg, "How Two Lobbyists Work the Washington Scene," *Science & Government Report* 13(19), November 15, 1983, p. 1; Florence Graves, "Hog Heaven," *Common Cause Magazine*, July–August 1986, pp. 17–23; Colin Norman, "How to Win Buildings and Influence Congress," *Science* 222, December 16, 1983, pp. 1211–13; Ken Schlossberg, "Earmarking by Congress Can Help Rebuild the Country's Research Infrastructure," *Chronicle of Higher Education*, January 24, 1990, p. A48; and "Testimony by Ken Schlossberg, President, Ken Schlossberg Consultants, Before the Committee on Science, Space and Technology, June 16, 1993."

research that otherwise should be supported through peer review. "So far as I know," Schlossberg wrote in a full-page editorial in the *Chronicle of Higher Education*, "nobody involved in the earmarking process has proposed that peer review be politicized or eliminated where research grants are concerned."[8] Earmarked facilities would enable weaker institutions to improve their research capabilities and then compete on more equal grounds for peer-reviewed funding. The elite research institutions simply would not support expensive facilities programs as long as the federal budget was constrained, such that facilities funding would come at the cost of student financial aid and research. Moreover, until the federal government established a meaningful research facilities program, earmarking was the only alternative open to institutions, particularly the have-not schools, to receive federal money.

Nevertheless, as Schlossberg later acknowledged, when it came to earmarking strictly research projects as opposed to facilities, "I have done that. It's usually happened when I have represented an institution on a facility issue, and they have some grant that they've been pursuing, and they've had trouble getting it." Furthermore, when asked if he would continue to pursue earmarks even if a federal facilities program were established, Schlossberg replied, "Yes. Because I don't think the world is perfect in any respect. . . . Congress has always retained to itself the right to intervene . . . that it thinks that a particular project is worth doing, either faster than an agency wants to do it, or because an agency doesn't want to do it."[9] So, despite the assertion that earmarking was a specific remedy for a particular problem, Schlossberg and Cassidy's true position was that of an entrepreneurial, commission-based, fee-for-earmarking, lobbying firm: when a university client approached them for help on a project that was politically feasible and likely to be successfully funded, they usually accepted.

In 1984, Gerald Cassidy bought out his partner and formed the firm of Cassidy and Associates, which has become one of the largest, most influential, and most aggressive lobbying firms in Washington; its specialty is working the appropriations process and obtaining academic earmarks. Cassidy immediately expanded his staff of lobbyists, hiring numerous former staffers who had served powerful and key members of Congress or who had staffed the most important congressional committees, especially the appropriations committees. Other Cassidy lobbyists have included Frank Rose and Elvis J. Stahr, Jr., former presidents of the universities of Alabama and Indiana, respectively; Gen. Paul X. Kelley,

8. Ken Schlossberg, "Earmarking by Congress."
9. Interview with Kenneth Schlossberg, September 27, 1991.

former Marine Corps commandant; Robert K. Dawson, former associate director of OMB; Robert Farmer, a chief Democratic party fund raiser and party treasurer; Jody Powell, who served as press secretary in President Carter's administration; and Sheila Tate, a press secretary for President Bush.[10]

To pay for all of this talent, Cassidy's fees charged to his university clients total hundreds of thousands of dollars a year. Boston University's president, John Silber, recounted that his school paid the firm "somewhere in the neighborhood of $400,000 a year." Michigan Technological University paid Cassidy $20,000 a month plus expenses to obtain an earmark worth $1.75 million. "We've been very satisfied" said Dale Stein, the university's president. Other agreements include a $90,000 fee paid by Columbia University for a $1 million earmark and a $254,000 fee paid by the Rochester Institute of Technology for a $1.75 million earmark. In 1991, the University of Hawaii hired Cassidy for a $520,000 two-year contract. "It's extraordinarily cost-effective," observed David Yount, the university's vice president for research, "if you think about the amount the university has paid and the amount the university has received." During the four preceding years, Cassidy received $636,000 in fees and obtained some $33 million in earmarks for the school.[11]

Although Cassidy's efforts often result in success, bringing multi-million-dollar earmarked projects to various universities, Cassidy and other Washington lobbyists are usually careful to take on or to recruit as clients schools that are either already or potentially politically well connected. Thus, if earmarking is offered as a remedy to the bias of peer review, the selection of clients to receive earmarks is also biased. The reason for this caution is that success breeds higher fees and improves business, while the fact and image of failure lowers them and damages business. "We're very, very selective," observed Cassidy. "For every

---

10. Daniel S. Greenberg, "Working on Capitol Hill for Science and Profit," *Science & Government Report* 15(20), December 1, 1985, p. 1; June Watanabe, "UH Hires D.C. Lobbyist; Some Regents Upset," *Hawaii Star-Bulletin*, September 11, 1986; Dan Morgan, "As Federal Funding Tightens, Lobbyists Find a Surer Way," *Washington Post*, June 18, 1989; Brooks Jackson, "Fund-Raiser Goes to Washington as Lobbyist, Democrats' Party Treasurer," *Wall Street Journal*, February 14, 1989.

11. *Academic Earmarks – Part III*, Committee on Science, Space, and Technology, U.S. House of Representatives, September 21 and 22 and October 6, 1994, p. 298; David Rogers, "Lobbying Firm Gets $1 Million in Fees from Institutions Seeking Federal Grants," *Wall Street Journal*, May 30, 1991; and Colleen Cordes, "Washington Lobbyists Continue to Sign Up University Clients, Capitalizing on Academe's Demand for Political Expertise," *Chronicle of Higher Education*, October 9, 1991, p. A31.

client we contract with, we probably send away at least one. We have to really believe that the project is fundable."[12]

Two earmarks of these fundable projects involved Loyola College and Loyola University. In 1989, Loyola College in Maryland selected Cassidy and Associates to represent its interests for a fee of $10,000 a month because Cassidy had worked for several other Jesuit institutions. At the time, Loyola hoped to build a computing center, but it had raised only about $5.5 million of the projected $13.5 million required. Cassidy's firm soon repackaged the computer center, calling it a "Center for Advanced Information and Resource Management Studies," and found money for the project in the federal government's National Defense Stockpile Transaction Fund, a budget account whose intended purpose had nothing to do with supporting academic research. According to a Senate appropriations subcommittee report, the new center would provide "specialized management education and training" and would manage "these and other federal systems management problems on a government-wide basis." The university received $3 million from the Stockpile Fund for the center, with much of the credit deservedly belonging to Sen. Barbara Mikulski (D-MD), an adjunct professor at Loyola, and Rep. Steny Hoyer (D-MD), both of whom served on the appropriations subcommittees that provided budgets for the fund.[13] Cassidy's function was to work with the parties involved, namely, the university and the members and their staffs, and show how the parts of the political and budgetary process could be put together to create the earmark.

Another Loyola University, that of Chicago, also hired Cassidy. The firm's lobbyists then asked Rep. Dan Rostenkowski (D-IL) to help the school fund its Center for Commerce and Industrial Expansion. Rostenkowski, then chair of the House Ways and Means Committee, had graduated from Loyola, and on the university's behalf he approached House Defense Appropriations Subcommittee Chair Rep. John Murtha (D-PA) for the project. With Murtha's intervention, Loyola received $24 million for its business school in 1991. To pay for the earmark, every domestic discretionary program in the federal budget was cut. The project's initial funding came from the category of the federal budget called "defense discretionary spending," which supported the Defense Department, a category with sufficient money to accommodate the earmark's cost. Loyola, however, worried that as a result it could then be called upon to conduct military research. So the cost of the center's funding

12. Daniel S. Greenberg, "Working on Capitol Hill for Science and Profit," *Science & Government Report* 15(20), December 1, 1985, p. 1.

13. Dan Morgan, "As Federal Funding Tightens, Lobbyists Find a Surer Way," *Washington Post*, June 18, 1989.

was transferred to the Department of Education, an agency classified as domestic discretionary in the federal budget. That earmark, however, exceeded the mandatory budget caps agreed upon in the 1990 Budget Enforcement Act for that budget category, so to bring domestic spending back under the cap, a rare across-the-board budget sequester or cut was triggered, which required a reduction of .0013 percent in all domestic discretionary accounts. To fund the Loyola earmark, virtually every discretionary domestic program in the budget was cut.[14]

If many of Cassidy's client schools are already represented in Congress by powerful and influential members, why do universities hire such lobbyists? Cassidy and other earmarking lobbyists are able to see the connections between clients, politicians, and the legislative process. "These people know how it works in Washington," observed one university vice provost for research, who nominally directed federal relations for that school. "I'm in experimental science, and these things boggle my mind." "They taught us things about how to deal with Congress," recounted Thomas Scheye, provost at Loyola College in Maryland, of Cassidy's assistance. Citing the lack of resources to hire full-time, in-house federal relations experts, William J. Byron, president of Catholic University, noted that "the vast majority of colleges and universities cannot count on that type of well-informed, persistent representation. Nor can they rely on an elected official's staff to know of all legislative opportunities. . . ." John Silber, president of Boston University, justified his hiring of Cassidy because of the "amateur hour in our own shop" and the deficiencies of Boston University's in-house lobbyists. Ken Schlossberg offered a similar justification for his firm's being hired when he observed of Columbia University that "they're not here [in Washington] full time. . . . We sit down with them and discuss what their government relations program is. . . . Then we try to come to some sort of assessment of strengths and weaknesses and how they can improve their government relations program."[15] In the early 1990s, as shown in Table 5, Cassidy and Associates could claim more than forty

14. Martin Tolchin, "Lawmaker's Aid to School May Skew Federal Budget," *New York Times*, April 3, 1991; George Hager, "Tiny Sequester Hits," *Congressional Quarterly Weekly*, April 27, 1991, p. 1042.
15. Morgan, op. cit.; William J. Byron, S.J., "Why Universities Employ Lobbyists," *Washington Post*, August 3, 1989; *Academic Earmarks – Part III*, Committee on Science, Space, and Technology, U.S. House of Representatives, September 21 and 22; October 6, 1994, p. 298; Daniel S. Greenberg, "How Two Lobbyists Work the Washington Scene," *Science & Government Report* 13(19), November 15, 1983, p. 1. Also on lobbyists, see Bruce C. Wolpe, *Lobbying Congress: How the System Works* (Washington, D.C.: Congressional Quarterly, 1990).

Table 5. *Higher education clients of Cassidy and Associates*

Albion College
Babson College
Bentley College
Boston College
Boston University
Buena Vista College
California Community Colleges
Clark-Atlanta University
Columbia University
Farleigh Dickinson
Florida Institute of Technology
Gonzaga University
Hahnemann University Hospital
Illinois Eastern Community College
La Salle University
Lehigh University
Lewis and Clark College
Loma Linda University
Loyola Marymount University
Miami-Dade Community College
Marquette University
Medical College of Wisconsin
Michigan Technological University
Monterey Institute of International Studies
New Jersey Institute of Technology
Northwestern University
Polytechnic University of New York
Rochester Institute of Technology
Saint Joseph's University
Saint Norbert's College
Saint Xavier College
Tougaloo College
Tri-State University
Tufts University
Tufts University Veterinarian School
University of the Arts
University of Detroit Mercy
University of Hawaii
University of Pennsylvania
University of San Francisco
University of Southern Mississippi
University of Saint Thomas
University of Vermont

Source: Washington Representatives (New York: Columbia Books Inc., 1993 and 1996).

universities and colleges as its clients, each paying some $10,000 a month in fees.

The elite lobbying firms are quick to point out these advantages when they actively recruit new clients. In 1989, for example, both the firms of Cassidy and Associates and Ken Schlossberg Consultants unsuccessfully attempted to recruit the same reluctant client, the University of Virginia, whose presidents, Robert M. O'Neil and John T. Casteen III, had elected to abide by the AAU moratorium on earmarking. Both firms sent representatives to meet with the university's officials, both promised to bring the university earmarked funds, and both noted their previous victories in obtaining earmarks. Numerous newspaper clippings gave reference to these accomplishments. Cassidy promised help in expanding the university's astronomy center, and Schlossberg promised the same for its neurobiology project.

Schlossberg's written material listed his services and accomplishments and stated what the client should expect from the legislative process:

> During the entire time [I have lobbied for earmarks], I have helped secure over $200 million for several dozen facilities of all kinds at fifteen institutions. . . . Our rule of thumb is to expect the process to require at least one Congress, meaning two sessions, or two years. During the first year, we develop the proposal until we are completely satisfied with it, a task that may take up to as much as three months. . . . If all goes well, we will achieve an initial authorization or appropriation during the first year . . . and a subsequent appropriation in the second year. If the size of the sought-after funding is substantial, then full funding may require several years of additional appropriations.[16]

Schlossberg went on to cite his successful earmarks, including those for the University of Nevada at Reno and Wake Forest University, and sent copies of his newspaper editorials in favor of earmarking. The charge for a $10 million earmark would be $10,000 a month for two years.

Once hired by a university, the lobbyists and the schools that employ them are aware that the direct inducements they can offer members of Congress to support their projects are of a special nature. Universities, unlike corporations and unions, rarely operate political action committees (PACS); fewer than thirty university PACs have been identified.[17] Universities also generally refrain from actively engaging in electoral politics, and they avoid making financial contributions to candidates for

---

16. Letter from Ken Schlossberg to Dennis Barnes, University of Virginia, May 10, 1989.

17. For a list of university PACs, see Douglas Lederman, "Political Action Committees Help Lawmakers Who Help Universities," *Chronicle of Higher Education*, April 18, 1997, p. A29. Also see Phil Kuntz, "Colleges and Universities Give Little But Advice," *Congressional Quarterly Weekly Report*, April 15, 1989, pp. 820–4.

public office. The repercussions from taking a partisan stand in any given election would be particularly damaging for public universities, which are always at the mercy of governors and state legislatures.

Instead, lobbyists of all types who represent universities rely upon other attachments and loyalties to gain access to the political process. The case of Georgetown University is particularly illustrative of how universities may employ various inducements to aid them in influencing members of Congress. What makes Georgetown so interesting is that, being located in the District of Columbia, it lacks a voting member to represent it in Congress, as well as the obvious geographical links and associations that serve other colleges and universities when they approach their congressional delegations. First, as Rep. Vic Fazio (D-CA) observed, Georgetown, a parochial school, "tends to work through Catholic members, or those who are close to Catholic schools." Former House Majority Whip Tony Choelho (D-CA), a once-aspiring Jesuit priest, declared himself a "close friend" of Georgetown's. Other members, such as Sen. Patrick J. Leahy (D-VT) and Rep. Thomas J. Bliley, Jr. (R-VA), a member of the House Appropriations Committee, graduated from Georgetown, while others, including Sen. Ted Stevens (R-ALK), a member of the Appropriations Committee, and former Rep. Dan Rostenkowski, chair of the House Ways and Means Committee, have received honorary degrees. All of these members have been approached for favors by Georgetown, as have many of the Georgetown alumni who work as congressional staff. In the case of Rostenkowski, Georgetown awarded the degree virtually at the same time it sought provisions in tax legislation that was being considered by his Ways and Means Committee. In addition, committee members receive special care when they seek attention at the university's hospital and medical center, and they may be given tickets to university athletic events. The children of the members may also receive extra consideration when they apply for admission to Georgetown. In addition to these benefits and special ties, members are aware that, after leaving Congress, many of their colleagues join universities as faculty or even become university presidents. These incentives appear to be cumulatively successful; Georgetown received more than $109 million in earmarks from 1980 to 1996, despite the lack of a single voting member of Congress to represent it.[18]

Finally, although universities themselves avoid making financial contributions to politicians, their lobbyists do not. Between 1979 and 1995,

---

18. David S. Cloud, "Georgetown Wins Friends and Funds on Hill," *Congressional Quarterly Weekly Report*, June 4, 1988, pp. 1502–5.

Gerald Cassidy and his wife, Loretta, donated $346,000 in campaign contributions, more than any Washington lawyer or independent lobbyist. In 1995 the couple donated $42,200, ranking them fifth on the list of contributors. In addition to making direct campaign contributions, Cassidy and some of his nonacademic clients have contributed substantially to chaired professorships named for members of Congress, while also donating to and attending numerous testimonial dinners and events honoring the members. Although Democratic candidates received all of Cassidy's donations, his partisan leanings have not hindered his ability to work with Republican members of Congress in obtaining earmarks for their constituent schools. If Cassidy has been associated with Democratic causes, his chief assistant, James Fabiani, is connected to the Republican party, having worked for Rep. Silvio O. Conte (R-MA) and having served on the Dole for President National Finance Committee. To appeal to Republicans, Cassidy's firm also hired Sheila Tate, the former press secretary to Nancy Reagan and President George Bush. In 1996, the firm's contributions, as distinct from the personal contributions of Cassidy and his wife, to members of Congress reached $416,734, with 62 percent designated for Democratic members and 38 percent for Republicans. This amount earned the firm fourth place on the *Washington Post*'s list of contributions by legal and lobbying firms.[19]

Other lobbying firms also depend upon special relations with universities and members of Congress to maintain their businesses. In some cases, senior officers of the lobbying firms have attended the client university. The firm of Ryan McGinn, for example, whose senior vice president, Michael Fulton, attended West Virginia University, includes several West Virginia universities as its clients, as shown in Table 6. Similarly, the firm of Broydrick & Associates was founded by William Broydrick, a Catholic, who began his business by serving Jesuit clients. In another case, the firm Tapestry Consultants' principal officer, Rosemarie Piepenhagen, graduated from George Mason University, which became a Tapestry client. New, small firms often take on as their first

---

19. Ruth Marcus, "Lobbyists: Where the Money Went," *Washington Post*, May 7, 1996; "Contributions from Lawyers, Lobbyists," *Washington Post*, December 15, 1997. Cassidy's Democratic party identification is consistent with observations about the dominance of Democratic lobbyists in the health and labor policy areas. See Robert H. Salisbury, John P. Heinz, Robert L. Nelson, and Edward O. Laumann, "Triangles, Networks, and Hollow Cores: The Complex Geometry of Washington Interest Representation," in Mark P. Petracca (ed.), *The Politics of Interests* (Boulder: Westview Press, 1992), p. 136.

Table 6. *Other lobbyists and their higher education clients*

Advocacy Group
Arizona State University
University of Arizona
Georgia State University
New Mexico State University
Sam Houston State University
University of Utah
Dowling College
Florida State University
    Board of Regents

Broydrick & Associates
Loyola University of Chicago
Marquette University

Delchamps/Capital Link
Alabama School of Math and Science
Spring Hill College

FBA Incorporated
Florida State University System
St. Petersburg Jr. College
University of Alaska
University of Texas
University of Nevada, Las Vegas

Jefferson Group
University of Miami
Virginia Commonwealth University
Embry-Riddle Aeronautical College
Bethume-Cookman College

Jordon Burt Berenson & Johnson
New York University
University of Miami
Florida State University
University of Tulsa
University of Medicine and Dentistry
    of New Jersey

Patton, Boggs & Blow
George Mason University
Loyola University of New Orleans
University of Arizona Foundation
Johns Hopkins University
University of Maryland
Villa Julia College

Ryan McGinn
Fairfield University
John Carrol University
Kent State University
Shepard College
Texas A&M University
University of Detroit Mercy
West Virginia University
Wheeling Jesuit University
Xavier University

Sagmore Associates Inc.
Indiana State University
Indiana University
Indiana University, South Bend

Tapestry Consultants
George Mason University

Whitten & Diamond
Southeastern University
Temple University

Source: Washington Representatives (New York: Columbia Books, Inc., 1993 and 1996).

client their founder's alma mater or rely upon other special ties. Furthermore, the members of these firms have usually benefited from experience in Washington, generally serving as congressional staff. In these positions, the lobbyists-to-be also develop relations with future university
clients.

The Byrd Amendment

Not everyone has been pleased by the success of earmarking lobbyists
like Cassidy and Associates. In 1987, West Virginia University hired the
firm to secure funding for its National Resource Center for Coal and
Energy. Gratified by the $15 million earmark, the university's president,
Neil Bucklew, next hired Cassidy to help obtain $18 million for a mate-
rials center. The firm recommended taking the money for the center
from the National Defense Stockpile Transaction Fund, an account administered by the Department of Defense, and aided West Virginia in
writing the project's prospectus. In 1989, a representative of the firm
and a delegation from the university approached Sen. Robert C. Byrd
(D-WV) for assistance. Byrd, the powerful chair of the Senate Appropriations Committee, asked the Cassidy lobbyist to wait outside his office
while he spoke privately with the university representatives. As Byrd
later recalled, "My constituents don't need a go-between to get my attention."[20] Byrd then agreed to help, and he wrote a letter in support of
the earmark to Dennis DeConcini (D-AZ), one of his appropriations
subcommittee chairs – whose son-in-law was a former Cassidy employee – thus effectively ensuring its approval. Soon after that, however,
Byrd read a *Washington Post* story that outlined how Cassidy and Associates had used that same budgetary source to fund numerous costly earmarks while charging significant fees to clients for their services. As an
outraged Byrd ordered his staff to retrieve the letter, he directed that
$16.2 million in other earmarks be struck from the FY 1990 Treasury,
Postal Service appropriations bill, which contained the Stockpile Transaction Fund, and he expressed his displeasure with the lobbying firm on
the Senate floor.

While presenting the Interior appropriations bill to his colleagues for
approval on the Senate floor, Byrd offered an amendment, which became law, requiring that all persons or organizations receiving federal
contracts with the aid of a lobbyist report the lobbyist's name, fee, and
source of that fee. Furthermore, these lobbyists could no longer be paid

---

20. Chuck Alston, "Sen. Byrd Launches Crusade Against Influence Peddling," *Congressional Quarterly Weekly Report*, August 5, 1989, p. 2010.

with federal funds derived from the grants. "The perception is grow-ing," declared Byrd,

> that the merit of a project, grant, or contract awarded by the Government
> has fallen into a distant second place to the moxie and clout of lobbyists
> who help spring the money out of appropriations bills for a flat fee. . . .
> There are also accounts of lobbyists who create projects that receive ear-
> marked appropriations. . . . They are arrogant about their ability to shake
> the appropriations money tree – for a flat fee.[21]

This behavior, Byrd argued, justified the enactment of a truth-in-lobby-ing law, and anyone attempting to lobby an executive or a legislative branch official would be covered by these new requirements.

Byrd was doubly incensed. First, as chair of the Appropriations Com-mittee, he resented the negative publicity the committee received regard-ing influence peddlers and their manipulation of the appropriations ac-counts. "I said to my subcommittee people," Byrd remembered, "now that I know how it's being done, we'll scrap the project. . . . I was angry that I was being used by the lobbyists." Second, Byrd was appalled by how, as he saw it, lobbyists were acting as a buffer or an unnecessary layer between members of Congress and their constituents. At the time when Byrd ordered the Cassidy representative to wait outside of his of-fice, he turned to West Virginia University President Bucklew:

> I then began to express to the university people my indignation and anger. I
> asked them: "Why do you think you have to employ a lobbyist? I said I
> was for anything that benefits West Virginia, and that I was always going
> to be supportive. I'm on the Appropriations Committee – If I can't do it,
> nobody can."[22]

As Byrd properly noted, he was more than willing and able to help his home state universities; by 1996, West Virginia University had received more than $120 million in earmarks through Byrd's influence. What Byrd objected to was the implication that his constituents required the aid of lobbyists, who were paid for with federal funds before they could come to him for assistance. On the same day that Byrd presented his amendment on the Senate floor, West Virginia University canceled its contract with Cassidy and Associates.

The Byrd amendment proved to have little effect in limiting the lobby-ing activities of such firms as Cassidy and Associates. Universities sim-ply pay their lobbyists' fees with nonfederal funds, and the reporting requirements became subject to broad interpretation as to what consti-

---

21. *Congressional Record Weekly Report*, July 26, 1989, p. S8779.
22. Dan Morgan, "Byrd Drops Home-State Effort in Anger Over Lobbyists' Role,"
    Washington Post, July 31, 1989.

tutes lobbying. Ironically, the enactment of the new law actually produced more business for the firms, as, said a Cassidy spokesperson, "We counsel [universities] how the Byrd amendment papers should be filed."[23] Furthermore, in response to a *New York Times* editorial that cheered on Byrd's efforts and denounced Cassidy and Associates, "which earned large fees by peddling projects," Cassidy defended his actions by writing, "I am convinced that the message of an individual group of citizens is more likely to be heard . . . if it is shaped by someone who understands the legislative and regulatory process."[24] Finally, Byrd's attack on lobbying could not be conceived as opposition to the practice of academic earmarking, certainly not by one of its greatest practitioners. Byrd's willingness, however, to confront Cassidy presaged future congressional inquiry into the behavior of such lobbyists and encouraged members of Congress who opposed academic earmarking.

The Rise of Consortium Earmarks

Aside from aiding a single client to obtain an earmark, one of the more creative and seemingly obvious innovations in lobbying is to help a coalition or consortium of several institutions share an earmark. Much of the politics in Washington involves building coalitions; the greater the number of people who share the same interests, the more likely they will be able to secure the votes or the influence needed to achieve their goals. When a single school tries to obtain an earmark, it usually relies upon one or two powerful members of Congress to gain funding for its project. But when several schools band together, the number of potentially supportive and powerful members increases, thus making it easier to secure the earmark.

Those schools conducting agricultural research were the first to make serious use of the consortium funding arrangement, though for relatively small amounts of money. Institutions such as Texas A&M served as the headquarters campus for a five-member consortium created to conduct riceland mosquito research. Texas A&M was the primary recipient of the earmark, as the Texas delegation championed the project,

23. Jeffrey H. Birnbaum, "Overhaul of Lobbying Laws Unlikely to Succeed Thanks to Opposition of Lobbyists Themselves," *Wall Street Journal*, May 30, 1991. Also see Dan Morgan, "Lobbyist-Reporting Bill Grew from Universities' End Run," *Washington Post*, September 25, 1989; Morgan, "Lobbying Reports: Few and Flawed," *Washington Post*, July 3, 1990; and Jeffrey H. Birnbaum, *The Lobbyists* (New York: Times Books, 1992), pp. 185–7.
24. "Lobbyists, Unmasked," *New York Times*, August 15, 1989, and Gerald S. J. Cassidy, "Letter: On Lobbying, a New Disclosure Law Is Desirable," *New York Times*, August 25, 1989.

and, demonstrating how earmarks become institutionalized in the budget, the earmark continued from its inception in FY 1982 to FY 1993. During these twelve years, the cost of the project totaled some $5 million. The earmarked money was shared by the consortium members, with funds allocated on a per project basis. Some internal evaluation of the individual projects was undertaken by the faculty at the member institutions, thus enabling them to claim that the projects were indeed reviewed for merit, despite the fact that only member schools were designated to receive the earmarked funds.

One of the first lobbyists to employ this basic rule of coalition politics to obtain large-scale earmarks was Newton O. Cattell. Cattell, who formerly worked for Pennsylvania State University and AAU, had become by the mid-1980s the director of the Midwestern Universities Alliance. The Alliance, in turn, consisted of five universities – Indiana, Minnesota, Purdue, Missouri, and Wisconsin – all of which are also members of AAU. For Cattell, AAU's efforts to denounce members of Congress who engaged in earmarking were self-defeating, particularly as AAU failed to police its own ranks during the moratorium by suspending earmarking universities. "Until they do penalize," he said, "they are paper tigers." AAU members observed this hypocrisy among the universities and viewed AAU's position as an act of arrogance. "We look really bad when we try to lecture the Congress. We're not going to be able to tell them to stop, and it's silly to try."[25] Instead, Cattell sought earmarks for his Alliance and, championed by the efforts of Rep. John Meyers (R-IN), the Alliance obtained millions of dollars in earmarked funding for the Midwestern Superconductivity Consortium and the Midwestern Plant Biotechnology Consortium.

Yet, even as they were pursing earmarks, Cattell and the presidents of the five universities tried to justify their activities by defining an acceptable earmark. The projects would not be funded from the appropriations bills that supported NSF or NIH; the projects had to serve the midwestern region and more than one midwestern university; and within the region, schools would have to compete among themselves for the funds, with the Alliance establishing the peer review panels.[26] Nevertheless, as Cattell acknowledged, "All money is fungible. . . . So any money we take out of the pool could conceivably come out of NSF or NIH. . . . We are arbitrary in our definition of earmarking and AAU is arbitrary in its definition."[27] Moreover, Cattell and the Alliance could afford to urge that NSF and NIH be protected, as their earmarking advocate, Rep.

25. Interview with Newton O. Cattell, October 25, 1989.
26. "Midwestern Universities Alliance Regional Programs," January 25, 1989.
27. Interview with Newton O. Cattell, October 25, 1989.

Meyers, channeled the Alliance's earmarks through his own subcommittee, which handled the Energy and Water appropriations subcommittee bill. As long as Meyers succeeded in earmarking DOE's budget, the Alliance could appear magnanimous and principled.

Consortium earmarks have grown in size and number throughout the 1990s, and they represent the ability of lobbyists and their clients to package together very expensive earmarks. One of the most costly consortia of the 1990s has been the Consortium for International Earth Science Information Network (CIESIN), which bundled the University of Michigan, Michigan State, Saginaw Valley State University in Michigan, the University of California at Santa Barbara, the University of Maryland, Utah State University, and the Polytechnic University in New York. More than $100 million has been directed at this consortium, $73 million in FY 1993 alone, principally with the help of Rep. Bill Traxler, (D-MI), who chaired one appropriations subcommittee and who served as the second-ranking majority member on another. Other consortia have been established to create rural policy institutes, fund textile and sewn products research, study arid lands, and undertake hazardous substance research for the Gulf Coast. All of these consortium arrangements, funded from a host of appropriations bills, provide political strength and cover for the institutions involved without subjecting their activities to external competitive review.

The Rise of the Full-Service Firm: Lobbyists and Earmarking

By the mid-1990s, many of the lobbying firms for which earmarking constituted the bulk of their business had begun to expand their operations to provide a full range of services for their clients. Lobbying firms merged with law firms and operated under consulting arrangements with both law firms and other lobbying groups. Cassidy and Associates, the bellweather of academic earmarking outfits, became The Cassidy Companies. Primarily owned and operated by Gerald Cassidy with the aid of his lieutenant, James Fabiani, the firm expanded to include separate firms conducting public opinion research, public relations, and two government relations companies, one of which remained Cassidy and Associates. In addition to this diversification, the firm includes a marketing branch consisting of consultants who are paid a 10 percent commission for bringing new clients to Cassidy.

Whereas Cassidy and the other major lobbying firms once specialized solely in earmarking and working the appropriations process, they have extended their activities to lobbying on other types of legislation of concern to higher education, monitoring federal regulations, defending student aid budgets, and protecting funding for university medical research centers. In 1995, Cassidy reported that only 19 percent of its revenues were derived from academic earmarking.[28] To be sure, this diversification has been due to the increasingly limited federal budget and the initial efforts of the Republican-controlled Congress in 1995 to restrict academic earmarking. Nevertheless, even in the mid-1990s, every significant lobbying firm offering its services to a higher education client still claimed the ability to secure academic earmarks.

These lobbyists function as more than simply middlemen. They provide their clients with a creative understanding of the federal government that sometimes even congressional staffs, with their high rate of turnover, fail to grasp. Consulting lobbyists such as Cassidy and Associates have educated university presidents, members of Congress, and staff in the mechanics of obtaining earmarks. They assist in packaging the project to be earmarked, provide help in drafting legislation, identify funding sources, and guide the project throughout the legislative and budgetary process. Perhaps most important, they actively solicit university clients and encourage them to seek earmarked funds.

At the same time, few if any sanctions have been successfully imposed on these lobbyists to restrain their activities. Restrictions that involve financial constraints ultimately run afoul of Supreme Court rulings that protect First Amendment rights, while reporting requirements, such as those contained in the Byrd amendments, apparently have little effect. As long as the funding opportunities remain in the federal budget, these firms will continue to pursue academic earmarks for their clients.

28. T. R. Goldman, "Cassidy's Big Adventure," *Legal Times*, October 2, 1995, p. 1; Peter H. Stone, "From the K Street Corridor," *National Journal*, February 4, 1995, p. 305.

6

Congress and the
Distribution of
Academic Earmarks

The rise of academic earmarking paradoxically coincides with a time of ever-increasing pressure on Congress to balance the federal budget, even by limiting its distributive spending. Distributive spending, whereby funds are allocated in pork barrel fashion to congressional districts and states, is more likely to occur when the budget is expanding, a period in which the cost of individual projects is hidden by increases in budgetary increments and a healthy collection of revenue. The budget deficits of the 1970s and 1980s and the fiscal conservatism of Presidents Jimmy Carter and Ronald Reagan, however, ushered in a period of increasingly restrictive budgeting. Constraints came, for example, in the form of such procedural rules as reconciliation to control entitlement growth, the enactment of the Gramm–Rudman–Hollings sequestration legislation, the imposition of pay-as-you-go provisions, and a variety of spending caps and "fire walls" placed on appropriations that have been extended through the 1990s.

To many observers, the efforts to control deficits during these years appear to have restrained, if not reduced, distributive spending. After President Reagan complained in his 1988 State of the Union Address about pork barrel projects, including academic earmarks, "tucked away behind a little comma here and there," in the FY 1988 omnibus budget bill, the administration promised it would release a list of such items. Nevertheless, OMB, which periodically monitors these projects, identified only $3 billion worth of pork in the $1 trillion budget. According to John Palmer of the Urban Institute, "the role of pork in the budget has declined. It just isn't a significant budget item anymore – if it ever was." A similar estimate was offered by Charles Schultze of the Brookings Institution, who declared that pork accounted for "no more than $10 billion, no really big bucks in a $1 trillion budget." Political scientist R. Douglas Arnold concurred that "the impact of the congressional quest for local benefits on federal expenditures seems to be diminishing." By

119

1995, Robert Stein and Kenneth Bickers concluded in their study of distributive spending that funding for most of these programs had fallen "sharply" since the 1970s and that the total was "fiscally modest."[1]

Despite these conclusions, the fact remains that virtually a completely new type of distributive spending, academic earmarking, developed during this period. While these earmarks, valued in the hundreds of millions of dollars on an annual basis, clearly have limited macrobudget or macroeconomic effects, their existence in both number and cost runs counter to these overall observations about the presence of distributive politics.

Congress and Academic Earmarking

To understand the rise of this new form of distributive spending, it is necessary to look to Congress, for academic earmarking is ultimately a congressional affair. University presidents and their lobbyists may solicit earmarks, but for these projects to become a reality, members of Congress must sponsor them and vote their approval. Members do so because just as university presidents respond to a variety of incentives and ambitions to seek earmarks, and by their actions legitimize earmarking for their institutions, members of Congress are subject to powerful incentives to fund these projects. The actual distribution of earmarks among the members nevertheless reflects the hierarchical nature of the congressional committee system. The primary beneficiaries of academic earmarking overwhelmingly tend to be senior members and those who chair the powerful appropriations subcommittees. Through their participation in academic earmarking, these influential and senior members help to legitimize earmarking by the entire Congress. At the same time, this concentration of earmarked dollars among subcommittee members influences both the equitable distribution of such projects among universities and their effectiveness in promoting an institution's research competitiveness.

1. "Budget Chief Withdraws Special-Projects Directive," *Wall Street Journal*, July 11, 1988; Paul Blustein, "U.S. Budget Increasingly Free of Pork-Barrel Spending," *Washington Post*, March 21, 1988; Rich Thomas, "Is the Pork Barrel a Must? *Time*, January 18, 1988, p. 24; John W. Ellwood, "Comments," in Gregory B. Mills and John L. Palmer (eds.), *Federal Budget Policy in the 1980s* (Washington, D.C.: Urban Institute Press, 1984); Charles L. Schultze, "Comment," in Mills and Palmer; R. Douglas Arnold, "The Local Roots of Domestic Policy," in Thomas E. Mann and Norman J. Ornstein (eds.), *The New Congress* (Washington, D.C.: American Enterprise Institute, 1981); R. Douglas Arnold, *The Logic of Congressional Action* (New Haven: Yale University Press, 1990), p. 133; Robert M. Stein and Kenneth E. Bickers, *Perpetuating the Pork Barrel* (Cambridge: Cambridge University Press, 1995), p. 10.

Furthermore, just as earmarking is ultimately a congressional affair, it is an affair specifically of the House and Senate appropriations committees. Except in a handful of cases, members and lobbyists who seek academic projects ultimately place their requests with the chairs of the thirteen House and Senate appropriations subcommittees, which have originated the more than $5 billion in earmarks. The congressional authorizations committees, however, generally have been left out of the earmarking process for two reasons. First, authorizations may create agencies and programs, but appropriations provide the money that funds them. So members and lobbyists view the approval of the authorizations committees as unnecessary in obtaining an earmark, even if many members of these committees resent being bypassed in the formal legislative process. This resentment, as will be seen in the next chapter, is a major source of dissent within Congress over academic earmarking.

Second, pragmatically speaking, members of Congress are more likely to obtain an earmark in one of the thirteen appropriations bills that must be passed each year to keep the government operating than in authorizations that are often multiyear and do not require annual attention by Congress. Moreover, since the early 1980s, Congress has enacted a declining number of authorizations bills. Due to budget constraints there have been fewer new programs to enact. The big budget battles of the Reagan years, which continued throughout the Bush presidency and into the Clinton administration, consumed Congress, leaving it little time to pass authorizations bills, as suggested by a decline in the number of votes taken on authorizations.[2] Federal programs have often been kept alive through appropriations bills and omnibus continuing resolutions. Special rules granted by the rules committees permit the appropriations committees in effect to authorize programs. DOE, for example, whose budget has supported numerous academic earmarks, has not been reauthorized since 1979, yet its programs continue to be maintained and funded primarily through appropriations. In any case, academic earmarking is largely associated with the appropriations process and the members who dominate that process.

The Incentives to Earmark

Academic earmarking falls into a class of public spending that political scientists characterize as "distributive" and "particularistic." These terms describe a situation in which federal spending benefits particular

---

2. Lawrence J. Haas, "Unauthorized Action," *National Journal*, January 2, 1988, pp. 17–21. The number of votes taken on authorizations legislation in the House fell from 216 in 1978 to 123 in 1984 and in the Senate from 121 in 1975 to 36 in 1984.

congressional districts and states, while the costs of these often economically inefficient but politically rewarding projects are spread throughout the nation through general taxation. Classic examples of distributive projects, often labeled as "pork barrel projects," are military bases, highways, and dams. With their limited benefits, distributive politics are said to overwhelm concern for programs that benefit the general population, as well as the allocation of resources based on merit.[3]

Members of Congress are subject to a variety of incentives to provide their constituents with distributive projects, where, again, benefits are localized and costs generalized. By bringing academic earmarks back to their congressional districts or states, members attempt to satisfy at least three basic ambitions that political scientists have long noted guide the behavior of members[4]: to gain reelection, to engage in what they understand as good public policy, and to exercise power within Congress. Additional incentives are also at work that tend to be either institutional or personal in their appeal.

First, many members of Congress obviously do earmark research funds to strengthen their reelection chances, claiming credit for obtaining visible public works projects for their constituents. Indeed, critics claim that this is the overwhelming reason that earmarking exists. "There is the root cause of earmarking," declared Robert Rosenzweig, president of AAU. "It is in the political interests of members of Congress to help their constituencies and it is in the institutional interests of university presidents . . . to find ways to help their congressmen to help their constituencies."[5]

Second, some members view earmarking as a way of making good public policy. They argue that such projects will enhance their home state's or district's economy, in the manner of Silicon Valley in California, Route 128 in Massachusetts, the Research Triangle in North Carolina, or Silicon Gulch in Texas, all of which developed around major research universities. In this case, academic earmarking is regarded as

3. The literature on distributive politics is vast. See, for example, David R. Mayhew, *Congress: The Electoral Connection* (New Haven: Yale University Press, 1974); Kenneth A. Shepsle and Barry R. Weingast, "Political Preference for the Pork Barrel: A Generalization," *American Journal of Political Science* 25 (1981): 96–111; Barry R. Weingast, "A Rational Choice Perspective on Congressional Norms," *American Journal of Political Science* 23 (1979): 245–62; Keith Krehbiel, *Information and Legislative Organization* (Ann Arbor: University of Michigan Press, 1991), especially Chs. 1 and 2.

4. The classic statement on incentives is Richard F. Fenno, Jr., *Congressmen in Committees* (Boston: Little, Brown, 1973), Ch. 1.

5. "Testimony of Robert M. Rosenzweig, Former President, Association of American Universities, United States House of Representatives, Committee on Science, Space and Technology, June 16, 1993," p. 4.

more than bringing home pure pork barrel projects that are often financially inefficient and economically ineffective. These academic projects may produce research with economic benefits that not only help the home district, but also potentially enhance the economic well-being of the entire nation.

Sometimes it is difficult to draw a line between the desire for reelection, the most obvious incentive to earmark, and the wish to carry out what the member regards as good public policy. Consider briefly the case of Rep. Wes Watkins (D-OK), a junior member of the House Agriculture Appropriations Subcommittee during the 1980s. Derisively called "Mr. Rural Development" by his colleagues for his incessant efforts to obtain resources for his district, Watkins carefully kept track of his projects, academic and otherwise, on a map in his office, all obtained as part of a broader plan to improve economic conditions in his district and to ensure his reelection. Assigned to multiple subcommittees, as are most members of the appropriations committees, Watkins secured academic earmarks from a variety of budgets and for a variety of purposes. In the FY 1990 Energy and Water appropriations bill, for example, Watkins obtained a $3 million earmark for an Advanced Technology Center at Oklahoma State University, a school in his district. At the same time, he successfully championed the university's efforts to gain projects from the agriculture appropriations bills. Just as Watkins's pursuit of academic earmarks and other economic development projects benefited his constituents, he, in turn, was rewarded by the absence of a serious challenger for his seat in Congress from 1976, the year of his initial election, through 1990, when he left Congress to run for governor of the state.[6] Clearly, for Watkins and other members, assisting constituents combines the rewards of making good public policy and enhancing one's chance for reelection.

Third, in another form of the "good government, good public policy" argument, some members find compelling the charge that federal research funds are inequitably distributed as a result of peer review and that earmarking helps to correct this problem. Thus, for these members, earmarking is both a corrective public policy and a logical extension of their responsibility to oversee the various executive agencies. Earmarking in this case may be seen as a form of congressional pressure on the federal bureaucracy to produce more geographically equitable results in funding decisions rather than meeting explicit constituency and reelection needs.

6. David S. Cloud, "For 'Mr. Rural Development,' Small Ideas Go a Long Way," *Congressional Quarterly*, September 30, 1989, pp. 2548–9.

Fourth, some members contend that it is their constitutional right and even their institutional obligation to play a direct role in allocating federal research money through the legislative process. Though Congress may determine that the federal government's research agencies should make most of these granting decisions, even if this involves the use of merit review, it remains the members' prerogative as the public's elected representatives to intervene when they think it is proper.

These concerns for equity in the distribution of funds and the members' duty to oversee the bureaucracy are evident in Rep. William H. Gray's (D-PA) defense of academic earmarking in an editorial column in the *Washington Post*. Gray, who had served as chair of the House Budget Committee, noted:

> Proponents of earmarking often cite the Constitution to make their argument that members of Congress are elected precisely to decide where federal dollars should go, while on the other hand, no one votes for the bureaucrats who sit in judgement on peer review committees. . . . What would it mean if Congress were to abandon the practice of earmarking? . . . [F]ederal research funds would remain in the hands of a precious few elite institutions. . . . I don't believe that's in the national interest.[7]

For Gray, earmarking is a constitutional right, a congressional duty, and good public policy.

Fifth, members may find that the simple exercise of power may provide an incentive to earmark. Richard Fenno characterized the appropriations committees, where nearly all academic earmarks originate, as "power" and "prestige" committees, whose members are able to exercise considerable influence within Congress. Bringing home federal money is more than simply a reelection ploy; it reflects the member's status within Congress. Moreover, one aspect of how members on the appropriations committees exercise their power, or, as Fenno says, "nurse their ambitions" within the Congress, is through their ability to reward friends and colleagues with earmarks and other favors. The appropriations committees, certainly prior to the Republican capture of Congress in 1994, have been renowned for their bipartisanship, moderation and cooperation among members, and the sharing of political perks such as academic earmarks.[8]

Sixth, a further incentive for chairs of the appropriations subcommittees to earmark is that by providing their colleagues with such rewards

---

7. William H. Gray III, "Pork or Providence? A Defense of Earmarked Funds for Colleges," *Washington Post*, February 27, 1994.

8. Fenno, op. cit., p. 4.

and favors, sometimes called "side payments," they encourage these colleagues to vote for the chairs' legislative initiatives. As John Ellwood and Eric Patashnik pointed out, "pork, doled out strategically, can help to sweeten an otherwise unpalatable piece of legislation." Indeed, at least one analysis of the distribution of academic earmarks found that the more projects a member received, the more likely the member would vote to support the bill in question.[9]

Seventh, aside from these institutional, policy, and reelection incentives, members may have personal motives for earmarking. These include the desire to aid a university from which members graduated or attended, or a parochial institutions with which members may have some special affiliation, such as shared religious or ideological values. Catholic universities and colleges, and even an institution without a congressional district such as Georgetown University, have received substantial assistance in obtaining earmarks from Catholic members, even when the school was located outside the members' districts. Earmarks may enable members to gain recognition from universities and colleges in the form of prestigious honorary degrees, lectureships, professorships, positions on institutional governing boards, and even buildings named in their honor, such as the Jamie L. Whitten National Center for Physical Acoustics at the University of Mississippi. Of the fifteen members leaving the Senate at the end of 1996, six indicated they would begin regular or part-time professorships, with two members teaching at university institutes named in their honor.[10] Members have also honored each other with earmarked academic buildings and centers, such as the Carl Albert center at the University of Oklahoma and the Barry Goldwater center at the University of Arizona. Therefore, providing services and benefits for universities and colleges in the form of earmarks, even if these institutions are not in a member's district or state, may be reward-

9. John W. Ellwood and Eric M. Patashnik, "In Praise of Pork," *The Public Interest* (Winter 1993), p. 21; Diana Evans, "Appropriations Committee Earmarks and Vote-Buying in the U.S. Senate," paper prepared for the 1996 American Political Science Association convention, August 29–September 1, 1996; Evans, "Policy and Pork: The Use of Pork Barrel Projects to Build Policy Coalitions in the House of Representatives," *American Journal of Political Science* 38 (1994): 894–917; Richard Munson, *The Cardinals of Capitol Hill* (New York: Grove Press, 1993), especially Ch. 3.

10. On Catholic schools' influence, see, for example, David S. Cloud, "Georgetown Wins Friends and Funds on Hill," *Congressional Quarterly Weekly Report*, June 4, 1988, p. 1502; Helen Dewar, "Retiring Senators Look Beyond the Beltway," *Washington Post*, December 29, 1996. On members' careers after the 1992 elections, for example, nine retired or defeated members assumed permanent or temporary positions with universities and colleges as professors, lecturers, or members of the boards of regents. Lucy Shackelford, "Where Are They Now?" *Washington Post*, June 14, 1993.

ing in ways that are not directly connected to the member's reelection ambitions.

The Appropriations Committees and
the Legitimization of Earmarking

Although members have a variety of incentives to earmark, they must have the influence and power to do so. Few in Congress, however, exercise as much power as members of the appropriations committees, and especially those who chair the committees and subcommittees. As a result of their institutional prerogatives, these chairs largely determine which members will receive projects and at what cost to the budget. Not surprisingly, chairs often reserve many of these earmarks for their own use, having reached the point in their careers when they often believe they deserve the rewards of their important positions. As indicated in Table 7, the allocation of earmarks among subcommittees is divided among ten of the thirteen subcommittees, though not equally. These decisions have also led to the concentration of academic earmarks in a relatively small number of geographical regions, states, and universities. Rather than increasing equity in the allocation of federal research funds, academic earmarking may actually intensify their concentration.

Table 7. *Distribution of earmarks by appropriations subcommittee, FY 1980–96*

Subcommittee	Dollar value	Percent of total	Number of earmarks	Percent of total
Defense	$1,463,116,000	28.5%	376	10　%
Agriculture	1,287,486,032	25.1	2,199	59
Energy & Water	871,837,000	17.0	273	7
Veterans-HUD-Ind	588,288,000	11.5	386	10
Commerce-Justice	291,735,600	5.7	191	5
Treasury-Postal	176,977,000	3.4	45	2.0
Labor-HHS-Ed	151,456,000	3.0	54	2.0
Interior	150,533,000	3.0	115	3
Transportation	134,070,000	2.6	68	2
Foreign Operations	10,900,000	.2	2	.001
Total	$5,126,398,632	100%	3,709	100%

Powers of the Chair

By the late 1980s, the practice of academic earmarking had become synonymous with the names of such appropriations committee chairs as Senators Mark O. Hatfield (R-OR), Robert C. Byrd (D-WVA), and Barbara Mikulski (D-MD) and Representatives John P. Murtha (D-PA) and Robert Traxler (D-MI). The involvement of these members with earmarking coincided with the beginning of the earmarking controversy in 1983, the explosion of earmarking during the late 1980s and early 1990s, and the decline of earmarking, though not its elimination, during the middle and late 1990s.

Through the procedural rules of the subcommittees and the federal budgetary process, these chairs set the size and level of various academic earmarks. They do so by controlling the subcommittee staffs, by marking up the drafts of the appropriations bills, and by setting the agenda for subcommittee meetings.[11] Special requests for funding from members, including earmarks, are submitted to the chair. Sometimes these requests consist of letters from the members to the chair, and in some cases the chair requires members to complete an application for each project. Rep. Richard J. Durbin (D-IL), for example, employed such an application, as shown in Figure 2, when he became chair of the agriculture appropriations subcommittee in 1992. In 1993, Rep. Bob Carr (D-MI), chair of the Transportation appropriations subcommittee, issued an "investment criteria" questionnaire that members had to submit before their projects would be considered. With the assistance of the staff, the chair determines which of these many requests will be included in the markup of appropriations bills. The markup is important because at this point the chair can allocate the subcommittee's full spending budget, requiring members who did not receive projects to produce a revenue offset to fund their projects. This usually means taking money away from another member, a very difficult task indeed. Members are generally allocated projects by the chair on the basis of seniority, committee assignment, and party. Members of the subcommittee, for instance, are more likely to receive an earmark than are nonmembers. Full committee chairs, of course, also

11. On the powers and influence of chairs, see Richard F. Fenno, Jr., *The Power of the Purse: Appropriations Politics in Congress* (Boston: Little, Brown, 1966); John A. Ferejohn, *Pork Barrel Politics: Rivers and Harbors Legislation, 1947–1968* (Stanford: Stanford University Press, 1974), especially Ch. 9; James D. Savage, "Saints and Cardinals in Appropriations Committees and the Fight Against Distributive Politics," *Legislative Studies Quarterly,* 16 (August 1991): 329–47.

Proposal for Special Research Grant

Principal Researcher Name	Address	Date

Participating Institution(s)

Brief Description of Proposed Research

Need for the Research

	Estimated Costs of Not Doing the Research

Where Is Similar Research Being Conducted	Others in Scientific Community That Endorse This Research

Proposed Federal Cost Share by Year

1. 2. 3. 4. 5. Total

Non-Recurring Costs Included Above	Overhead Costs Included Above

Source and Amount of Non-Federal Funds

Committee Use Only

Proposed by	Endorsed by
☐ Individual _____	☐ Individual _____
☐ Association _____	☐ Association _____
☐ Member _____	☐ Member _____
☐ Delegation _____	☐ Delegation _____

RETURN TO: Subcommittee on Agriculture, Rural Development, FDA and Related Agencies
Room 2362 Rayburn Building
Washington, DC 20515
202-225-2638

Figure 2. Proposal for special research grants.

exercise similar influence over full committee staff and committee agendas.

The Legitimization of Earmarking

Even before earmarking became a subject of concern within the higher education community in 1983, it had powerful practitioners and protectors. When President Jean Mayer of Tufts University, assisted by the lobbying firm of Schlossberg and Cassidy, began his quest for earmarks to support his nutrition center in the late 1970s, he turned to the Massachusetts congressional delegation led by Rep. Thomas P. "Tip" O'Neill (D-MA), the speaker of the House of Representatives, and Sen. Edward Kennedy (D-MA). O'Neill also later aided Boston College, his alma mater, and Boston University in securing their earmarks in the early 1980s. Meanwhile, several of the earmarks for Tufts were funded in the House Agriculture Appropriations Subcommittee, where Jamie L. Whitten, the formidable chair of both the subcommittee and the full appropriations committee, once proclaimed that members who engaged in earmarking were "performing a public service."[12]

If members who favored academic earmarking could point to any precedent to justify their actions, it was Whitten's subcommittee. Subcommittee chair from 1949 to 1992, Whitten, known to his colleagues as the "permanent secretary of agriculture," ruled that department's budget with an iron hand. The son of a farmer, Whitten firmly believed that agriculture was the economic backbone of the nation, and that members of Congress, and he in particular, knew more about the needs of the country's farmers than the bureaucrats and appointed political leaders of the department. This knowledge extended to determining the agency's research agenda and making adjustments when deemed necessary by earmarking. Still, at the time of the early Tufts projects, the amount of academic earmarking was small in comparison to what it would become. During FYs 1980–2, the total earmarking in the federal budget amounted to an estimated $39 million, with nearly all of this total emanating from Whitten's subcommittee.[13] Between FY 1980 and FY 1996, however, the total amount within the agriculture bill alone was 1.3 billion.

12. Mark Crawford, "USDA Grants Program Threatened," *Science*, July 1, 1988, p. 21.
13. David Rapp, *How the U.S. Got Into Agriculture, and Why It Can't Get Out* (Washington, D.C.: Congressional Quarterly Press, 1988), Ch. 5. Also see Eric Pianin, "Whitten's Limitless Longevity," *Washington Post*, November 6, 1991, and Pianin, "Rep. Whitten on Verge of Seniority Record," *Washington Post*, January 4, 1992.

With the blessing of the Speaker of the House and the chair of the House Appropriations Committee, other members soon took the lead in earmarking money for their home universities and colleges. Members learned from each other what was necessary to obtain a project, and they were aided by aggressive lobbyists and university presidents who called upon them to secure earmarks. Yet, even as earmarks were allocated to subcommittee members and others within Congress, the bulk of the projects went to the home districts and states of such subcommittee chairs as Hatfield, Byrd, Murtha, Traxler, and Mikulski.

Senator Mark O. Hatfield

When the Republicans took control of the Senate in 1980, the chair of the Appropriations Committee and of the Energy and Water Appropriations Subcommittee fell to Mark Hatfield. A moderate conservative from Oregon, Hatfield allowed his subcommittee to be a growing source of earmarks, with a generous supply going to his home state schools. Between FY 1980 and FY 1996, Oregon received more than $261 million in projects, the second highest total going to any state, with the majority of the earmarks bound for Oregon generated by Hatfield's efforts. In particular, Hatfield's earmarks in the Energy and Water bill benefited the University of Oregon, which received $46 million in projects, and the Oregon Health Sciences University, which obtained $105 million in earmarks.

Although Hatfield was inevitably successful in obtaining earmarks, they sometimes caused considerable controversy. Hatfield was subjected to criticism within Oregon when it became known that the Health Sciences University had offered to admit his daughter to the school by a special acceptance policy, leading two admissions officers to resign in disgust. Meanwhile, Hatfield's attempt to aid a university outside of Oregon caused him further embarrassment. In 1991 the *Oregonian*, the leading newspaper in the state, reported that Hatfield violated Senate rules by failing to report a $9,265 gift of art given to him by the president of the University of South Carolina, James B. Holderman. At the time, Holderman was seeking a $16.3 million earmark for an engineering center from Hatfield's subcommittee. In addition to the art, Hatfield received $15,000 worth of gifts between 1983 and 1987, as well as a full scholarship valued at $15,000 for his son to attend South Carolina. As a result of the controversy, Holderman resigned his presidency and the earmark was virtually eliminated in the subcommittee. The earmark, however, was restored to full funding in a House–Senate conference committee. Hatfield later apologized to the Senate after an ethics investigation but succeeded in gaining reelection in 1992.[14]

Senator Robert F. Byrd

In 1986 control of the Senate shifted again, with the Appropriations Committee chairmanship eventually being assumed by Robert F. Byrd (D-WVA), who, through extensive press coverage, became perhaps the most famous earmarking member of Congress. Purposely stepping down as Senate majority leader in 1989 to became the chair of the appropriations committee and of the Interior Department's appropriations subcommittee, Byrd fully intended to use this position unabashedly to direct federal spending to his home state. "What helps West Virginia," Byrd once noted, "helps the nation."[15] A master of Senate rules and history, Byrd inspired caution, if not fear, in colleagues who might challenge him on some legislative action, lest they lose their own desired projects. Declaring that the members were cowed by Byrd, Sen. John McCain (R-AZ) proclaimed that "I see fear and intimidation on the part of some of my colleagues who fear losing their pork."[16]

Byrd, in any case, rarely lost an opportunity to aid the universities and colleges back home. West Virginia University, with its Robert C. Byrd Health Sciences Center, has been the primary recipient of Byrd's efforts, having obtained more than $125 million in projects since 1985. Byrd's generosity extends to other in-state schools. Among the most widely publicized of Byrd's earmarks have been those benefiting Wheeling Jesuit College, an institution with no doctoral students and an en-

14. Richard L. Berke, "Hatfield Failed to Tell Senate About Art Gifts Worth $9,265," *New York Times*, March 9, 1991; Berke, "For Hatfield, a Shining Image Tarnished by Ethics Charges," *New York Times*, June 3, 1991; Ronald Smothers, "Former University President Pleads Guilty to Gift Charge," *New York Times*, May 29, 1991; Lloyd Grove, "The Senator at the Stake," *Washington Post*, March 9, 1995; Helen Dewar, "Ethics Panel Rebukes Hatfield," *Washington Post*, August 13, 1992. When Hatfield voted against the balanced budget amendment in 1995, some conservatives demanded that he be stripped of his appropriations committee chair. Yet others argued that the real reason he should be punished this way was his pork barrel activity and because "he has been awarded with ethics investigations of his relationships." In Gordon S. Jones, "The Real Reasons to Punish Sen. Hatfield," *Washington Times*, March 7, 1995.

15. Lawrence J. Haas, "Byrd's Big Stick," *National Journal*, February 9, 1991, pp. 316–20; Helen Dewar and Eric Pianin, "Senate Is Power Source for a 'Coal Miner's Son,'" *Washington Post*, June 24, 1993.

16. Adam Clymer, "Victor of Budget Battle, Byrd Invokes an Army of Kings, Poets and Patriots," *New York Times*, March 2, 1993.

rollment of 1,400. This school has received earmarks ranging in value from at least $34 million to over $40 million, all for an institution whose annual budget is just $14 million. The college obtained a Classroom of the Future project on computer training and a National Technology Transfer Center funded from the NASA budget. "This is not what so many of you folks glibly call pork," Byrd said of the earmarks, "it's infrastructure."[17] During the period FY 1980–96, West Virginia received no less than $190 million in earmarks, the eighth largest amount obtained by a state, and West Virginia University received the fourth largest total of any university or college.

Representative John P. Murtha

Pennsylvania is the leading beneficiary of academic earmarking among all the states, and Rep. John P. Murtha (D-PA) is the source of most of these projects. Between FY 1980 and FY 1990, the year when Murtha became the chair of the Defense Appropriations Subcommittee, the state received some $57 million. By FY 1996, the state's total reached at least $450 million. Murtha, with the support of Rep. Joseph McDade (R-PA), the ranking member of the subcommittee, had turned the defense appropriations bill into a major source of academic earmarking, with his home state obtaining the largest share. Commenting on critics of his earmarking, Murtha described how he ran his subcommittee:

> We know as much about defense as anyone in that Defense Department. . . . Everybody's got a few parochial interests and a few systems they're interested in and so forth, but we've got a professional staff and they make good recommendations. . . . [T]he political reality is, you're obviously interested in certain programs in your own district, and what you can do for your area. You try to attract industry.[18]

Murtha's efforts to attract industry included aiding Pennsylvania's institutions of higher education. In the first five years of his chairmanship, Murtha's subcommittee earmarked approximately $1 billion in academic projects, with much of this amount directed to Pennsylvania. The University of Pittsburgh, Murtha's alma mater, and Pennsylvania State University in particular benefited from Murtha's efforts, but virtually every significant institution of higher education in the state of Pennsyl-

17. Mary Jordan, "For a Little College, a Big Helping Hand," *Washington Post*, June 24, 1992.
18. Lawrence J. Haas, "Murtha, the Insider," *National Journal*, August 11, 1990, pp. 1947–51; Colleen Cordes, "King of the Earmarks," *Chronicle of Higher Education*, November 2, 1994, p. A49.

vania received some sort of academic earmark. One institution's earmark, which stood out from the rest and received significantly adverse publicity, was a $10 million project designated for Marywood College, which was approved by Murtha for a school in McDade's district. This small Catholic college, with an enrollment of 3,000 mostly undergraduate students in the humanities and liberal arts operating on an annual budget of some $30 million, received an unspecified $10 million earmark of "major importance" funded by the Department of Defense. Neither the department nor the college had requested the money from either Murtha or McDade. "It's not like I knew a year ago we were going to get this," observed Sister Mary Reap, the college president.[19] Finally it was determined that the earmark would fund a family service institute to study problems of military families.

Just as Murtha aided his friends, including Republicans like McDade, he also punished those who criticized his earmarking. In 1994, Murtha announced that President Clinton's FY 1995 budget request for $1.8 billion in Department of Defense–funded university research would be cut in half. This reduction in largely peer-reviewed support could prove highly disruptive to schools that had been expecting, if not dependent on, defense funding. MIT, for example, estimated that Murtha's $900 million cut could cost MIT $40 million, and the University of Michigan projected that its federal research base would drop by more than 10 percent.

Moreover, Murtha threatened to hold hearings on the indirect cost rates received by universities as reimbursement for the administrative expenses incurred while conducting federal research. Indirect costs, which are in effect a surcharge added to a researcher's grant, had become a subject of great embarrassment for the elite universities. Previous hearings held by Rep. John Dingell (D-MI), chair of the House Commerce Committee, revealed that a number of these universities had misused these reimbursements, sometimes for frivolous purposes unrelated to university research. Further hearings on indirect costs directed by another angry committee chair could only cause the research universities more trouble.[20]

The budget cuts and the hearings were intended to intimidate those university presidents and members of Congress who objected to Murtha's

---

19. John Lancaster, "Legislators Use Earmarks to Bring Home Bacon," *Washington Post*, December 6, 1991; Lancaster, "Clearing Up a $10 Million Mystery," *Washington Post*, December 16, 1991.
20. See, for example, Dingell's letter, "Rectifying How Tax Dollars Are Spent," to the *New York Times*, February 17, 1992, and Mary Jordan, "House to Expand Research-Cost Probe," *Washington Post*, January 30, 1992. The *Chronicle of Higher Education* covered this story extensively in 1991 and 1992.

earmarking, which included $18 million for a University of Pittsburgh project in the FY 1995 defense bill's report. After heavy lobbying by the university research community the Senate voted to limit Murtha's $900 million cut to $80 million. Eventually, with Murtha's concurrence, Clinton's request was reduced by $200 million in a House–Senate conference committee. Murtha also refrained from holding hearings, relying instead on budget cuts to make his point that "a member knows better than anyone else what would go well in his district."[21]

Representative Bob Traxler and Senator Barbara Mikulski

When in 1989 Rep. Bob Traxler (D-MI) and Sen. Barbara Mikulski (D-MD) became chairs of the House and Senate Veterans Administration–Housing Subcommittee and the Urban Development–Independent Agencies Appropriations Subcommittee (VA–HUD), respectively, they took charge of a spending bill that had been kept almost free from academic earmarks. Their predecessors, Rep. Edward P. Boland (D-MA) and Senators William Proxmire (D-WI) and Jake Garn (R-UT) aggressively avoided earmarking their bill, defending in particular the NSF budget.

Traxler and Mikulski radically changed the subcommittees' position on earmarking. When comparing his stance on earmarking to Boland's, Traxler observed, "We're not identical twins. I have a great sensitivity to the members' requests and needs. I want to be in every way helpful in fulfilling these national needs that are specific to localities. This is the function of Congress. This is the appropriations process."[22] The State of Michigan, which had never obtained an earmark prior to 1989 from the subcommittee, received over $90 million in projects from this source during the six years of Traxler's reign as chair. In addition, while also serving on the Agriculture Appropriations Subcommittee, Traxler delivered more than $77 million in earmarks to his alma mater, Michigan State University, which named Traxler to a position on its board of trustees. A major portion of these earmarks benefited a project known as the Consortium for International Earth Science Network (CIESN),

---

21. Colleen Cordes, "The Power of Pique," *Chronicle of Higher Education*, June 29, 1994, p. A21; Scott Jaschik, "Defense Budget Approved by House Would Halve President's Request for University Research," *Chronicle of Higher Education*, July 6, 1994, p. A24; Scott Jaschik, "Cut in Military-Research Budget for 1995 Upsets Universities, but They Are Thankful It Wasn't Larger," *Chronicle of Higher Education*, October 5, 1994, p. A30; "Savage Cuts in Defense Research," *Washington Post*, July 28, 1994; Eric Schmitt, "House Battle Threatens Big Research Universities with Loss of Millions," *New York Times*, August 17, 1994; "Research Funding Rumpus," *Washington Post*, July 10, 1994.
22. Phil Kuntz, "Just One More Project, Please . . .", *Congressional Quarterly Weekly Report*, July 22, 1989, p. 1866.

which Rep. George Brown (D-CA) declared was "awarded without adequate competitions and virtually no congressional oversight. NASA itself has little idea where this funding is going." During the same period, Mikulski sent a conservatively estimated $44 million to universities in her home state. Among the most costly of her projects was the Christopher Columbus Center of Marine Research in Baltimore, whose budget included an eventual $54 million contribution from the federal government. The project was funded from the NASA budget. As *Nature* magazine noted, "The space agency is now in the marine research field, whether it likes it or not." Beneficiaries of the earmark include the University of Maryland at College Park and the University of Maryland at Baltimore County, where Mikulski sometimes lectures. Commenting on these and other projects, the senator pronounced that "these earmarks represent sound national policies."[23]

One thing that Traxler and Mikulski did avoid was earmarking the NSF's peer-reviewed programs. "I early on made my position known relative to NSF," Traxler observed, "and no member approached me [for an NSF earmark]. We think that system works very well, and we're very pleased with it." Instead, the two subcommittee chairs funded their academic projects from such agencies as the Environmental Protection Agency and NASA.[24]

Representative Robert L. Livingston

Although Rep. Robert L. Livingston (R-LA) is not as well known a practitioner of earmarking as, say, Senators Hatfield or Byrd, he deserves special mention. Livingston's term as chair of the House Appropriations Committee has been marked by significant reductions in academic earmarking since the Republicans took control of Congress in 1994, as well as the relegitimization of academic earmarking by the Republican leadership as an acceptable activity of Congress.

Armed with their Contract with America, the Republican party in 1994 achieved control over both houses of Congress for the first time since 1956. Overjoyed with their victory, the Republicans pledged to balance the budget and greatly reduce domestic spending by passing a budget resolution that would have cut discretionary spending by 23 percent in real terms over seven years. To assist the House leadership in car-

23. Christopher Anderson, "In Space, No One Can Hear You Oink," *Nature*, October 10, 1991, p. 406; Phil Kuntz, "Mikulski's 'Change Purse,'" *Congressional Quarterly Weekly Report*, September 23, 1989, p. 2467.
24. Kuntz, "Just One More Project, Please . . .", and "Traxler's Legacy: Small Print Spelled Big Bucks," *Washington Post*, April 16, 1993.

rying out this task, Speaker Newt Gingrich (R-GA) selected Livingston to be House Appropriations Committee chair over four more senior members who were considered too ideologically moderate. Gingrich also appointed seven highly conservative freshman members to stiffen the committee's resolve to bring federal spending under control. Meanwhile, the seventy-three newly elected House Republicans organized a group called the New Federalists to monitor the funding levels in the thirteen appropriations bills in order to keep the appropriators in line with their desire to reach a balanced budget.

Armed with these fiscal and ideological constraints, the Republicans did indeed greatly limit academic earmarking in the Appropriations Committee. To demonstrate his commitment to the goals of the Contract with America, Livingston called a meeting of the committee members and promptly displayed an alligator-skinning knife and two progressively larger knives to indicate what he would do to federal spending. "We are going to be curtailing new expenditures," Livingston later told reporters, "we're going to stop projects across the board. We're going to slow down the pork barrel. There's no doubt about it." Livingston and his Republican colleagues did indeed trim earmarking significantly in FY 1996. A freeze, for example, was placed on academic facilities earmarking in the agriculture appropriations bill, and the number of "special project" research grants was cut from 210 to 96. The total estimated earmarking in FY 1996 of $327.8 million was $200 million less than in FY 1995.

Nevertheless, Livingston's committee earmarked at least $22.3 million in FY 1996 for schools in Louisiana, including $3.3 million for Tulane University, where Livingston received his bachelor's and law degrees. Meanwhile, other senior Republicans in the House and Senate continued to earmark. Rep. Jerry Lewis (R-CA), chair of the VA–HUD Appropriations Subcommittee, earmarked $4.5 million for Loma Linda University in his district. Sen. Ted Stevens (R-AK), chair of the National Security Appropriations Subcommittee, earmarked $15 million for a supercomputer at the University of Alaska. The Republicans also allowed senior Democrats to receive projects. Livingston approved, for instance, a $4.8 million earmark for Rep. Richard J. Durbin (D-IL), the ranking member of the Agriculture Appropriations Subcommittee, for a coal gasification project at Southern Illinois University. What is important is not the size of these earmarks, but that they occurred at all. By securing earmarks for themselves, these high-ranking members, and others, signaled to their colleagues that such projects were acceptable spending items if committee support for their approval could be gained.

By the time of the 1996 elections, the Republican leadership had concluded that aiding members' reelection chances through appropriated pet projects was a legitimate activity. In July, Speaker Gingrich sent a memo to each appropriations subcommittee chair, asking them, "Are there any Republican members who could be severely hurt by the bill or who need a specific district item in the bill?" Academic earmarks may not be funded at the same high levels as they were during the early 1990s, but they have not disappeared. In fact, perhaps in response to Gingrich's efforts to aid Republican electoral chances, the dollar value of academic earmarks apparently increased by nearly 50 percent in FY 1997 over the previous fiscal year.[25]

Finally, it is worth noting that the Republican cuts in earmarks, though dramatic, continued a trend in the reduction of such projects that had begun in FY 1994, following the peak years of FY 1992 and FY 1993. To some extent, this decline may be explained by opposition to earmarking within Congress, which will be examined in the next chapter. A more fundamental reason for these reductions, however, may be that FY 1992 was also the peak year for discretionary spending by the appropriations committees. From a high of $513 billion in FY 1992, the committees' spending allocation has fallen in real dollars every year since then. Faced with this loss of resources, the committees have frozen or cut in real terms many agency budgets; therefore, it is not surprising that academic earmarks have also been reduced.[26]

The Concentration of Subcommittee Earmarks

The power exercised by the chairs of the appropriations subcommittees, as well as that of the rank-and-file members of these subcommit-

---

25. Andrew Taylor, "GOP Pet Projects Give Boost to Shaky Incumbents," *Congressional Quarterly Weekly Report*, August 3, 1996, p. 2169. Also see Allan Freedman, "Members' Pet Projects Survive Despite Tight Fiscal Limits," *Congressional Quarterly Weekly Report*, July 8, 1995, pp. 1990–2; George Hager, "Today's Appropriators Preside Over a Shrinking Empire," *Congressional Quarterly Weekly Report*, May 20, 1995, pp. 1365–82; Jeff Shear, "Pain's the Game," *National Journal*, January 14, 1995, pp. 108–11; Shear, "United They Stand," *National Journal*, October 28, 1995, pp. 2646–50; Richard Cohen, "Appropriators Losing Clout," *National Journal*, January 20, 1996, p. 130; Dan Morgan, "Tobacco Subsidies Under Attack," *Washington Post*, June 15, 1995.

26. The 602a spending allocations for the House Appropriations Committee, for example, have been: FY 1992, $513.1 billion; FY 1993, $506.1 billion; FY 1994, $500.9 billion; FY 1995, $510.7 billion; FY 1996, $487.3 billion; FY 1997, $490.3 billion. Some observers of earmarking predicted that earmarking would increase with the Republicans taking control of Congress. In a conflict between divided branches of government, the legislative branch would earmark to assert its presence. See Gary J. Andres, "Pork Barrel Spending – On the Wane?" *PS: Political Science & Politics*, January 1995, pp. 207–11. Andres argues that earmarking is more likely in an divided government, as "a lack of responsiveness by the administration for a member's distri-

tees, has affected the distribution of academic earmarks. Because earmarks are by definition political in nature, and because political power is unequally divided, so is the division of earmarks within the subcommittees. Although there is some debate among political scientists about the influence of leadership and senior positions in Congress on resource allocation, in the case of academic earmarking it is certainly true that a pyramidlike distribution of resources exists, with chairs and senior members receiving the bulk of committee benefits.[27] In 1993 the House Science, Space, and Technology Committee analyzed the allocation of FY 1992 earmarks to academic institutions and concluded:

> The only thing these schools seem to have in common is that a member of Congress, usually a member of the House or Senate Appropriations Committee, has decided that a particular project at a particular school is worthy of federal support. In short, they all have friends in high places. . . . Seventeen of the top twenty states receiving academic earmarks have Senators and/or Representatives who were Appropriations Committee Chairs or Subcommittee Chairs or Ranking Members. . . . The top twenty states, represented on the Appropriations Committees by just twelve Senators

butional priorities begets frustration, and frustration begets earmarks." Andres forgets to consider that members must have the necessary resources to engage in earmarking. In fact, the idea of "distributive politics," as outlined by political scientists, (see footnote 2) is predicated on growing budgetary increments. For more on Andres, see Guy Gugliotta, "Earmarking Can Cap the Pork Barrel," *Washington Post*, September 5, 1995.

27. Some of the studies that explore the degree of influence of senior members and appropriators in the distribution of resources include John A. Ferejohn, *Pork Barrel Politics* (Stanford: Stanford University Press, 1974), Ch. 9; R. Douglas Arnold, *Congress and the Bureaucracy* (New Haven: Yale University Press, 1979; Michael K. Moore and John R. Hibbing, "Length of Congressional Tenure and Federal Spending: Were the Votes of Washington State Correct?" *American Politics Quarterly*, 24 (1996): 131–49; Carol F. Gross, "Military Committee Membership and Defense-Related Benefits in the House of Representatives," *Western Political Quarterly* 25 (1972): 215–33; Keith E. Hamm, "Patterns of Influence Among Committees, Agencies, and Interest Groups," *Legislative Studies Quarterly* 8 (1983): 379–426; in Barry S. Rundquist (ed.), *Political Benefits* (Lexington: Lexington Books, 1980), see Bruce A. Ray, "Congressional Promotion of District Interests: Does Power on the Hill Really Make a Difference?"; J. Norman Reid, "Politics, Program; Administration, and the Distribution of Grants-in-Aid: A Theory and a Test"; J. Theodore Anagnoson, "Politics in the Distribution of Federal Grants: The Case of the Economic Development Administration"; Richard Carlton, Timothy Russell, and Richard Waters, "Distributive Benefits, Congressional Support, and Agency Growth: The Cases of the National Endowments for the Arts and Humanities"; and Robert M. Stein and Kenneth N. Bickers, "Universalism and the Electoral Connection: A Test and Some Doubts," *Political Research Quarterly* 47 (1994): 295–317.

and thirty-four Representatives, received 78.7% of all apparent academic earmarks.[28]

In fact, of the $3.8 billion in earmarks that went to the top seventy-three recipient universities and colleges, as listed in Table 10, over $2.3 billion, or 61 percent, went to institutions in states represented by appropriations subcommittee chairs. Another $240 million, or 6 percent, is accounted for by the Massachusetts-based clients of Schlossberg and Cassidy, who benefited from the influence of Speaker O'Neill. Three percent, or $122 million, went to Georgetown University, with its own set of unique political connections. Virtually every other earmark for these schools may be attributed to a member of the House or Senate appropriations committee.

This concentration of resources is evident in Table 8. The table identifies the distribution of earmarks by state for the top five earmarking House and Senate appropriations subcommittees. In each case, ten states received the bulk of earmarked dollars allocated by the subcommittee, and in each case the top state was represented by a senior appropriations member, either a chair or a ranking member. In the Defense subcommittee, for example, 66 percent of all earmarks went to ten states, with a third of the funds going to just one state, Pennsylvania. This state's windfall represents the activities of Rep. John Murtha (D-PA) and Rep. Joseph McDade (R-PA), who have served as chair and ranking member of the subcommittee, respectively. In the case of Energy and Water, the distribution was influenced by Sen. Hatfield (R-OR), chair of the full Senate Appropriations Committee and member of the subcommittee; Sen. J. Bennett Johnston (D-LA), chair of the Senate subcommittee; and Rep. Tom Bevill (D-AL), chair of the House subcommittee. Similarly, for VA–HUD, Rep. Bob Traxler (D-MI), chair of the House subcommittee; Sen. Robert Byrd (D-WVA), full Senate Appropriations Committee chair; and Sen. Barbara Mikulski (D-MD) directed substantial earmarks to their states and districts.

So, even though chairs may allocate earmarks as side payments to subcommittee members and others throughout Congress to construct winning coalitions to pass their bills, they still reserve the clear majority of these projects for their own constituents.[29] When logrolling or trad-

---

28. Chairman George E. Brown, Jr., "Academic Earmarks: An Interim Report by the Chairman of the Committee on Science, Space, and Technology," August 9, 1993, pp. 4–6.
29. See footnote 8, as well as Diana Evans, "Policy and Pork: The Use of Pork Barrel Projects to Build Policy Coalitions in the House of Representatives," *American Journal of Political Science* 38 (1994): 894–917, and Evans, "Who's Calling the Shots? Vote-Buying and the Control of Pork," paper prepared for the annual meetings of the American Political Science Association, Chicago, August 31–September 3, 1995.

Table 8. *Apparent academic earmarks by state and selected appropriations subcommittee, FY 1980–96*

Defense

	State	Amount	Number of earmarks
1	Pennsylvania	$340,284,000	62
2	Florida	111,284,000	14
3	California	89,245,000	26
4	Alaska	82,340,000	7
5	Louisiana	75,950,000	73
6	Massachusetts	72,300,000	13
7	West Virginia	54,150,000	11
8	District of Columbia	52,150,000	9
9	New York	44,798,000	16
10	Illinois	43,196,000	15
	Total	$966,103,000[a]	

Agriculture, Rural Development

	State	Amount	Number of earmarks
1	Mississippi	$117,968,500	145
2	Texas	91,509,000	101
3	North Dakota	90,403,333	141
4	Iowa	87,671,500	110
5	Michigan	62,935,334	133
6	Washington	62,021,300	89
7	Oregon	60,040,133	118
8	Illinois	56,551,000	58
9	Arkansas	50,368,200	93
10	Pennsylvania	39,261,000	58
	Total	$679,468,800[b]	

Energy and Water

	State	Amount	Number of earmarks
1	Oregon	$113,400,000	16
2	Louisiana	108,750,000	16
3	New York	93,299,000	13
4	Alabama	66,530,000	12
5	Florida	60,572,000	16
6	South Carolina	50,127,000	10
7	Indiana	46,564,000	34
8	Massachusetts	44,050,000	12
9	California	30,500,000	8
10	Arizona	25,000,000	3
	Total	$638,792,000[c]	

(Continued)

Table 8. *(cont.)*

Veterans–Housing Urban Development–Independent Agencies		
State	*Amount*	*Number of earmarks*
1 Michigan	$93,383,000	26
2 West Virginia	70,562,000	26
3 Maryland	45,380,000	12
4 New York	42,850,000	22
5 Louisiana	26,920,000	20
6 North Carolina	19,233,000	11
7 Tennessee	18,800,000	7
8 Utah	16,530,000	7
9 Alaska	16,350,000	8
10 Georgia	14,693,000	12
Total	$364,701,000[d]	

Commerce-Justice		
State	*Amount*	*Number of earmarks*
1 New Hampshire	$34,028,000	5
2 Massachusetts	25,253,000	13
3 Iowa	23,251,000	10
4 South Carolina	19,283,000	14
5 Kentucky	16,762,000	10
6 Florida	16,279,500	7
7 Hawaii	15,909,500	9
8 Georgia	13,884,000	6
9 Oregon	12,394,000	4
10 Texas	10,052,000	3
Total	$187,106,000[e]	

[a]Represents 66 percent of all Defense earmarked dollars.
[b]Represents 53 percent of all Agriculture earmarked dollars.
[c]Represents 73.3 percent of all Energy and Water earmarked dollars.
[d]Represents 62 percent of all VA-HUD-IA earmarked dollars.
[e]Represents 64.1 percent of all Commerce-Justice earmarked dollars.

ing earmarks for votes does occur, for academic projects much of it takes place within the Appropriations Committee itself. Of the eighteen states and the District of Columbia listed among the top ten geographical recipients of earmarks, nine states are listed among the top ten in two subcommittees, and three states are listed among the top ten in three subcommittees.

What may explain this concentration among states is that some particularly "entrepreneurial" members used their multiple subcommittee assignments to obtain projects from more than one subcommittee, and in return for these projects they agreed to support the bills. For example, the State of Florida is among the top ten recipients on both the Defense and Energy and Water lists. During the 1980s, Rep. Bill Chappell (D-FL), an aggressive earmarker, chaired the Defense Subcommittee and was the third-ranking majority member of the Energy and Water Subcommittee. Florida consequently benefited twofold from Chappell's membership on the Appropriations Committee.

Aside from the congressional politics and discord this allocation of resources has generated within Congress, which will be considered in the next chapter, this concentration of dollars has significant consequences for the issues of equity and effectiveness of earmarking as an institution-building strategy.

The Distribution of Academic Earmarks

Perhaps the central issue in the debate over academic earmarking is that of equity. The argument offered in behalf of earmarking is that the merit review system is biased in favor of elite universities, with the result that research funds are distributed in an inequitable manner. Because there is also no meaningful federal facilities program, emerging academic institutions argue that they must seek earmarked funds to improve their scientific infrastructure to be competitive in obtaining research awards. Inequities found in the current system, therefore, are said to be remedied in part by earmarking.

This claim, however, also raises the issue of equity in the distribution of earmarked funds. If the peer or merit review system should be evaluated on the basis of equity, so should the allocation of earmarked dollars. When evaluated in terms of equity, earmarking is found to suffer from its own biases, for in Congress, which allocates earmarks, neither power nor the rewards of power are distributed equally. As a result, rather than promoting a more equitable distribution of resources, earmarking encourages its own concentration of funding, sometimes bene-fiting geographic regions, states, and universities that are already major recipients of merit-reviewed funds. In this way, these regions, states, and schools are double-dipping into the federal budget.

The data presented here provide some indication of how earmarking rates in terms of equitable distribution by state, institution, and geo-graphical region.[30]

States

Table 9 indicates that the vast majority of earmarked dollars were dis-tributed to a minority of states. Nearly 30 percent of earmarked funds went to institutions in only five states, and 47 percent went to ten states. These top ten earmarking states included five states that were also ranked among the top ten recipients of federal academic research and development (R&D) funds in FY 1994, allocated principally through the merit review process, namely, Pennsylvania, Massachusetts, New York, Michigan, and Texas. The top ten state recipients of these federal R&D funds also obtained 35 percent of all the earmarked dollars. Fur-thermore, the concentration of earmarked dollars is such that the top fifteen states obtained 62 percent of the total amount of $5.126 billion, the top twenty states received over 72 percent, and half of the states gained over 80 percent.

Meanwhile, the poorest states in terms of receiving R&D funds have received relatively few of these earmarks. Only one state of the top ten receiving earmarked dollars, West Virginia, ranked in the bottom ten in terms of federal R&D support. Moreover, the ten states re-ceiving the smallest R&D funding secured just 11.4 percent of the earmarked dollars, with six of these states being among the last ten beneficiaries. If equity is measured in terms of geography, then ear-marking tends to help the rich states get richer. If earmarking is in-tended to help the least-funded states become more competitive, they are not receiving earmarked dollars at a level at all comparable to that of well-funded states.

30. The methodology and analysis for this section is based on James D. Savage, *Trends in the Distribution of Apparent Academic Earmarks in the Federal Government's FY 1980–92 Appropriations Bills* (Washington, D.C.: Congressional Research Service, September 22, 1992), Report 92-726 SPR.

Table 9. *Apparent FY 1980–96 academic earmarks, ranked by state*

Earmark rank		$ Amount	Percent of funds (cumulative)	FY 1994 federal research rank
1	Pennsylvania	$450,317,000		5
2	Oregon	261,072,133		26
3	Florida	246,500,000		13
4	Massachusetts	246,396,000		3
5	Louisiana	236,312,000	28.1%	28
6	New York	222,628,333		2
7	Iowa	200,885,800		25
8	West Virginia	190,144,000		46
9	Michigan	184,964,334		9
10	Texas	174,368,500	47.1	6
11	California	172,530,833		1
12	Hawaii	159,292,000		33
13	Mississippi	157,478,500		37
14	Dist of Columbia	138,900,000		29
15	Illinois	135,916,000	62.0	7
16	North Dakota	130,228,333		48
17	Washington	109,305,300		11
18	Alaska	107,223,600		41
19	South Carolina	101,520,000		31
20	Maryland	99,301,000	72.7	4
21	Alabama	96,018,000		21
22	New Jersey	87,523,000		19
23	Indiana	81,207,800		22
24	Georgia	76,029,000		15
25	Wisconsin	74,682,000	80.8	12
26	Oklahoma	71,724,500		38
27	Nebraska	69,035,300		39
28	Arizona	60,096,000		23
29	Arkansas	59,778,200		40
30	Nevada	58,676,000	87.0	43
31	Ohio	57,159,500		10
32	Utah	53,445,600		27
33	New Hampshire	53,320,000		34
34	Kansas	53,073,400		35
35	North Carolina	50,506,000	92.2	8

(*Continued*)

Table 9. *(cont.)*

Earmark rank	$ Amount	Percent of funds (cumulative)	FY 1994 federal research rank
36 New Mexico	43,397,000		30
37 Minnesota	41,640,000		20
38 Connecticut	38,463,000		16
39 Tennessee	36,922,000		24
40 Missouri	35,715,000	96.0	17
41 Kentucky	31,459,000		32
42 Virginia	29,190,000		18
43 Idaho	25,117,633		47
44 Montana	24,508,700		45
45 Colorado	21,406,000	99.0	14
46 Rhode Island	20,936,000		36
47 Vermont	17,550,000		42
48 South Dakota	10,487,333		51
49 Wyoming	9,357,000		50
50 Maine	9,104,000		49
51 Delaware	3,588,000	100.0%	44
Total	$5,126,398,632		

Note: Institutional rankings are based on NSF's ranking of federal obligations for research and development to the states and the District of Columbia.
Source: Federal Support to Universities, Colleges, and Nonprofit Institutions: FY 1994 (Washington, D.C.: National Science Foundation, 1996), Table B-4.

Universities and Colleges

The distribution of earmarked dollars by academic institutions that have received at least $20 million in projects is shown in Table 10. This table reveals a concentration of earmarks similar to that of the states. The top ten schools received nearly a quarter of all earmarked money, while the top twenty obtained 36 percent of these funds, the top thirty received 46 percent, and just forty institutions benefited from over half of the $5.126 billion in earmarked dollars. Of the more than 387 universities and colleges identified as having received an earmark, the bottom 314 schools shared only a quarter of these dollars. While more and new institutions may have sought earmarks in the late 1980s and early 1990s, many institutions have received $1 or $2 million, with 25 percent of all earmarking institutions receiving less than $1 million during the period FY 1980–96.

Table 10. *Apparant FY 1980–96 academic earmarks, ranked by university or college: Institutions receiving at least $20 million*

Earmark rank		$ Amount	Percent of (cumulative)	FY 1994 federal rank
1	University of Hawaii	$159,292,000		71
2	University of Pittsburgh	151,720,000		19
3	Iowa State University	142,941,300		78
4	University of West Virginia	125,644,000		
5	Georgetown University	122,300,000		58
6	Oregon Health Science University	105,500,000		74
7	Louisiana State University	103,047,000		50
8	University of Alaska	102,783,600		99
9	University of Florida	81,491,500		47
10	Pennsylvania State University	81,107,000	22.9%	14
11	Oregon State University	79,443,133		65
12	Michigan State University	77,506,334		51
13	University of Rochester	73,527,000		26
14	University of Maryland	67,601,000		42
15	University of Nebraska	67,035,300		
16	Mississippi State University	63,815,500		
17	University of North Dakota	63,718,000		
18	North Dakota State University	62,081,333		
19	Baylor Medical College	61,102,000		33
20	Rutgers University	60,448,000	36.1	55
21	Washington State University	59,106,700		
22	Tufts University	57,446,000		80
23	Boston University	56,500,000		44
24	University of Mississippi	55,475,000		
25	Saginaw Valley State	55,470,000		
26	Indiana University	51,338,800		41
27	University of Illinois	47,738,000		25
28	University of Oregon	46,156,000		
29	Loma Linda University	45,500,000		
30	University of Wisconsin	43,932,000	46.2	8
31	University of Miami	42,074,000		40
32	Florida State University	41,977,500		92
33	University of Scranton	41,800,000		
34	University of Massachusetts	41,567,000		98
35	University of South Carolina	40,048,200		
36	University of Arkansas	38,556,200		
37	Columbia University	36,500,000		13
38	Kansas State University	35,535,000		
39	University of New Hampshire	35,247,000		
40	Tulane University	34,610,000	53.8	87

(Continued)

Table 10. *(cont.)*

Earmark rank		$ Amount	Percent of (cumulative)	FY 1994 federal rank
41	Wheeling Jesuit University	34,100,000		
42	Illinois Institute of Technology	33,700,000		
43	Northwestern University	33,054,000		30
44	Carnegie-Mellon University	32,610,000		53
45	Texas A&M	30,963,500		62
46	Clemson University	30,772,000		
47	California State University System	29,000,000		
48	Northeastern University	28,500,000		
49	University of Connecticut	28,433,000		83
50	University of Alabama	28,390,000	59.8	
51	New Mexico State University	28,287,000		94
52	Arizona State University	27,588,000		
53	Lehigh University	27,225,000		
54	University of Nevada, Reno	27,105,000		
55	University of Washington	26,773,600		2
56	University of Arizona	25,813,000		24
57	University of Southern Mississippi	25,252,000		
58	South Carolina Medical College	24,600,000		
59	Boston College	24,500,000		
60	University of Idaho	23,917,633	64.9	
61	Oregon Graduate University	23,673,000		
62	Iowa Public and Private University	23,500,000		
63	University of California, Davis	22,945,500		32
64	Xavier University (LA)	22,750,000		
65	Georgia Institute of Technology	22,533,000		70
66	University of Alabama, Birmingham	22,430,000		27
67	Rochester Institute of Technology	22,382,000		
68	University of Minnesota	22,028,000		16
69	Cornell University	21,634,333		10
70	University of Missouri	21,358,000		
71	University of Nevada, Las Vegas	20,814,000		
72	University of Kentucky	20,409,000		76
73	Wake Forest University	20,113,000	74.4	69
Other institutions		1,310,563,866	25.6	
Total		$5,126,398,632	100.0%	

Note: Institutional rankings are based on NSF's ranking of federal obligations for R&D to the top 100 institutions receiving support.

What these data also indicate is that many of the institutional recipients of earmarking benefited greatly from both the regular peer and merit review systems. Of the 73 schools identified as having received $20 million or more in earmarks, 40 are on the list of the top 100 recipients of federal academic R&D funding. Three schools on this list – the universities of Wisconsin and Washington and Cornell University – are actually among the top 10 recipients of peer- and merit-reviewed research funding. Two of the top 10 earmarking schools, the University of Pittsburgh and Pennsylvania State University, are ranked in the top 20 of the 100 recipients of federal academic R&D funding. In fact, 21 of the top 50 universities are also among the list of 73 major earmarking schools. Fewer than half of these top earmarking schools are unranked in terms of receiving federal R&D funds. These unranked institutions are perhaps the ones that might be considered emerging. This raises the question of whether most of these top earmarking schools are truly emerging, or merely exceptionally ambitious and are willing to double-dip into the federal budget in order to achieve their goals.

Regions

Historically, Congress has expressed concern for equity in the geographical distribution of funds rather than for equal research funding of individual universities.[31] The NSF enabling legislation, for example, notes the importance of geographical equity in the allocation of federal money. One way the agency acknowledges this is by providing data to Congress on the regional distribution of federal R&D funds, for which the United States and affiliated territories are divided into ten regions. Table 11 incorporates these divisions, indicates the distribution of earmarks by region, and compares each region's share of total earmarked dollars to its share of FY 1994 R&D funds.

One critical issue is whether earmarking could improve the competitiveness of the emerging regions. For this to happen, those regions of the country that receive the smallest amounts of R&D funds should benefit from a healthy share of the earmarked funds. This amount should be more than, and not simply equal to, the amount allocated to the more well-to-do regions if the poorer regions are to catch up. Table 10 shows that four of the regions received less than 10 percent of the total federal R&D funds for universities and colleges: West North Central, East

---

31. Thomas P. Murphy, *Science, Geopolitics, and Federal Spending* (Lexington: Heath Lexington Books, 1971), especially Ch. 2.

Table 11. *Apparent FY 1980–96 academic earmarks, by NSF geographical region*

Region	$ Earmarks	Percent of earmarked funds	Region's percent of FY 1994 federal research funds
New England			
Connecticut	$38,463,000		
Maine	9,104,000		
Massachusetts	246,396,000		
New Hampshire	53,320,000		
Rhode Island	20,936,000		
Vermont	17,550,000		
	$385,769,000	7.5%	10.0%
Middle Atlantic			
New Jersey	$87,523,000		
New York	222,628,333		
Pennsylvania	450,317,000		
	$760,468,333	14.8	16.6
East North Central			
Illinois	$135,916,000		
Indiana	81,207,800		
Michigan	184,964,334		
Ohio	57,159,500		
Wisconsin	74,682,000		
	$533,929,634	10.4	13.6
West North Central			
Iowa	$200,885,800		
Kansas	53,073,400		
Minnesota	41,640,000		
Missouri	35,715,000		
Nebraska	69,035,300		
North Dakota	130,228,333		
South Dakota	10,487,333		
	$541,065,166	10.6	5.8
South Atlantic			
Delaware	$3,588,000		
District of Columbia	138,900,000		
Florida	246,500,000		
Georgia	76,029,000		
Maryland	99,301,000		
North Carolina	50,506,000		
South Carolina	101,520,000		
Virginia	29,190,000		
West Virginia	190,144,000		
	$935,678,000	18.2	18.2

(*Continued*)

Table 11. *(cont.)*

Region	$ Earmarks	Percent of earmarked funds	Region's percent of FY 1994 federal research funds
East South Central			
Alabama	$96,018,000		
Kentucky	31,459,000		
Mississippi	157,478,500		
Tennessee	36,922,000		
	$321,877,000	6.3	3.8
West South Central			
Arkansas	$59,778,200		
Louisiana	236,312,000		
Oklahoma	71,724,500		
Texas	174,368,500		
	$542,183,200	10.6	7.1
Mountain			
Arizona	$60,096,000		
Colorado	21,406,000		
Idaho	25,117,633		
Montana	24,508,700		
Nevada	58,676,000		
New Mexico	43,397,000		
Utah	53,445,600		
Wyoming	9,357,000		
	$296,003,933	5.8	6.2
Pacific			
Alaska	$107,223,600		
California	172,530,833		
Hawaii	159,292,000		
Oregon	261,072,133		
Washington	109,305,300		
	$809,423,866	15.8	18.5
Total	$5,126,398,632	100.0%	98.8%[a]

[a]Remaining federal R&D funds go to the "outlying areas," such as Puerto Rico and Guam.

South Central, West South Central, and Mountain. Two of these regions, East South Central and Mountain, also received the smallest amounts of earmarked dollars. The number of earmarked dollars allocated to these regions is unlikely to change their relative status in obtaining federal funding. Two of these regions, however, West North Central and West South Central, did obtain a share of earmarked funding that is somewhat comparable to the amount received by the other regions.

Nevertheless, three of the nine regions – the Pacific, South Atlantic, and Middle Atlantic – received 48.8 percent of all earmarked dollars. Of these regions, Pacific received the largest amount of regular R&D funds and the second largest amount of earmarked funds, South Atlantic received the largest amount of earmarked dollars and the second largest share of R&D funds, and the Middle Atlantic received the third largest share of both earmarked and R&D funds. The consequence of earmarking is that the most well-to-do regions in terms of regular federal R&D funding, like the states and institutions, double-dip into the federal budget through academic earmarking.

These data, therefore, indicate that, contrary to the argument that earmarking increases the equity of R&D funding, the distribution of earmarked dollars is highly concentrated. Still, many emerging states, regions, and institutions did obtain a share of these dollars. The question remains whether the earmarked dollars were employed in an effective, efficacious, and strategic manner to promote a state's or institution's competitive research capabilities.

The Competitive Effect of Earmarking

Advocates of academic earmarking contend that earmarking corrects for the biases of the peer review system by allowing emerging institutions to receive the support they need to become competitive with established research institutions. Opponents of earmarking, however, argue that earmarked funds are simply wasted or that they do not support the same high-quality science that is funded through peer and merit review.

Of all the questions related to academic earmarking, that of the quality of the science funded through earmarking may be the most difficult to address. Opponents of earmarking properly note that earmarking lacks the accountability and evaluation associated with merit and peer review. Thus, assessments of earmarked projects are often anecdotal rather than systematic; it is always possible to identify both successful and failed projects.

The data, nevertheless, provide an objective, but necessarily inferential, assessment of the effect of earmarking on an institution's ability to compete for funds in a peer or merit review process by comparing an institution's and a state's federal receipt of R&D funds rank before and after receiving significant earmarked funds. Two important caveats must be taken into account when employing this method. First, some institutions may have had their earmarked dollars for only a few years. The actual spending of an appropriation may take several years, as in the construction of a new research lab. Second, in the collection of data on federal obligations for academic R&D, neither NSF nor the various agencies distinguish between peer-reviewed and earmarked funds. In other words, as an institution receives more earmarked dollars, its ranking actually increases. Thus, a higher rank may not be due to increased competitiveness, but rather to increased earmarking. Nevertheless, the NSF ranking remains the best indicator of institutional competitiveness. In any case, it is employed here merely as an indirect measure of the status of the research generated through earmarking in the absence of better measures of quality.

States

Table 12 identifies the total FY 1980–96 earmarked dollars received by each state, the first fiscal year in which those funds totaled $1 million or more, the state's federal research rank that year, that rank for FY 1994, and the change in rank. The table indicates that since receiving their first large earmark, sixteen of the states improved their rankings as recipients of federal research funds, twenty states experienced a drop in rank, and thirteen states experienced no change in rank.

The total earmarked dollars a state obtained had a positive, though limited, relationship to improved rank. Among the top ten states receiving earmarks, four increased their rank, two declined, and three experienced no change. Of the states ranked 11 through 20, only two gained in rank, while three declined and five remained constant. Meanwhile, among the ten states receiving the fewest earmarked dollars, those ranked 41 through 51, three gained rank, four lost, and three experienced no change. Thus, a positive change in ranking, and nearly at the same rate, was evident in the states receiving both the most and fewest earmarked dollars.

Most states, in any case, experienced little change in rank over time in terms of either gains or losses. Thirty-eight states experienced no more than a change of +2 or −2 or +1 or −1. The states with the greatest change – −14 for Oregon, −6 for North Dakota, and −4 for Oklahoma – are also among the biggest recipients of earmarked funds.

Table 12. *Change in federal research rank among states, FY 1980–96*

Cumulative FY 1980–96 earmark rank		$ Amount	Year of first $1 million earmark	Rank that year	FY 1994 research rank	Rank change
1	Pennsylvania	$450,317,000	1980	6	5	+1
2	Oregon	261,072,133	1983	24	38	−14
3	Florida	246,500,000	1985	15	13	+2
4	Massachusetts	246,396,000	1980	3	3	0
5	Louisiana	236,312,000	1985	31	28	+3
6	New York	222,628,333	1982	2	2	0
7	Iowa	200,885,800	1985	27	25	+2
8	West Virginia	190,144,000	1983	44	46	−2
9	Michigan	184,964,334	1985	9	9	0
10	Texas	174,368,500	1980	5	6	−1
11	California	172,530,833	1985	1	1	0
12	Hawaii	159,292,000	1983	32	33	−1
13	Mississippi	157,478,500	1985	38	37	+1
14	Dist Columbia	138,900,000	1984	28	29	−1
15	Illinois	135,916,000	1982	7	7	0
16	North Dakota	130,228,333	1980	42	48	−6
17	Washington	109,305,300	1985	11	11	0
18	Alaska	107,223,600	1990	41	41	0
19	South Carolina	101,520,000	1987	34	31	+3
20	Maryland	99,301,000	1987	4	4	0
21	Alabama	96,018,000	1986	24	21	+3
22	New Jersey	87,523,000	1980	23	19	+4
23	Indiana	81,207,800	1985	21	22	−1
24	Georgia	76,029,000	1985	18	15	+3
25	Wisconsin	74,682,000	1989	14	12	+2
26	Oklahoma	71,724,500	1980	34	38	−4
27	Nebraska	69,035,300	1984	36	39	−3
28	Arizona	60,096,000	1987	27	23	−4
29	Arkansas	59,778,200	1989	41	40	+1
30	Nevada	58,676,000	1986	42	43	−1
31	Ohio	57,159,500	1980	9	10	−1
32	Utah	53,445,600	1988	26	27	−1
33	New Hampshire	53,320,000	1983	36	34	+2
34	Kansas	53,073,400	1986	32	35	−3
35	North Carolina	50,506,000	1985	8	8	0
36	New Mexico	43,397,000	1985	29	30	−1
37	Minnesota	41,640,000	1992	19	20	−1
38	Connecticut	38,463,000	1987	12	16	−4
39	Tennessee	36,922,000	1990	22	24	−2
40	Missouri	35,715,000	1992	17	17	0
41	Kentucky	31,459,000	1989	34	35	−1
42	Virginia	29,190,000	1984	17	18	−1
43	Idaho	25,117,633	1989	47	47	0

(Continued)

Table 12. *(cont.)*

Cumulative FY 1980–96 earmark rank	$ Amount	Year of first $1 million earmark	Rank that year	FY 1994 research rank	Rank change
44 Montana	24,508,700	1991	47	45	+2
45 Colorado	21,406,000	1988	16	14	+2
46 Rhode Island	20,936,000	1986	31	36	0
47 Vermont	17,550,000	1987	39	42	−3
48 South Dakota	10,487,333	1990	51	51	0
49 Wyoming	9,357,000	1989	49	50	−1
50 Maine	9,104,000	1993	50	49	+1
51 Delaware	3,588,000	1995	NA	44	NA

Note: A plus sign and a number indicates the number of ranks gained. A minus sign and a number indicates the number of ranks lost. A zero indicates no change in rank. State ranks are based on NSF's ranking of federal obligations for R&D.
Source: Federal Support to Universities, Colleges, and Selected Nonprofit Institutions, various fiscal years (Washington, D.C.: National Science Foundation, 1980–94).

Universities and Colleges

A more interesting and significant result emerges when the focus turns to the earmarking effectiveness of institutions. Table 13 attempts to measure the effect of earmarking on institutional rankings. The figure of $40 million is used as a threshold, based on the assumption that over a possible seventeen-year time span, an institution that had received that level of additional, largely discretionary funding might be able to improve its competitive standing in some objective fashion, such as the receipt of competitive R&D funds. Moreover, the thirty-five universities that fit this category received 50.3 percent of the total dollar value of all earmarks throughout FY 1980–96. Also, the institutions that have accumulated $40 million or more in earmarks generally have done so over a number of years, and thus they are more likely to have digested these funds and maximized their use. Finally, the fewer the earmarked dollars an institution has received, the more difficult it becomes to assert that these funds played a significant role in boosting a school's ranking. To make such an assertion more plausible, the figure of at least $40 million appears reasonable. If these institutions have not succeeded in improving their status, then the effectiveness of earmarking for this purpose must seriously be questioned.

Table 13 identifies the universities and colleges receiving $40 million or more in earmarks for FY 1980–96, the dollar amount of those ear-

Table 13. *Change in federal research rank among institutions receiving $40 million or more in earmarks, FY 1980–96*

Cumulative FY 1980–96 earmark rank		$ Amount	Year of first $1 million earmark	Federal research rank that year	FY 1994 federal research rank	Rank change
1	University of Hawaii	$159,292,000	1983	70	71	−1
2	University of Pittsburgh	151,720,000	1991	15	19	−4
3	Iowa State University	142,941,300	1987	—	78	+22
4	University of West Virginia	125,644,000	1983	—	—	—
5	Georgetown University	122,300,000	1985	93	58	+35
6	Oregon Health Science University	105,500,000	1983		74	+26
7	Louisiana State University	103,047,000	1983	60	50	+10
8	University of Alaska	102,783,600	1990	—	99	+1
9	University of Florida	81,491,500	1988	42	47	−5
10	Pennsylvania State University	81,107,000	1983	19	14	+5
11	Oregon State University	79,443,133	1983	50	65	−15
12	Michigan State University	77,506,334	1988	49	51	−2
13	University of Rochester	73,527,000	1983	24	26	−2
14	University of Maryland	67,601,000	1990	41	42	−1
15	University of Nebraska	67,035,300	1985	—	—	—
16	Mississippi State University	63,815,500	1985	—	—	—
17	University of North Dakota	63,718,000	1986	—	—	—
18	North Dakota State University	62,081,333	1980	—	—	—
19	Baylor Medical College	61,102,000	1980	37	33	+4
20	Rutgers University	60,448,000	1980	76	55	+21
21	Washington State University	59,106,700	1986	—	—	—
22	Tufts University	57,446,000	1980	100	80	+20
23	Boston University	56,500,000	1984	42	44	−2
24	University of Mississippi	55,475,000	1988	—	—	—

(*Continued*)

Table 13. *(cont.)*

Cumulative FY 1980–96 earmark rank	$ Amount	Year of first $1 million earmark	Federal research rank that year	FY 1994 federal research rank	Rank change
25 Saginaw Valley State (MI)	55,470,000	1990	—	—	—
26 Indiana University	51,338,800	1986	49	41	+8
27 University of Illinois	47,738,000	1986	17	25	−8
28 University of Oregon	46,156,000	1987	—	—	—
29 Loma Linda University (CA)	45,500,000	1988	—	—	—
30 University of Wisconsin	43,932,000	1989	9	8	+1
31 University of Miami	42,074,000	1990	42	40	+2
32 Florida State University	41,977,500	1985	88	92	−4
33 University of Scranton	41,800,000	1988	—	—	—
34 University of Massachusetts	41,567,000	1986	—	98	+2
35 University of South Carolina	40,048,000	1987	—	—	—
Total	$2,578,233,000[a]				

Note: A plus sign and a number indicates the number of ranks gained. A minus sign and a number indicates the number of ranks lost. Blank spaces indicate an institution not ranked in the top 100 recipients of federal research funding.
[a]This total accounts for 50.3 percent of the dollar value of all academic earmarks.

marks, the year of the first earmark totaling $1 million or more, the institution's federal R&D rank that year, its rank in FY 1994, and the change in rank. Of the thirty-five institutions identified, thirteen improved their ranking and ten experienced a decline. The remaining twelve schools were unranked at the time of their initial $1 million earmark and they remain unranked, thereby limiting the basis for comparison in this manner.

Since receiving their first $1 million or more in earmarks, seven institutions increased their rank by eight or more places: Iowa State University, Georgetown University, Oregon Health Sciences University, Louisiana State University, Rutgers University, Indiana University, and Tufts University. Ten schools, however, failed, despite substantial earmarking, to register improvement, and their rank actually declined: the universities of Hawaii, Pittsburgh, Florida, Rochester, Maryland, and Illinois, as well as Michigan State University, Florida State University, and Boston University.

Strategically Productive and Unproductive Earmarks

One explanation for the variation in the ability of earmarking to improve institutional competitiveness may lie in the types of earmarks these universities receive. The data in Table 7 indicate that 82 percent of the congressional earmarks were associated with four House and Senate appropriations subcommittees: Defense, Agriculture, Energy and Water, and Veterans Administration–Housing Urban Development–Independent Agencies (VA-HUD).

This distribution may partially explain why some types of earmarks do not appear to change measurably a state's or institution's subsequent federal R&D rank. Although the Agriculture subcommittees, for example, appropriated 25.1 percent of all earmarked dollars, research funding by the Department of Agriculture amounts to only 3.9 percent of total federal R&D academic support in FY 1994, *including earmarks.* Although the Energy and Water subcommittees appropriated 17 percent of all earmarked dollars, research funding by the DOE accounted for only 5 percent of total FY 1994 federal academic R&D support. At the same time, while the Labor–Health and Human Services–Education subcommittees appropriated 2.9 percent of all earmarked dollars, research funding by the three major agencies in their bills provided 54.7 percent of total federal academic R&D. The VA–HUD subcommittees have appropriated 11.5 percent of all earmarked funds, and the research agencies in their bills provided 20.8 percent of total federal R&D dollars. In other words, the types of research facilities and projects generated by earmarked dollars may not necessarily translate into the kind of basic science that is likely to be competitively funded by the federal government in large amounts or that may enhance the general competitive capability of an institution.

An example from the State of Oregon may underscore the difference between strategically productive and nonproductive earmarks. Two of the leading beneficiaries of earmarking, courtesy of Senator Hatfield, are Oregon Health Sciences University (OHSU), the sixth leading recipient of earmarked funds, and Oregon State University (OSU), the eleventh leading recipient. Both institutions are public universities, and both have suffered through good and mostly bad state budget allocations. Yet, since FY 1983, OHSU has improved its ranking as a recipient of federal R&D funds from less than 100 to 74, an increase of 26 ranks. During the same time period, OSU fell from a rank of 50 to 65.

The difference between these two universities may be that during these years OSU almost exclusively pursued agricultural earmarks, playing up to its strength as a land-grant institution with a heavy agricultural emphasis. These earmarks, however, could do little to assist the university in competing for funding from the large, merit-reviewed federal research programs, such as those administered by NSF. The Department of Agriculture's competitive research budget, meanwhile, is relatively tiny, and most of its research dollars are allocated through earmarking and formula-driven programs. OHSU, in contrast, has sought out earmarks to enhance its ability to compete for the much more amply funded research programs in NIH and other agencies within the Department of Health and Human Services.

Simply put, to be a top ten or top twenty research university in the United States, an institution must be able to compete successfully for biomedical research funding, the largest source of federal academic R&D support, and for the research grants offered by NSF, the second largest source of federal R&D support. However, many earmarks simply do not contribute to institutions in this way. The universities that have demonstrated the most improvement in their R&D ranking, such as OHSU, Georgetown, and Tufts, have used their earmarks to achieve these goals, and they are clearly the great success stories of academic earmarking.

Thus, earmarking by itself appears to produce mixed results in strengthening an institution's ability to compete for federal research funds. At the institutional level, it appears likely that earmarks can be used as part of a careful strategic plan to improve a university's research capabilities. A variety of factors clearly influence the research capability of an institution, however, including the quality and vision of its leadership; the research abilities of its faculty; the scientific and disciplinary focus of the faculty's research efforts; financial support in terms of salaries, equipment, and staff; modern research facilities; a research-oriented library; and able graduate student research assistants. Earmarking may aid a university in remedying deficiencies in some of these areas. Moreover, when used as part of a well-considered and funded strategic plan firmly endorsed by the institution's leadership to build research centers of excellence, such as Tufts University's Nutrition Center, earmarks may indeed enhance an institution's ability to compete for much greater federal funding.

Nevertheless, even earmarks totaling $100 million or more do not guarantee competitive success. A number of institutions have obtained total earmarks of this amount and have failed to improve their relative standing, including the top two recipients of earmarks, the University of Hawaii and the University of Pittsburgh. As noted, many factors influence research capability, and earmarked funding is only one of them. Finally, this dramatic improvement in ranking for a small number of institutions – fewer than ten – has come at the cost of hundreds of millions of dollars, a price the federal government may often be unable to pay.

7

Congress, the President, and the Fight against Earmarking

The institutional and personal incentives to engage in academic earmarking are powerful. University presidents seek to leave a legacy of strengthening their schools and appeasing their boards of trustees, faculty, and alumni while enhancing their careers as university administrators. Members of Congress seek to aid their constituents, influence their colleagues, participate in making what they regard as good public policy, and promote their chances for reelection. In both instances, obtaining earmarks may further these ambitions. Thus, what is surprising is not that academic earmarking exists, but that, subject to macro budgetary constraints, it has not been more prevalent.

If, in the face of these incentives and ambitions, the opposition to academic earmarking had consisted solely of a handful of elite university presidents and their lobbyists, earmarking in the 1980s and 1990s would have been more extensive. Yet, academic earmarking has also been opposed by a small number of sometimes highly effective members of Congress with their own motivations and incentives. Moreover, although less effective within Congress but perhaps more visible publicly, Presidents Reagan, Bush, and Clinton have each spoken out against earmarking. Thus, academic earmarking has been contested, often sporadically but also sometimes very effectively.

Opposition to earmarking has clearly existed within Congress. It is worth recalling that academic earmarking began with university presidents and their lobbyists asking members for earmarks, not with members approaching presidents. Earmarking of academic facilities and research projects spread slowly within Congress, and it has been repeatedly attacked by various members of both political parties who have employed all available congressional rules and procedures in their efforts to limit or defeat earmarked projects. By doing so, these members have sometimes jeopardized their relations with colleagues to the point

159

of inviting reprisals from more powerful members, although reprisals and sanctions have rarely, if ever, been employed.

The motivations of those who stand against earmarking vary and are often interrelated. Some members argue that earmarking runs counter to good public policy, that is, it damages the ability of the federal government to set research priorities, undermines the quality of academic research, and constitutes nothing more than pork barrel politics. Sen. James Jeffords (R-VT), for example, has suggested that "The money should be competitive grants, that's the most effective and efficient way to maximize the money for research." "I think that what we have now," declared Rep. Robert Walker (R-PA), referring to the growth in earmarking, "is a system that is not being adequately peer reviewed, that is subject to political pressure, and ultimately results in getting bad science for big money." Rep. George Brown (D-CA) concurred and observed that "We want to spend all money that's intended for the purposes of research and development and the support of science in the most efficient way possible. You spend the money more efficiently when you do so as a result of a carefully reviewed process where the money goes to the best qualified recipient."[1]

There are also members who oppose earmarking because it threatens their committee prerogatives. Members of the various authorization committees in particular have asserted that the appropriations committees' control over academic earmarking undermines their right to engage in policy making and to allocate projects to enhance their own reelection efforts. Members bristle at legislation that blatantly distributes earmarks to a handful of members who usually serve on the appropriations committees. So, for example, while George Brown voiced his support for peer review, he also defended the right of authorizers to select projects for earmarks. "At the present time," Brown declared, "the number of members who are in a position to earmark funds for their districts can be counted on the fingers of your two hands, they are the senior members of the appropriations committees. The members of Congress, as much as they love the senior members of the appropriations committee, would like to have the opportunity to have worthwhile projects in their districts."[2]

So, just as members of the appropriations committees respond to their various incentives to earmark science projects, such as the desire to gain reelection, conduct good public policy, and exercise influence within the Congress, many of these same incentives promote opposition to earmarking by their colleagues who hold different formal positions in Congress.

1. Interview with Sen. James Jeffords, March 25, 1993; interview with Rep. Robert Walker, March 11, 1992; interview with Rep. George Brown, December 11, 1991.
2. Interview with Rep. George Brown, December 11, 1991.

Whatever success these opponents of earmarking have enjoyed is nevertheless surprising. The opponents are often in the minority on this matter, and they serve in an institution whose majoritarian biases, incentives, and rules favor earmarking, even if these earmarks numerically have benefited those who serve on appropriations committees. Distributive decision making based on impartial peer or merit review is an artifact of academic culture or of the administrative practices of executive branch research agencies, not of Congress. Within the legislative branch decisions are political in nature and concerns for merit and efficiency tend to be secondary at best. As a result, some political scientists have labeled members who oppose their colleagues' pork barrel projects as "saints," and others have posited that "a representative is only one vote in the legislature. . . . [O]ne vote is not likely to alter policy."[3]

Conflict within Congress over Academic Earmarking

Nevertheless, individual members have fought academic earmarks, sometimes successfully, and they have turned to a variety of institutional rules and procedures to counter the majoritarian biases and incentives favoring earmarking.

First, the prerogatives of seniority and of committee chairs, particularly in the appropriations subcommittees, have been used to prevent earmarks from even being considered in appropriations bills. Second, members have engaged in hard-fought floor fights to strike earmarks from bills. Third, members have employed House and Senate rules to delete earmarks from legislation. They have also proposed new rules that would be even more prohibitive against earmarks. Fourth, extensive committee hearings have been held in conjunction with media efforts to highlight the adverse consequences of earmarking. Nevertheless, the opposition to earmarking chronicled here has been episodic, uncoordinated, and often spontaneous. The members who oppose earmarking have never gathered together as a group to caucus and plan an organized fight against these projects, nor have the higher education associations attempted to initiate such a group. As a result, those efforts that have been most successful at stopping earmarks have been the individ-

---

3. For the description of members who oppose distributive projects as "saints," see David R. Mayhew, *The Electoral Connection* (New Haven: Yale University Press, 1974), p. 15. Quote from Barry R. Weingast, "A Rational Choice Perspective on Congressional Norms," *American Journal of Political Science* 23 (1979): 245–62. Both Mayhew and Weingast argued that saintly individual members would be unable to prevent their colleagues' projects, that they would be few in number within the legislature, and that their colleagues would punish them for their efforts.

ual actions of powerful members and bipartisan opposition that developed in response to what were regarded as egregious incidents of academic earmarking.

Fighting Earmarks in Appropriations Subcommittees

The most effective way to defeat an earmark is to prevent it from being considered in an appropriations bill or report. This ability to "bottle up" an earmark is one of the powers exercised by the chairs of the appropriations subcommittees. Even as these chairs determine which member will receive a project at what funding level, they also may exclude or greatly limit the earmarking that takes place in their subcommittees. Although earmarking is a practice associated with the appropriations process, as shown in Table 7, not all of the thirteen appropriations bills, or more properly the reports accompanying the bills, are equal in their number or cost of earmarking.

The difference in earmarked funding levels among the subcommittees is largely due to the position taken by their chairs and the ability of the chairs to use the rules of the budgetary process to deny members their earmarks.[4] In the VA–HUD subcommittee, Chairmen Jake Garn (R-UT)

---

4. The ability of individual subcommittee chairs to prevent or limit earmarking in their bills and reports stems from the rules of the budgetary process. Under the current process, the appropriations committees are allocated an amount of money to spend, which is called the "602a allocation." This money is further divided into 602b allocations for the thirteen subcommittees. The allocation sets a ceiling on the total amount of money the subcommittee can spend for outlays and budget authority. The rules prohibit the subcommittee from exceeding their ceilings, and a point of order may be called on the floor against any bill violating the ceiling; to override the point of order in the Senate requires sixty votes. After the 602b allocations have been determined by the chairs, the subcommittee chair has the prerogative to propose how the entire allocation should be spent. This takes place in what is called the chair's "markup." The chair marks up the bill, perhaps using the full allocation, before presenting it to the subcommittee members for their concurrence. Before the chair begins marking up, the subcommittee members, as well as any member who desires a project, submits requests to the chair. With the aid of the staff, the mark is pieced together, and it may be presented to the subcommittee members as late as the afternoon before the subcommittee meets to vote on its bill. So members usually have very little time to organize to defeat or revise the chair's mark. Moreover, since the 602b allocation must be respected throughout the entire budgetary process, the bills are insulated from floor amendments for projects that do not contain revenue offsets. So members who are denied projects must cut someone else's project or budget to provide offsetting revenues to fund the desired earmark. Such efforts invite the wrath of the members whose funded programs are targeted as offsets, so such substitution is rare. Moreover, members who vote in favor of amending the chair's mark in this way risk alienating the chair's goodwill when they seek funding for their own projects. Thus, the chair's mark is a powerful procedural tool that enables the subcommittee chair to prevent or greatly limit academic earmarks.

and William Proxmire (D-WI) in the Senate and Edward Boland (D-MA) in the House opposed academic earmarking in their bills, which registered just two identifiable earmarks during the period FY 1980–9. "If decisions about who shall do research and where it shall be done are made by Congress," Proxmire wrote in a newspaper editorial he co-authored with his Senate colleagues Jeff Bingaman (D-NM) and John Danforth (R-MO), "with . . . almost complete indifference to the relative quality of the work, we will be well on the road to mediocrity, at best, in our research enterprise."[5] Commenting on Boland's position on earmarking, his subcommittee staff director noted, "I can't recall instances where other members on that subcommittee requested earmarks. It was clear to all that Mr. Boland opposed earmarks for academic institutions."

In the Labor–Health and Human Services–Education (Labor–HHS) subcommittee, Rep. William Natcher (D-KY) and, to a lesser extent, Sen. Lawton Chiles (D-FL) were opponents of earmarking. The Labor–HHS bill is particularly important, for it is the largest source of academic research funding, principally through its budget for the Department of Health and Human Services (HHS). Natcher, who proved to be the most effective enemy of academic earmarking in Congress, was the second most senior member of the House Appropriations Committee during the 1980s and later became chair of the full committee from 1992 until his death in 1994. What troubled Natcher about earmarks was not that they represented bad science or poor public policy, but rather that they had rarely received prior authorizations. A stickler for following legislative protocol, Natcher demanded that before his committee would appropriate funds for a program or project, it first had to receive proper authorizations. Those members looking to secure an earmark almost never took the time to follow this traditional law-making procedure and bypassed the authorizations committees by going directly to the appropriations committees.

If Natcher had opened HHS's programs in NIH to earmarking, the extent and cost of earmarking could easily have doubled or tripled during the late 1980s and early 1990s. Yet, as the subcommittee staff director observed, "It's the policy of the subcommittee chair [to decide whether earmarks will be allowed]. Natcher doesn't like it and defeats the Senate in conference." In the conference committee over the FY 1990 bill, for example, where the differences between the House and Senate were resolved, Natcher refused to fund six projects worth $4 mil-

---

5. Jeff Bingaman, John C. Danforth, and William Proxmire, "Research Funds Shouldn't Have a Pork-Barrel Fate," *Los Angeles Times*, June 2, 1986.

lion included in the Senate bill, which were supported by the new Senate subcommittee chair, Tom Harkin (D-IA). The Senate simply acceded to Natcher's implacable stand against such unauthorized projects.

These members' opposition to earmarking in their subcommittees affected the behavior of other subcommittees, even those that allowed earmarking. The House Energy and Water Subcommittee funded a nuclear medicine project in FY 1987 at the request of a member who failed to obtain Natcher's approval. That project led to more requests to the subcommittee. Energy and Water received fifteen proposals for similar projects in FY 1989 and four new requests for academic earmarks of all types valued at more than $200 million in FY 1990. Consequently, the subcommittee chair, Rep. Tom Bevill (D-AL), ordered a freeze on new earmarks for FY 1989 and FY 1990 due to the cost of these projects. After this brief hiatus, this subcommittee, whose nominal responsibility is funding such agencies as DOE, went into the business of supporting the biomedical earmarks Natcher refused to consider. Between FY 1991 and FY 1993, Bevill's subcommittee forced DOE to fund more than $171 million in biomedical research facilities at the expense of the budgets for regular DOE programs. Meanwhile, as early as 1988, DOE complained that its budget for Basic Energy Sciences, the source of support for basic academic research, had to be reduced to make room for the subcommittee's academic earmarking.[6]

As the higher education associations came to realize, earmarks are easiest to defeat when the appropriations subcommittee chair prevents them from becoming part of a bill or report. Once an earmark has reached that stage, defeating it becomes infinitely more difficult. By employing the budget process as they did to prevent or greatly limit academic earmarks, subcommittee chairs such as Natcher, Boland, Garn, and Proxmire prevented hundreds of millions of dollars in earmarks from being funded.

Fighting Earmarks on the Floor

Between 1983 and 1996, seven major skirmishes flared up over academic earmarking on either the House or Senate floor, where members tried to defeat these projects. These efforts typically pitted members of the authorizations committees against members of the appropriations committees. The authorizers usually had two reasons to oppose ear-

6. Department of Energy, "Budget Highlights, FY 1989," February 1988, p. 9. "The net decrease in overall funding for BES [Basic Energy Sciences] reflects the fact that the request does not include funds for major university construction projects such as those added by Congress to this budget in recent years."

marking: first, they argued that earmarking constituted poor public policy and questionable science; second, they resented being left out of the decisions as to which members, including themselves, received earmarks. In the latter case, they objected to the appropriators hoarding the earmarks for themselves, thereby denying the authorizers the opportunity to bring projects back to their own constituents and hindering their own reelection chances. The appropriators, in turn, were tenacious in protecting their earmarks and what they considered to be their jurisdictional turf in the face of hostile authorizers, and usually they outfought or outwitted their opponents. This combination of conflicting attitudes, status positions within Congress, and complex incentives underpinning the politics of academic earmarking is evident in the following review of some of these floor debates:

1983. In 1983 the earmarking debate centered on the $10 million worth of earmarks obtained by Columbia and Catholic Universities. Yet, it is often forgotten that during that same year the House defeated $43 million in earmarked projects. During the conference over the FY 1994 Labor–HHS appropriations bill, Representative Natcher refused to support $38 million in earmarks for Boston University and the University of New Mexico that had been proposed in the Senate version of the bill. Still, Rep. Jim Wright (D-TX), then House majority leader, inserted these earmarks, and an additional $5 million for Barry University, in the FY 1984 continuing resolution. When the bill reached the floor, Rep. Robert Michael (R-IL), the House minority leader, immediately attacked the projects, declaring that they constituted "out-and-out pork and ought to be defeated." Natcher claimed that they "violated every law in the book." The House consequently voted down the earmarks by a vote of 286 to 122.[7] In this case, the opposition of a senior member of the appropriations committee helped to defeat these projects.

1985. The Senate version of the FY 1986 Defense appropriations bill included $65.5 million in earmarks. These projects were sponsored by Senators Robert Dole (R-KS) for Wichita State University, Don Nickels (R-OK) for Oklahoma State University, Alfonse D'Amato (R-NY) for Rochester Institute of Technology and Syracuse University, Edward Kennedy (D-MA) for Northeastern University, Paul Laxalt (R-NV) for the University of Nevada, and Ted Stevens (R-ALK), the chair of the subcommittee. The Syracuse earmark in particular drew the criticism of members. Sponsored by D'Amato, a graduate of Syracuse, the project

---

7. *Congressional Record*, November 8, 1983, pp. H31479–80.

was attacked by Sen. Warren B. Rudman (R-VT), who declared, "I am an alumnus of Syracuse University and I oppose it! I want that clearly understood by all the piranha in this room!" Despite the efforts of Rudman, Sen. William Proxmire (D-WI), and others, an amendment to defeat the earmarks failed by a vote of 55 to 35.[8]

Significantly, when the bill came to the floor, another project had been added to it: a $10 million earmark for Cornell University. Appropriations Chair Sen. Mark Hatfield (R-OR) sponsored the earmark for the purchase of a supercomputer for the New York university because the supercomputer would be built in his home state of Oregon. Yet, in a widely noted response, Cornell's president, Frank Rhodes, rejected the earmark on the principle that it violated the peer review process.[9]

The Department of Defense balked, in any case, at spending the money for the other earmarks. Ironically, the bill also included a provision requiring that all universities be allowed to compete for research funds, and agency officials feared that they would be violating that rule. Secretary of Defense Casper Weinberger wrote to Senate Majority Leader Bob Dole that distributing the money without open competitive review would "jeopardize" the "preeminence that our nation's universities enjoy." Because the earmarks were contained in the bill's nonbinding report rather than in the bill itself, Weinberger refused to fund the projects.[10]

1986. In response to Weinberger's refusal to fund these earmarks, the sponsoring senators, as well as sympathetic House members, came back the following year and added language to the FY 1986 supplemental appropriations bill itself, rather than to the advisory subcommittee report,

---

8. George C. Wilson, "Funneling Funds by Formula," *Washington Post*, May 15, 1986.
9. On Cornell, see Colin Norman, "Congress Approves Deals for Ten Universities," *Science*, January 17, 1986, p. 211. Also, on January 20, 1986, President Frank Rhodes wrote a letter to the Cornell faculty explaining why he rejected the earmark: "I determined that Cornell could not accept a funding award if it circumvented established merit review procedures. . . . I believe merit review is fundamental to the success of the whole federal system for supporting science because the alternative – what is commonly called 'pork barrel funding' – will ultimately unermine and weaken national support for science. If the gateway to federal support is political influence – often with the help of paid lobbyists – science, industry and the nation will soon be the poorer."
10. Wilson, op. cit. Weinberger letter cited in *Congressional Record*, June 5, 1986, p. S6890. Also see Colin Norman and Eliot Marshall, "Over a (Pork) Barrel: The Senate Rejects Peer Review," *Science*, July 11, 1986, p. 145; Janice Long, "Congress Persists in Approving Funds for Specific Universities," *Chemical and Engineering News*, January 20, 1986, pp. 14–15; Long, "Funding Bill Stirs Academic Research Issue," *Chemical and Engineering News*, June 16, 1986, p. 12.

thereby legally requiring the money to be spent. By this time, however, the earmarks totaled $80 million for ten projects.

When the bill reached the floor, Sen. John Danforth (R-MO) offered an amendment to eliminate the projects. Pleading his case, Danforth declared to this colleagues, "When research money is designated for universities on the basis of political influence, when it is designated on the basis of who has pull, when it is designated on the basis of lobbying instead of merit and instead of competition, that is wasteful spending of limited defense resources." Other senators joined in support of Danforth. Jeff Bingaman (D-NM) warned that earmarking jeopardized the nation's future, declaring that "we will be well on the road to mediocrity, at best, in our research enterprise." "University pork," Jim Sasser (D-TN) observed, "is just as much pork as public works is pork in some instances."[11]

Danforth's amendment had its opponents. Russell Long (D-LA) spoke against it, criticizing the peer review process:

> I do not know of anything here for Louisiana. . . . But if Louisiana is going to get something, I would rather depend upon my colleagues on the Appropriations Committee than on one of those peers. I know a little something about universities; I have a couple of college degrees. I know something about college professors. . . . [T]hey have their brand of politics, just as we have ours; and they have their old-boy network, just as we have our old-boy network.[12]

Ted Stevens added that earmarking constituted "fairness." Danforth's amendment nevertheless passed on a voice vote.[13]

The earmarking senators, however, refused to surrender. Just two weeks later, Dole secured Speaker Thomas P. O'Neill's (D-MA) agreement to add the projects to the conference version of the continuing resolution, as O'Neill enthusiastically supported the Northeastern project in his home state. With the force of the conference bill behind them, the appropriators secured sufficient votes to overturn Danforth's amendment, defeating it by a vote of 56 to 42. Six Republicans and four Democrats changed their votes to support the earmarks. Thus, in a legislative struggle over two fiscal year budgets, the persistence and deal-making of those members seeking earmarks prevailed over their opposition.

Meanwhile, a similar debate took place in the House when Rep. Robert Walker (R-PA) offered an amendment to the Energy and Water

---

11. *Congressional Record*, June 5, 1986, pp. S6892, S6894, S6895.
12. Ibid., p. S6897.
13. Ibid., pp. S6892–93.

appropriations report language to delete eight earmarks valued at $69.7 million. In proposing his amendment, Walker declared, "These are not only projects that have been set aside in a political kind of way; they have come out of the hide of other deserving projects all across the country. Political determinations are made about science rather than good academic scientific decisions." In response, Rep. Tom Bevill (D-AL), subcommittee chair, proclaimed, "With regard to this business of peer review that we hear about, nobody ever knows where the peers come from. We are being asked for Congress to delegate its responsibility to these peers. . . . I think it is ridiculous for us to sit up here and let the administration tell the Congress where the money has to go and how it has to be spent."[14] Walker's amendment was defeated on a largely party-line vote of 315 to 106.

1988. Sen. Sam Nunn (D-GA), chair of the Armed Services Committee, offered an amendment to the FY 1989 Defense appropriations bill that would force the deferring of funding for $46 million in earmarks until the Department of Defense evaluated the merits of each project. As Nunn proclaimed to his colleagues, "I have had numerous schools in my own state ask the Senate Armed Services Committee to designate certain set asides for their school. We have refused to do that . . . while at the same time we have increased university [peer-reviewed] funding." Nevertheless, Nunn complained, the appropriations committee failed to support this new $25 million peer-reviewed facilities program, but instead earmarked the $46 million. "If we accept the earmarking identified," Nunn continued, "the pressures on every senator to take care of his state's universities will be enormous. Is that what we want? To pit our schools against one another at the pork barrel?"[15] Despite opposition from such members as Sen. J. Bennett Johnston (D-LA), who defended his earmark for Tulane University, Nunn's amendment won on a voice vote. Later, Secretary of Defense Frank Carlucci informed Congress that the $46 million would be spent on competitive facilities and fellowship awards. In this rare instance, Nunn's status within the Senate as Armed Services Committee chair enabled him to defeat the intentions of the defense appropriations subcommittee.

Another floor fight occurred in the House. In that chamber, a bill to extend the $750,000 authorization for the Taft Institute for Two-Party Government, which conducts seminars for elementary and high school

14. *Congressional Record*, July 23, 1986, pp. H4766, H4770, H4768.
15. Carol Matlack, "A Harder Sell for Home-State Colleges," *National Journal*, November 5, 1988. For the floor debate, see *Congressional Record*, September 30, 1988, pp. S13870–83.

teachers, quickly became encrusted with nineteen earmarks worth $66 million, targeted primarily for academic institutions. Although the original bill was only three lines long, it emerged from conference with seventeen projects intended for the members of the conference committee. Funding for some of these projects included $2 million for the University of Mississippi Law School, $4 million for St. Joseph's College in Philadelphia, and $4.5 million for Voorhees College in South Carolina.

A rule that would allow consideration of the conference report was overwhelmingly defeated on a bipartisan vote of 256 to 131. The projects were widely denounced as pork barrel for the members of the committee and as a reason for the American people to distrust Congress. Furthermore, added Rep. William Goodling (R-PA), "I do not say that as a matter of fact some of [the earmarks] would not pass the grants process, but they should have to go through that process. Why should we just automatically say forget the grant process?" Only a few members spoke in favor of the projects contained in this small, politically vulnerable, and poorly packaged legislation.[16]

1992. Rep. George Brown, Jr. (D-CA), chair of the House Science, Space, and Technology Committee, challenged the FY 1993 Energy and Water appropriations conference report when it reached the floor. As the bill was being considered in its final form, the subcommittee chair, Tom Bevill, offered the motion that the House adopt the section containing $94 million in academic earmarks. Brown framed his objection to these projects as an attempt by the majority of members who did not sit on the appropriations committee to assert their own prerogative to determine how Congress spent federal money. Bevill and his allies, meanwhile, tried to portray Brown's opposition to the earmarks as an attack on members' rights in favor of agency peer review. "Support your committees," argued Bevill. "Do not get into this peer business and do not get into this business of letting the administration decide where these projects are going to go." In response, Rep. Harris Fawell (R-IL) countered, "We all know what has happened. Some privileged members sitting on a conference committee feel they can just take these types of liberties with the taxpayers' money. . . . If ever we are going to take a stand, it should be here." Fawell, a member of the House Science and Technology Committee, as well as the bipartisan congressional group called Porkbusters Coalition, whose members opposed earmarks as examples of wasteful spending, later declared that "As a result of

16. *Congressional Record*, October 13, 1988, p. H30461.

pork-barreling, mediocre research is funded, while high-quality science is not."[17]

In a surprising defeat for Bevill, the House voted down the earmarks by vote of 203 to 157. The fight over these projects did not end with this vote, however. The appropriators struck back by including these same projects in another piece of appropriations legislation, the FY 1993 Defense appropriations bill, with the cooperation of the subcommittee chair, Rep. John Murtha (D-PA). Brown was outraged. On the floor, Brown warned the appropriators that they would find their "names spread [unfavorably] not only in the national press but in every local newspaper in their districts." Brown, in turn, was goaded by Rep. Bob Traxler (D-MI), chair of the VA–HUD appropriations subcommittee. Reflecting on the fact that Congress passed relatively few authorizations bills that could provide the vehicle for earmarks, Traxler queried Brown: "Could the gentlemen tell me where the authorization bill is for science and technology? You see, it has been in the Senate for now, I think, several months. . . . I am trying to find out where your authorization bill is." Between September and October, when the House considered the two appropriations bills, the appropriators rounded up enough votes to defeat Brown. The provision in the defense bill containing the earmarks passed 250 to 171.[18]

Summary

Of the floor fights reviewed here, four were successful, at least temporarily. In 1983 three earmarks were stripped from a continuing resolution; in 1988, the funding of Defense-funded earmarks was deferred and effectively defeated; in 1988, the earmarks in the Taft Center reauthorizations bill were defeated; and in 1992, the earmarks in the Energy and Water bill were deleted, only to be added later to the Defense bill.

Only one of these floor fights – over the defense earmarks in 1988 – truly constituted a defeat for the appropriations committees, and that was brought about by the highly respected chair of the Senate Armed Services Committee, Sam Nunn. In the case of the continuing resolution, Representative Natcher, an appropriations subcommittee chair, helped to lead the fight against projects, many of which would normally have fallen under the jurisdiction of his subcommittee. So a defeat of these projects would not have been considered a challenge to the appropriators. In the case of the Taft bill, an authorizations bill, the appropriators

17. Ibid., September 17, 1992, p. H8714.
18. Ibid., October 5, 1992, pp. H11387, H11391.

were not challenged. When they were confronted, however, more often than not, the appropriators found a way to get their projects funded, even if this meant shifting the projects from one subcommittee bill to another.

These floor fights amply demonstrate the difficulty of assembling voting majorities to defeat projects approved by the appropriations committees. When successful, these floor fights required, at a minimum, the leadership of prominent members, usually chairs and the ranking members of committees with direct jurisdictional interest in these earmarks. Such was the case when Nunn, with the aid of Sen. John Warner (R-VA), the ranking member of his committee, united against the Defense earmarks. In another instance, however, when Robert Walker, ranking member of the House Science Committee, unsuccessfully led a floor fight in 1986, he lacked the support of his committee chair, Don Fuqua (D-FL), thus reducing the vote over these earmarks to a partisan one and therefore losing. Yet even the chair and the ranking member of a committee could ultimately fail, as in 1992, when appropriators succeeded despite the unified opposition of George Brown and Walker.

Fighting Earmarks with Rules and Procedures

For the average member of Congress who chairs neither a committee nor a subcommittee of jurisdiction, nor perhaps even belongs to the majority party, the task of assembling voting majorities to defeat earmarks on the floor is a daunting, if not hopeless, task. As a result, some members realize that their best way to eliminate these projects is to employ congressional rules of order that do not require majority assent. Nevertheless, although members may utilize such rules to defeat earmarks, they encounter significant opposition from defenders of earmarking when they threaten to extend the rules specifically to counter these projects. This occurred in 1989, for instance, when an opponent of earmarking successfully employed House rules to defeat some earmarks, but other members failed to expand existing Senate rules to defeat even more earmarks.

On November 15, 1989, Rep. Steve Bartlett (R-TX) called a point of order against the FY 1990 Defense appropriations bill, thereby cutting $61.2 million in earmarks from the legislation. The bill had been brought to the floor by the formidable subcommittee chair, Rep. John P. Murtha (D-PA). Murtha had a special interest in the bill, as it included $15 million for Lehigh University and $13 million for the University of Scranton, both located in Murtha's home state. Bartlett, however, objected to the relevant provisions in the report that contained the earmarks, contending they violated House Rule XVI since they were not germane to the subject matter in the bill. Immediately recognizing that Bartlett was correct, Murtha conceded the point of order.[19]

On November 9, 1989, Sen. John Danforth introduced a resolution (S. Res. 206), cosponsored by Senators Sam Nunn and Terry Sanford (D-NC), to establish a rule that could forever eliminate academic earmarking. Danforth's proposal required the Senate's presiding officer to rule in favor of a point of order that a senator could call against any noncompetitive research project, thus striking the earmark from the legislation. A three-fifths vote would be required to overturn the presiding officer's ruling. The proposal was then sent to the Senate Rules Committee for review.

Unfortunately for Danforth and his allies, the chair and the ranking member of the Rules Committee, Wendell Ford (D-KY) and Ted Stevens (R-ALK), respectively, were earmarkers of long standing, and they vehemently opposed the rule. Indeed, Stevens, ranking member and later chair of the Senate Defense Appropriations Subcommittee, sponsored one of the most infamous of all earmarks: over $40 millon was earmarked from the Office of Naval Research and NASA budgets to fund the University of Alaska's project to generate electricity from the aurora borealis. One skeptical physicist noted that to collect the energy would require an antenna stretching from Mount McKinley to Mount Fuji, and then it would power nothing more than a microwave oven. In any event, when Ford finally agreed to hold hearings on the rule in June 1990, Danforth testified that earmarking "turns the university research grants into pork barrel." He then recited the story of how the Defense Department was forced to fund a project, despite the department's determination that the university was "incompetent to do the research. But we in Congress gave them the dough anyway." Danforth went on to assert that fully 17 percent of Department of Agriculture and nearly 15 percent of DOE academic research funding had been earmarked in FY 1989.[20]

Ford countered that peer review amounted to little more than a "good old boy network." That network, Ford said, dominated the peer review panels, and as a result, twenty universities received 60 percent of all federal research funds. When other schools apply for funds, "the doors slam in [their] face. The rest of us don't have a chance." The rule should

19. Interview with Rep. Steve Bartlett, January 26, 1990; James D. Savage, "Saints and Cardinals in Appropriations Committees and the Fight Against Distributive Politics," *Legislative Studies Quarterly* 16 (August 1991): 340.

20. Susan Cohen, "Pork in the Sky," *Washington Post Magazine*, November 10, 1991; Timothy J. Burger, "Chairman Barbecues Anti-Pork Measure," *Roll Call*, June 25, 1990, p. 7.

be opposed, declared Ford, because it "limits your ability to help your own." Testifying against the rule, Michael Crow, representing Iowa State University, argued that earmarking enabled universities to "respond rapidly to the demand for action in R&D" to meet public needs. Given the lack of a federal facilities program, this was the only opportunity for schools to equip themselves appropriately. Not surprisingly, the Rules Committee refused to report the resolution to the Senate.[21]

Fighting Earmarks in Congressional Hearings

In January 1991, Rep. George Brown (D-CA) became chair of the House Space, Science, and Technology Committee. Under Brown's direction, the committee conducted the most complete set of congressional hearings ever held on the subject of academic earmarking. Brown was greatly aided in his efforts by the ranking committee member, Rep. Robert Walker (R-PA), one of earmarking's most determined foes. Brown and Walker repeatedly took to the House floor to denounce earmarks that appeared in various pieces of legislation. Meanwhile, Brown's hearings received extensive coverage in the scientific and higher education media, as well as in national news magazines such as *U.S. News & World Report*, in newspapers such as the *Washington Post*, the *Boston Globe*, and the *Minneapolis Star Tribune*, and in television on C-SPAN.[22]

Brown's interest in academic earmarking stemmed from his own efforts to obtain a project for the University of California at Riverside, which was in his district. The project, priced at approximately $5 million, consisted of constructing a facility for the Department of Agriculture's Salinity Laboratory on the campus. Despite Brown's pleas, the

21. Burger, op. cit.; Colleen Cordes, "Senate Is Not Expected to Limit Earmarking of Funds for Colleges," *Chronicle of Higher Education*, June 27, 1990, p. 1; "Testimony of Dr. Michael M. Crow, Director, Office of Science Policy and Research, Iowa State University of Science and Technology, Regarding Senate Resolution 206," June 21, 1990.

22. For news coverage, see, for example, Curt Suplee, "The Science Chairman's Unpredictable Approach," *Washington Post*, October 15, 1991; Eric Pianin, "'Academic Pork' Fills Favored School Larders," *Washington Post*, September 23, 1992; Eliot Marshall, "George Brown Cuts Into Academic Pork," *Science*, October 2, 1992, p. 22; Richard Saltus, "Mass. Leads in Landing 'Earmarked' Funds," *Boston Globe*, February 13, 1993; Greg Gordon, "'Pork Barrel' Grants for Colleges Set Off a Bitter Controversy," *Star Tribune*, October 24, 1993; Thomas Toch and Ted Slafsky, "The Scientific Pork Barrel," *U.S. News & World Report*, March 1, 1993, pp. 58–9. For additional references to Brown and Walker on the floor, see, for example, *Congressional Record*, October 2, 1991, pp. H7719–22; August 10, 1994, pp. H7320–1; August 18, 1994, pp. H8624–5; and September 12, 1994, H905–3.

powerful chair of the House Appropriations Committee and its agriculture appropriations subcommittee, Jamie Whitten (D-MS), refused to fund the project. Whitten's refusal was hardly based on the principle of defending the peer review process. His problem was simply that the subcommittee bill was already packed with projects for members of the appropriations committee, and there was virtually no other money to spend at the time for other requests. As a senior member of the House Agriculture Authorizations Committee, Brown was incensed by Whitten's response. By the time he came to chair his own committee, Brown was determined to fight earmarking, initially because he believed the honor, prerogatives, and relevance of the authorizing committees in the legislative process were at stake and increasingly because he considered that the rapid growth of earmarking harmed the quality of academic science.[23]

As Brown had observed, during the preceding years, members who did not serve on the Appropriations Committee were usually ineffective in their opposition to earmarking. Floor fights were difficult to win, and could easily be interpreted as an attack not just on earmarking, but on the appropriators themselves, the chairs of the appropriations subcommittees, and even the majority party and majority leaders. Efforts to expand the rules to defeat earmarks had failed, if for no other reason than that they were ignored by the appropriators.

Brown's strategy for opposing earmarking consisted of "shining a light" on the adverse consequences of earmarking in highly publicized hearings held in 1993 and 1994. The science committee's immediately preceding chairs, Don Fuqua and Robert Roe, also held hearings, but they primarily addressed the issue of establishing new federal facilities programs, were limited to a single day, and received little publicity. Brown's hearings were different.

What set Brown's hearings apart was that for the first time a significant number of earmarking institutions were called before Congress to justify the scientific contributions of their projects. Earmarking's opponents had long claimed that earmarking required virtually no accountability on the part of the institutions that received federal money in this manner. As some members complained, universities could spend their earmarked money on virtually anything they wanted, regardless of what was stipulated in the various appropriations subcommittee reports. Sometimes a subcommittee would go through the motions of asking an agency to comment on the merits of a proposed project prior to awarding the funds. Yet, as in the case of the House Agriculture Appropria-

23. Interviews with Rep. George Brown, December 11, 1991, and January 23, 1995.

tions Subcommittee, staff could not recount a single instance when agency recommendations against a particular project resulted in its not being funded.[24] Occasionally, some projects were evaluated after they had been funded, but again, these post hoc reviews had little if any effect on the continued funding of a project. In contrast, Brown and his staff called upon fifty universities to report on the status of their earmarked projects, and in some cases requested that the presidents of these institutions testify before the committee.

On June 16, 1993, in a meeting of his full committee, Brown declared, "Today, we begin the first of a series of hearings on academic earmarking – or for the less squeamish – the 'science pork-barrel.'" "Pork-barreling is of course an age-old political practice," Brown continued.

> For example, President Lyndon Johnson used a mixture of threats and pork in order to secure the votes he needed to pass the 1964 Civil Rights Bill. . . . It is my opinion that academic earmarking has proliferated to the extent that the pork has turned rotten. . . . The political problem with earmarks is that they are typically inserted in an appropriations bill or report with minimal discussion or public record, thereby bypassing not only merit-review, but also the hearings and authorization process. . . . Earmarks are of course, allocated not on the basis of need (as many would suggest), but in fact in direct proportion to the influence of a few senior and influential members of Congress.

Brown claimed that the level of earmarking had "spiraled out of control" and that it had "reached the point where it is distorting scientific and agency priorities and causing serious inefficiencies in the use of scarce research dollars."[25]

After Brown's introduction, the various speakers presented their testimony. The first to speak was Robert Rosenzweig, the former president of AAU. Rosenzweig, who had led higher education's fight against earmarking in the 1980s, had by this time become quite skeptical about the ability of either Congress or academia to restrain their earmarking appetites. Nor was he sanguine about the use of authorizations committees to conduct their own review of potential earmarks. Such a process would only "enlarge the number of members who have leverage on behalf of their constituencies. . . . It pains me to say it, but the genie, I fear, is out of the bottle, and it is notoriously hard to put it back."[26]

---

24. "U.S. Department of Agriculture Research and Extension Priorities, Hearing Before the Subcommittee on Department Operations and Nutrition, Committee on Agriculture, Statement of James D. Savage to the Committee, March 25, 1993," p. 70.
25. *Academic Earmarks – Parts I and II*, Committee on Science, Space, and Technology, U.S. House of Representatives, June 16 and September 15, 1993, pp. 4 and 6.
26. Ibid., p. 24.

Also testifying was Chancellor Joe Wyatt of Vanderbilt University, who had become higher education's primary spokesperson against earmarking. Earmarking, he warned, "effectively thwarts any effort to establish national priorities as part of a national policy on research and technology. . . . The country deserves to hear a debate on the Nation's interest in research, not after-the-fact defenses for earmarks or rationalizations of particular universities' lobbying fees. . . . Is this . . . what we want to say to our graduate students, that it doesn't matter how good their ideas or diligent their work, that it only matters whether their university is paying the right lobbyist $50,000 every month?"[27]

Also present were defenders of earmarking: Charles McCallum, president of the University of Alabama at Birmingham: David Gute, interim director of Tufts University's Center for Environmental Management; and William Polf, deputy vice president of Columbia University. All three justified the earmarks their institutions received on the basis of their scientific quality, their contribution to the nation's research effort, and their function as a necessary remedy for their institutions' infrastructure needs, given the absence of federal facilities programs.

During the question-and-answer session, however, Brown and his committee members caused these speakers more than a little discomfort. After the three described the high quality of their earmarked projects and universities, Brown noted that "now, all of you have presented convincing evidence that your institutions are institutions of the highest merit, highest quality, outstanding, amongst the top in the United States, and yet one of the arguments in support of earmarking is that this is the way you redress the disadvantage that the poor and deprived and the unsuccessful have against the rich and successful like you all represent." Only Gute responded directly to Brown, claiming that Tufts really was not a rich institution.[28]

Ranking committee member Walker asked the three if they would be satisfied with a system that resulted in "100 percent of the money for federal research being done through an earmark process." Each of the three quickly replied no. Then Walker pushed his point further: if 100 percent of funding should not be earmarked, then why not 10 percent or 20 percent? In a feeble response, McCallum answered, "I just am not knowledgeable enough about all the intricacies of Congress. . . . I think that has to be left with those whom we elect as our representatives."[29]

---

27. Ibid., pp. 60–79.
28. Ibid., pp. 148–9.
29. Ibid., p. 153.

Later, Rep. Xavier Becerra (D-CA) questioned President McCallum about how much consultation the University of Alabama had with DOE, the agency that was forced to fund the earmarked project designated for the university. Did the school ever alert the agency to the purpose or scope of the project? "Not that I know of," replied McCallum. The university had determined on its own that the project was beneficial and had worked through its lobbyists to obtain the earmark.[30]

In another set of hearings, President John Silber of Boston University testified before the committee. During the preceding decade, more than any other university leader, Silber had skillfully and combatively defended earmarking. In his testimony, Silber lashed out at earmarking's opponents, claiming that the "big players among universities . . . virtually own that system. . . . [T]heir distinguished faculty . . . become judges in their own cases." "The 'haves,'" he continued, "constitute an informal cartel," and earmarking threatens "to break the cartel by placing other institutions in a position to compete on an equal or nearly equal footing."[31]

In a heated exchange with Rep. Martin Hoke (R-OH), Silber was questioned about the national need for Boston University's Center for Photonics Research, a $29 million earmark. After Silber claimed that this earmark was necessary for the nation's research effort, Hoke pointed out that both the Commerce and Defense (DOD) Departments funded such research, and then he asked why Boston University had not obtained funding from these agencies through the normal review process. Silber responded that the university did submit an application that deserved agency approval. Hoke then charged that "DOD initially refused to fund this proposal . . . citing that it was superficial and not unique. The faculty were 'rather unknown in the field of Photonics' and that DOD already supported 'many excellent photonic centers.'" As a result of Boston University's failure to submit a winning proposal, Hoke argued, it bypassed DOD's review and obtained funding through earmarking. Hoke questioned Silber further on his testimony, in which Silber claimed that the idea for the photonics center emerged from DOD's Critical Technologies List. After pointing out that no such idea could be found on the DOD statement, Silber was forced to concede that "well, it didn't grow out of that list," leaving Hoke to observe, "It is clear that you have decided that there is an agenda of Boston University's which is a higher agenda and a greater priority than the agenda of the United

---

30. Ibid., p. 158.
31. *Academic Earmarks – Part III*, Committee on Science, Space, and Technology, U.S. House of Representatives, September 21 and 22 and October 6, 1994, p. 243.

States Congress, and that if that means going around and getting to a funding source that somehow is able to circumvent the regular legislative process that you are going to do that."[32]

Finally, throughout these hearings, representatives of the executive agencies charged with overseeing the nation's research agencies testified that earmarking damaged the agencies' ability to set priorities and to manage their budgets. Each of the agency officials reported that while the appropriations subcommittees designated earmarks, they had not provided additional funds to support those projects. Thus, reductions were forced in other programs and projects to fund the earmarks. At DOE, for example, the agency was forced to support numerous earmarked projects that were "outside the mission of the Department." "The benefits derived by the Department from academic earmarks are limited because they generally are not produced by research activities directly related to Departmental missions," Martha Krebs, director of the Office of Energy Research, testified. Between 1990 and 1993, the appropriations committee ordered DOE to finance more than $171.8 million in earmarks for biomedical facilities for just ten universities that had nothing to do with DOE's core mission.[33] According to Jonathan Cannon, assistant administrator for administration at the Environmental Protection Agency, "earmarks are not subject to competitive peer review, thus putting in jeopardy our goal of high quality science and engineering. They also undercut the Agency's goal of seeking to increase the competition for its resources." All representatives reported that their agencies opposed earmarking.[34]

The Science Committee's inquiry into academic earmarking extended beyond the hearings. Brown requested fifty universities that had received earmarks in FY 1992 to respond in writing on whether their projects underwent any type of agency review and authorization. As the committee later noted in its "Interim Report," "the responses reveal an amazing amount of confusion about what peer review is and what it means to have an 'authorized' program, a point that we would have hoped most university presidents would remember from their high school civics classes."

The universities justified their projects on the grounds that they underwent some form of peer review, but they failed to mention that these reviews were only a form of competition limited to the institutions al-

---

32. Ibid., pp. 295–6. On other photonics earmarks, see Ernest Sternberg, *Photonic Technology and Industrial Policy* (Albany: State University of New York Press, 1992), Ch. 5.
33. Ibid., pp. 25–31.
34. Ibid., p. 37.

ready designated to receive the earmarks. After examining these projects the report found, "there is little or no competition in awarding the money." The universities proved to be evasive in evaluating the scientific results of their earmarks and determining whether these projects enabled them to compete more effectively for peer-reviewed grants. They also claimed that they deserved their earmarks given the absence of federal facilities programs. Yet, as the report concluded, despite this absence, in 1991 institutions of higher education undertook $5.2 billion in new facilities construction. Furthermore, although the federal government's direct funding of facilities programs was lacking, the committee pointed out that indirect cost recovery in 1988 provided universities with potentially $1 billion in facilities money. Brown's committee, nevertheless, supported increased funding for NSF's facilities program.[35]

In 1994, the House Science, Space, and Technology Committee passed a bill reauthorizing NSF. This legislation included a provision declaring that any institution engaging in earmarking would be barred from receiving facilities funding from the agency for five years. During the consideration of the bill, Rep. Sherwood Boehlert (R-NY) offered an amendment that would have banned an earmarking institution from receiving *any* funding from NSF, not just from its relatively poorly funded facilities program. Brown, however, thought the amendment "too draconian," and it was defeated 11 to 10 in the committee. The version that did pass expressed the committee's hostility toward earmarking, but the bill later failed to pass in the Senate. The following year, when the Republicans took control of Congress and Robert Walker became chair, the committee did include the sanction of a funding ban in its version of the NSF authorization. This bill, however, also failed to become law.[36]

Presidents and Earmarking

The Reagan, Bush, and Clinton administrations have all opposed academic earmarking, largely on the grounds that earmarking is wasteful spending, produces dubious research, and undermines the executive branch's ability to set priorities. These concerns are usually expressed by

35. "Academic Earmarks: An Interim Report by the Chairman of the Committee on Science, Space, and Technology, Chairman George E. Brown, Jr., August 9, 1993," pp. 15, 18–19.
36. See the "Additional View" in the Science, Space, and Technology Committee Report for H.R. 3254, the National Science Foundation Authorization Act of 1994, Report 103-475. Comment on Brown's position on the sanctioning provision comes from committee staff. For the provisions in the Walker version, see the Report for H.R. 1852, the National Science Foundation Authorization Act of 1995, Report 104-231, p. 7. Also interview with Rep. Robert Walker, March 11, 1992.

agency officials or by the director of the White House Office of Science and Technology Policy (OSTP) and sometimes by the president himself. All three presidents, for example, have denounced earmarking in their State of the Union Addresses. Not surprisingly, in this context, academic earmarks have been highlighted to justify an augmentation of executive power by way of the line-item veto. Bill Clinton actually employed the veto, while George Bush exercised the sanctions afforded to him through the budgetary process to try to defeat, unsuccessfully, academic earmarks contained in congressional appropriations bills.

The Reagan Administration

Some proponents of earmarking have blamed the beginning of the practice on the Reagan administration. In 1983, Reagan's OSTP director, George Keyworth, included funding for a materials center at Lawrence Berkeley Laboratory in Reagan's FY 1984 budget proposal, despite the lack of a peer-reviewed evaluation for the project. A DOE facility, the lab is managed by the University of California. Some university presidents seized upon the materials center as justification for their own earmarks. When defending his earmarking, for instance, Catholic University President Rev. William J. Byron claimed that the materials lab motivated him to obtain his own project, stating that "At the starting line of this race, there had been no peer review at all."[37] The practice of academic earmarking, however, as in the case of the Tufts projects, preceded the materials center controversy. Moreover, the planning for the famous Columbia and Catholic earmarks occurred in advance of congressional consideration of the materials center. The first-stage funding for Byron's vitreous center project eventually came from the DOE lab's budget.

In any case, the Reagan administration attacked earmarking, principally in public pronouncements. Such agency officials as Erich Bloch, director of NSF, and Secretary of Defense Casper Weinberger denounced the practice. Most prominently, President Reagan criticized earmarks in his State of the Union Addresses. Following an appeal for the line-item veto, Reagan's 1988 address included the observation that "Over the past few weeks, we have all learned what was tucked away behind a lit-

---

37. Kim McDonald, "Insulate Science from Politics, Presidents Urge," *Chronicle of Higher Education*, November 2, 1983, p. 12. For more on the Catholic earmark, see "Testimony of Rev. William J. Bryon, S.J., President, The Catholic University of America, Presented to the Energy and Water Development Subcommittee of the House Appropriations Committee, on Behalf of Catholic University's Vitreous State Laboratory, April 5, 1984."

tle comma here and there. For example, there's millions for such items as cranberry research, blueberry research, the study of crawfish, and the commercialization of wild flowers." After the speech, James Miller, the director of OMB, issued a directive ordering the various executive agencies to ignore the nonbinding reports that listed Congress's desired earmarks.[38]

Defenders of blueberry and cranberry research also responded to Reagan's speech. "Frankly, I don't see what's so funny about cranberry research," stated Rep. Don Bonker (D-WA), whose district included a number of cranberry farmers. The research on this topic was to be conducted at the Blueberry-Cranberry Research Center at Rutgers University, and both of New Jersey's senators, Bill Bradley (D-NJ) and Frank Lautenberg (D-NJ), wrote Reagan in defense of the earmarks. Within a few months, due to the objections of the New Jersey delegation and others affected by the ruling, OMB's Miller withdrew his directive against the earmarks.[39]

The Bush Administration

President Bush's opposition to earmarking was greatly encouraged by his OSTP director, D. Allan Bromley, the coauthor of the 1986 Packard–Bromley report that had supported increased federal funding of academic research facilities. Bromley ordered his staff to conduct a survey of all types of congressional earmarks for research and development projects, academic and otherwise. This survey was the first of its kind carried out by the White House. The totals of $809.6 million for FY 1991, $992.8 million in FY 1992, and $1.712 billion for FY 1993 were widely distributed to the press and to congressional opponents of earmarks, who used the figures in committees and in floor debates over earmarking. Bromley also worked with OMB Director Richard Darman to include language in the federal budget reiterating the administration's opposition to earmarking, for "not only does this practice result in a less optimal allocation of R&D resources, but, there is no evidence that it improves the breadth, depth or quality of the Nation's R&D infrastructure."[40]

---

38. Text: Put on Your Work Shoes, We're Still on the Job: The State of the Union," *Los Angeles Times*, January 26, 1988.
39. Juices Flow Over Cranberry Remarks," *Milwaukee Journal*, January 27, 1988; "Budget Chief Withdraws Special-Projects Directive," *Wall Street Journal*, July 11, 1988; Colleen Cordes, "Berry Research Center at Rutgers, Ridiculed by Reagan, Will Get Federal Funds After All," *Chronicle of Higher Education*, July 20, 1988, p. 1.
40. Interview with D. Allan Bromley, January 16, 1992. "Congressional R&D Earmarks in FY 1992 Appropriations," Executive Office of the President, Office of Science and

In March 1992, OMB submitted to Congress a set of rescissions that cut existing spending by $5.7 billion, among which were a number of academic earmarks, including some thirty agriculture projects. Among these earmarks were $3.1 million for a poultry center at the University of Arkansas; $1.5 million for water pollution research conducted by Iowa State, Kansas, and Nebraska Universities; and $39,000 for celery research at Michigan State University. While a line-item veto, which Bush did not possess, cuts proposed spending, a rescission enables a president to eliminate existing expenditures if Congress approves the rescission within 45 days of its submission. By terminating these various projects, Bush challenged Congress during an election year to end what he charged was pork barrel spending.

The Democrats who ran Congress responded by repackaging the rescission list and even engaged the president in a bidding war by increasing the total cut by several hundred million dollars. More important, with regard to the academic earmarks OMB identified, the new list subtracted the agriculture projects and added thirty-four academic research grants worth $2 million that had been peer reviewed by NSF and NIH. These projects were selected not for their cost but rather to ridicule the types of activities that peer review panels funded. An NSF project, for example, studied the behavior of middle-class lawyers in small firms, and an NIH grant examined why people were afraid to go to the dentist. Sen. Robert Byrd (D-WVA), the mastermind behind the switch, emphasized this point by declaring, "There's waste at both ends. . . . There's enough blame to go around, but it's not just the fault of Congress." Outflanked by Byrd and the Democrats, with their own larger rescissions list and the argument that they could cut at least as much waste as the president, Bush eventually signed the rescission bill. As a result, peer-reviewed as well as congressionally earmarked projects were subject to termination.[41]

Technology Policy, January 23, 1992. The updated figures for FY 1993 were released in a letter from Bromley to Congress on January 14, 1993. In March 1993, Senator James Jeffords (R-VT) used the OSTP report as the basis for offering S.Con.Res.18, a sense of the Senate bill that called for the funding of merit-reviewed projects before noncompetitive projects; the bill did not come to a vote. *The Budget for Fiscal Year 1991* (Washington, D.C.: Office of Management and Budget, 1990), p. 90. For more on Bromely, see D. Allan Bromley, *The President's Scientists* (New Haven: Yale University Press, 1994), pp. 87–9.

41. For a list of the first set of Bush's rescissions, see "Rescissions and Reasons," *Washington Post*, March 23, 1992; Colleen Cordes, "Bush Seeks to Block Spending on Earmarked Projects," *Chronicle of Higher Education*, April 1, 1992, p. A27. Jack Anderson and Michael Binstein, "The President's Pork List," *Washington Post*, April 5, 1992; Eric Pianin, "Sen. Byrd's 'Pork Barrel' Revenge?" *Washington Post*, May 22, 1992; Letter from Sen. Barbara A. Mikulski to Dr. Burton Richter, President, Ameri-

In one more challenge to Congress, the Bush administration in 1989 proposed that the Department of Agriculture's (DOA) competitive research programs be expanded from $50 million to $100 million. Initiated by the agriculture research community and spearheaded in the administration by DOA Assistant Secretary Charles Hess, a University of California at Davis professor, the administration proposal directly confronted Rep. Jamie Whitten (D-MS), the chair of the House Appropriations Committee. Whitten, of course, was a champion and an expert practitioner of academic earmarking, and any serious expansion of competitive funding would come at the expense of Whitten's micro management of the DOA budget by earmarking. The National Research Initiative, as DOA called the competitive grants expansion, was eventually funded at $73 million for FY 1990. Whitten struck back, however, by cutting the indirect cost rate universities could receive on competitive grants from the already low figure of 25 percent in FY 1989 to just 14 percent in FY 1990. The Bush administration might get its competitive grants program, but the universities would pay a heavy price for their efforts to constrain earmarking.[42]

The Clinton Administration

The Clinton administration has also opposed academic earmarking. The initial report of Vice President Al Gore's National Performance Review, for example, called for the "minimization" of such projects and cited a $100,000 earmark for the University of Hawaii to study how beagles detect brown tree snakes as an instance of questionable spending. Meanwhile, John H. Gibbons, the director of OSTP, repeatedly testified before Congress in favor of merit review and against earmarking. When President Clinton asked Congress for the line-item veto in his 1995 State of the Union Address, he justified the need for the veto by pointing to

can Physical Society, May 26, 1992; George Hager, "Democrats Keep Tight Rein on Rescissions Process," *Congressional Quarterly Weekly Report*, May 9, 1992, pp. 1238–9; Hager, "Rescissions Top Bush's Target, Change What Will Get Cut," *Congressional Quarterly Weekly Report*, May 23, 1992, pp. 1433–5; Walter Pincus, "Parliamentary Fight Awaits Bush Cuts," *Washington Post*, March 22, 1992. Also see the House debate over the rescissions and a list of affected projects in *Congressional Record*, May 7, 1992, pp. H3039–56.

42. Interview with Charles Hess, March 23, 1993; Christine M. Matthews, *National Research Initiative of the U.S. Department of Agriculture* (Washington, D.C.: Congressional Research Service, April 25, 1991), Report 91-435 SPR; Board on Agriculture, National Research Council, *Investing in Research: A Proposal to Strengthen the Agricultural, Food, and Environmental System* (Washington, D.C.: National Academy Press, 1989).

two "pet spending projects": "There was $1 million to study stress in plants, and $12 million for a tick removal program that didn't work. It's hard to remove ticks . . . but . . . if you'll give me the line-item veto, I'll remove some of that unnecessary spending."[43] Both of these pet projects were, of course, academic earmarks.

Clinton appeared to be moving in the opposite direction, however, when he advocated the continued funding of an earmark while on the campaign stump in Iowa in 1995. Noting that the Republican-controlled Congress threatened to terminate an earmark on pork research for Iowa State University, Clinton defended the project declaring, "We need more agricultural research, not less."[44]

Nevertheless, in the first use of the line-item veto in 1997, President Clinton vetoed no fewer than five academic earmarks contained in FY 1998 appropriations legislation. Clinton's various veto messages described the justification for denying funding for these earmarks:

> In the Commerce, Justice appropriations, Clinton vetoed $5 million intended for Montana State University's research on constructing environmental "green" buildings because, "by diverting scarce resources to a nonfederal facility, this project damages [the National Institute of Standards and Technology's (NIST)] ability to choose projects for their national benefit and technical merit."[45]

> An earmark valued at $10 million for the University of Arizona's Steward Observatory telescope project was vetoed in the VA–HUD appropriations because it "duplicates . . . an on-going project. . . . Given that NASA is already investing in a superior capability in the Keck II facility, NASA should not fund the Arizona project."[46]

> Four projects in Agriculture appropriations were vetoed. An earmark for the University of Alaska valued at $250,000 for dairy cattle feed research was vetoed because the Department of Agriculture "currently funds a large amount . . . of research on the nutritional requirements of dairy cows that addresses farmers nationwide, whereas this grant focuses on the specific

43. Al Gore, *Creating a Government That Works Better and Costs Less* (New York: Plume Books, 1993), p. 17; "Remarks by the President in State of the Union Address," Office of the Press Secretary, The White House, January 24, 1995; interview with John H. Gibbons, July 15, 1993.

44. John F. Harris, "Clinton Urges More Money for Pork Research in Iowa," *Washington Post*, April 26, 1995.

45. Cancellation of Dollar Amount of Discretionary Budget Authority, Report Pursuant to the Line Item Veto Act, P.L. 104-130," Cancellation No. 97-82, December 2, 1997.

46. Cancellation of Dollar Amount of Discretionary Budget Authority, Report Pursuant to the Line Item Veto Act, P.L. 104-130," Cancellation No. 97-71, November 1, 1997.

... issues facing the dairy industry in Alaska." A $140,000 tomato research project at Ohio State University was vetoed because it was not requested in the president's budget, since the budget "emphasizes high priority programs in the national interest and competitively-awarded research ... to support only the highest quality research." Another project for Ohio State, $50,000 for genome plant research, was vetoed because the university "could conduct this research using its federal Hatch Act formula funds, or the principal investigator could compete for the $40 million available in FY 1998 through the National Science Foundation for plant genome research." A $600,000 earmark for the poisonous plants laboratory at Utah State University was vetoed because "these funds would provide for planning of this facility and would require additional future appropriations for construction ($4.8 million)."[47]

Thus, these earmarks were vetoed, according to the White House, because they denied executive branch agencies their right to determine national funding and research priorities; they diverted scarce funds from competitively funded research programs; they were planning funds that essentially constituted "the camel's nose in the tent," which would require future, larger-scale construction spending; they were not subject to the merit standards of competitively awarded grants; they duplicated existing projects at a reduced level of quality; and, in some cases, alternative funding sources were available to those universities engaged in earmarking. Although the Supreme Court declared the line-item veto unconstitutional, and although the number of academic earmarks vetoed was few, President Clinton's use of the veto has been the most forceful assertion of the executive branch's desire to restrain academic earmarking.[48]

Finally, it is worth noting that the issue of academic earmarking did play a role in two of the Clinton administration's major legislative initiatives. In both cases, charges were made that members received academic earmarks as the price of their votes to support the North American Free Trade Agreement (NAFTA) of 1993 and the crime bill of 1994. Among the projects offered to supporters of NAFTA, Rep. Gerald Solomon (R-NY) claimed in a meeting of the Rules Committee, were "research centers and university grants," including $10 million for a Center for Western Hemispheric Trade that would benefit a school in

47. "Cancellation of Dollar Amount of Discretionary Budget Authority, Report Pursuant to the Line Item Veto Act," P.L. 104-130, Cancellation No. 97-79, Cancellation 97–80, Cancellation 97-81, and Cancellation 97-78. November 20, 1997.

48. Heather Bourbeau and Adrienne Roberts, "Line-Item Veto Put to the Test," *Financial Times*, January 9, 1998.

Rep. Jake Pickle's (D-TX) district. The project was included in the final version of the agreement.[49]

In the case of the crime bill, one academic earmark received a great deal of negative television and newspaper coverage, which characterized the project as typical of congressional vote-buying schemes. The Republicans attempted to undermine public support for the crime bill by claiming that it was little more than pork, and they employed as their primary evidence a $10 million criminal justice center at Lamar University in Texas. The project was championed by Rep. Jack Brooks (D-TX), who, at the time of its insertion into the crime bill conference report, hooted, "If it's pork, it'll be tasty!" This remark made the Republicans' case easy, and before the Democrats could pass the bill they were forced to drop the project, as well as a $1 million earmark for Sam Houston University sponsored by Rep. Charles Wilson (D-TX).[50]

The Fight against Academic Earmarking

Congressional opposition to earmarking has prevented hundreds of millions of dollars in projects from being funded and, more important, has ensured that most major merit-reviewed programs in the federal government, particularly in NSF and NIH, have remained insulated from earmarking. Members have defeated earmarks through the sagacious employment of rules during the appropriations process and by defeating politically vulnerable bills during floor debates. Moreover, by the mid-1990s, due primarily to the difficulty of stopping earmarking within Congress, those members who opposed earmarking increasingly went outside Congress, turning to the media to take their case to the public. Although the effect of the press on congressional deliberations and the actual level of earmarking is debatable, the press overwhelmingly portrayed earmarking as wasted expenditures.[51]

---

49. Solomon made his charge against Pickle on November 11, 1993. The data on the center were provided by Solomon's office by fax, November 24, 1993.
50. Dale Balz, "Clinton Isn't Sweating This One Alone," *Washington Post*, August 17, 1994; Sue Anne Pressley, "A Symbol of 'Academic Pork,' Lamar U. Feels Aggrieved," *Washington Post*, August 20, 1994; Brooks quoted in Katherine Q. Seelye, "The Man Who Tried for Bacon," *New York Times*, August 20, 1994.
51. Interview with George Brown, January 23, 1995. "There has been considerable public attention focused on the activities of the [House Science] committee," stated Brown. "If we speak of how this resulted in any real drop in earmarking, I doubt it." Furthermore, this media coverage had no effect on Brown's reelection efforts: "I received no electoral benefit from it. I don't think it had any effect electorally. It was on the periphery of the campaign. My opponent did not make an issue of it."

Two decades of experience, however, has demonstrated that with a few exceptions, the fragmented and uncoordinated opposition offered by individual members of Congress and a handful of authorizations committees has been insufficient to beat the resourceful and tenacious appropriations committees. When an isolated bill was stripped of its earmarks, the appropriators simply moved the projects to another bill that had more support. When rules were proposed that would enable members to declare points of order against earmarks, they were bottled up in committee. When the Reagan administration refused to distribute funds to an earmark contained in a nonbinding appropriations subcommittee report, the appropriators simply included the project in the bill itself. When the Bush administration attempted to eliminate existing earmarks through rescissions, the appropriators merely switched projects, forcing Bush to accept the cutting of peer-reviewed grants, all in the name of deficit reduction.

Finally, despite the conflict between members that took place over academic earmarking, rarely were sanctions imposed on members who opposed these projects. Members were threatened, but actual penalties were not assessed. Both Steve Bartlett, who called the point of order against John Murtha's earmarks, and George Brown, who led the fight against earmarking in the House in the early 1990s, reported that although retribution was mentioned to them on a number of occasions, as Brown said, "Good common sense remains that if you threaten a colleague, it will backfire on you."[52] Not only was Brown not punished for his fight against earmarking, in 1990 he obtained a $5.3 million earmark for a salinity laboratory at the University of California at Riverside from the very appropriations committees he so often opposed.

---

52. Ibid. Brown reported that even when Rep. John Murtha cut funding for academic research in the FY 1995 defense appropriations bill, "I don't consider that was an effort to punish me. It did not impact on my district."

8

The Future of
Academic Earmarking

In 1985, Richard C. Atkinson, then chancellor of the University of California at San Diego, published an article that firmly defended the peer review process. Atkinson argued that a strong peer review system strengthened the ability of the academic science community to preserve its independence in the face of its powerful federal sponsor. By uniting around peer review, the community would provide "an effective demonstration that science is not just another special interest lobby," while "preserving scientific autonomy not only for science but for society. And it would give to the scientific community a good deal of the political and moral authority required to negotiate issues of genuine national importance."[1] In an interview conducted several years later, Atkinson continued to defend peer and merit review, and he was even more forceful in his denunciation of academic earmarking:

> I just think [earmarking] is the wrong way to make scientific decisions. . . .
> Obviously the Congress can pork barrel in lots of ways, but I think when it
> gets down to the business of granting funds for research projects and the
> like, that it's a disastrous path. I mean I just think it's pathetic to go in that
> direction. I think that when you look at the decisions that the Congress has
> made . . . the pork barrel decisions are atrocious: I'd say they are a ninety
> percent waste of funds.[2]

Could Atkinson conceive of a situation in which the University of California would, on the basis of principle, engage in earmarking? "Well,"

---

1. Richard C. Atkinson and William A. Blanpied, "Peer Review and the Public Interest," *Issues in Science and Technology*, Summer 1985, pp. 111–12. Also see Richard C. Atkinson, "Science Gets Political: Congress' Pork-Barrel Grants Threaten Our Progress," *Los Angeles Times*, March 29, 1987.
2. Interview with Richard C. Atkinson, March 12, 1992.

Atkinson replied, "if I really thought the game were over and that . . . one could no longer depend on intellectual values."[3]

What makes Atkinson's advocacy of merit review so significant is that not only was he the chancellor of an elite research university, an institution that regularly is ranked in the top ten recipients of federal research funds, he was also the former director of NSF. This is the federal research agency that, especially under the leadership of Erich Bloch, had been the most vocal critic of academic earmarking. Given Atkinson's position within the nation's science community, these comments were both natural and expected.

What was neither natural nor expected, and an example of how difficult it is to predict the future of academic earmarking, is that within a year of the interview, Atkinson approved his campus's pursuit of an earmark. In the FY 1993 Transportation appropriations bill, the University of California at San Diego received $1.6 million to fund its advanced composites technology transfer bridge project. Atkinson defended his earmark as something special: "Unlike 'earmarked research projects,' this consortium initiative seeks to develop a mechanism for facilitating university–industry technology research in a timely, collaborative manner." As part of his explanation, Atkinson claimed that the project had been "reviewed" by congressional staff and "evaluated and endorsed by executive agencies and the White House."[4] What Atkinson could not claim is that the project underwent merit review – that it had been subjected to open competition with project proposals submitted by other universities. Like any other earmark, the project was funded by a direct appropriation. By 1996 Atkinson had become president of the entire University of California system, and in that year he allowed five of the system's nine campuses to obtain earmarks for FY 1997 valued at some $2.653 million.

Perpetuating the Academic Pork Barrel

The Institutional Incentives to Earmark

The Atkinson decision exemplifies the argument presented in this book: that academic earmarking stems from choices made by institutional leaders who are influenced by a variety of incentives, norms, and sanctions. The dynamics of these institutional settings, with their personal, professional, and constituent ambitions, may lead these decision makers to solicit or fund earmarks. University presidents respond to their per-

---

3. Ibid.
4. Letter from Richard C. Atkinson to James D. Savage, September 27, 1993, p. 2.

sonal and institutional ambitions by seeking earmarks to improve their universities' research capabilities. Members of Congress act on their ambitions to gain reelection and exercise power within Congress by assisting their local universities. These presidents and members also usually contend that earmarking constitutes good science and public policy.

What becomes apparent in the case of academic earmarking, however, is that universities and Congress offer competing inducements. Neither institution is completely uniform in its support of earmarking, and its opponents are visible and vocal within higher education and Congress. If either of these institutional settings freely accepted the practice of earmarking, the number and dollar value of such projects clearly would be much greater.

Understanding these institutional contexts, with their competing incentives and norms, sets the stage for viewing academic earmarking as a collective action problem, where the classic issue is how to limit or prevent defection from the group. In the case of academic earmarking, the collective action problem is how the group, primarily consisting of research universities or those with research ambitions, can induce or constrain other universities from earmarking, which is regarded as a threat to the dominant policy of peer review. Within academia, virtually every president must decide whether to break ranks with those schools and higher education associations that oppose earmarking and free-ride. Free riding also means that these institutions double-dip by competing for merit-reviewed money even as they solicit earmarks. The cost of earmarking is often borne by merit-reviewed research budgets.

To limit or prevent defection from the group, opponents of earmarking can use several procedures. Presidents may attempt to dissuade their colleagues by personal appeals and suasion, by offering alternative facilities funding as a form of side payments, and by imposing sanctions such as denying earmarking schools membership in prestigious associations.

In Congress, members may attempt to dissuade their colleagues from earmarking through personal appeals, defeating earmarks in committee or on the chamber floor, excluding earmarks from the chair's markup of a bill, employing rules and points of order against earmarks, enacting new facilities programs, and holding hearings to highlight publicly the adverse consequences of earmarking for science.

These incentives and sanctions, however, have at best mixed success. Within higher education, persuasion is highly idiosyncratic in its effect, is difficult to measure, and has failed to prevent many significant defections. Despite long-term lobbying efforts, the higher education community repeatedly failed to gain support from either Congress or the executive branch for meaningful new facilities programs. Thus, efforts to offer schools side payments to encourage them not to earmark proved to be ineffective. Finally, the leading opponents of earmarking consciously refrained from imposing sanctions, such as terminating memberships in associations. As Chancellor Atkinson candidly observed, "Scientific pork barreling cannot be halted unless the scientific community disciplines those who engage in it."[5] Yet, the sole penalty that exists within this community is the annual listing of earmarking universities published by *Chronicle of Higher Education*. Even this monitoring activity is resented because the higher education associations themselves have been embarrassed by their failure to prevent their members from earmarking.

Within Congress, those members who oppose earmarking are faced with something of a reverse collective action problem. Normally, such a problem refers to a group controlling defectors. Yet, members opposing earmarking are usually in the minority; they are essentially defectors who are attempting to influence the behavior of the group. Consequently, they often are forced to employ insurgent strategies to realize their goal. Committee markup procedures, floor fights, the use of and attempts to create rules and points of order, as well as public hearings, have all been mobilized against earmarking. Nevertheless, because these members are often the minority in a majoritarian-biased institution, their ability to restrict earmarking has been noteworthy, but sporadic and limited to the exploits of a handful of committee and subcommittee chairs and senior members. In addition to these individual efforts, the dollar value of earmarks approved by Congress most likely dropped during the mid-1990s because of the overall reduction of discretionary funds in the federal budget.

The Institutional Failure of Earmarking

Despite the inability to control individual earmarks, the peer review system remains the dominant policy in allocating federal dollars for academic research. This is so for two reasons. First, support for peer and merit review remains strong within academia. In spite of the absence of any meaningful penalties for earmarking, many universities have refrained from the practice, and others that could obtain more projects have limited their requests.

The second reason that earmarking remains a "small revolution" is that it has yet to challenge peer review with an institutionalized process of its own. Earmarking occurs when a unique coalescing of interests, often brought about by entrepreneurial contract lobbyists, mobilizes to obtain a project. Earmarking is an individual, somewhat spontaneous act that ultimately depends upon the patronage of a powerful member

---

5. Atkinson and Blanpied, op. cit., p. 111.

of Congress, especially an appropriations subcommittee chair. Indeed, even if a university is supported by such a member, when that member retires or is defeated, the school must find a new patron. Once Rep. Bob Traxler (D-MI) retired, for example, the level of earmarks for Michigan schools dropped significantly. Obviously, this produces special uncertainty about federal funding. In contrast to peer review, little is routinized and regular about earmarking other than that a few schools and states benefit disproportionately from the practice.

At the same time, only a few defenders of earmarking and critics of peer review recognize that the current distribution of federal funding for academic science is due not only to the peer review system, but also to the government's reliance upon project grants rather than upon institutional formula funding. Charles McCutchen, an otherwise successful scientist, claimed that peer review "is at best a treacherous servant" when he failed to publish an article in a desired journal. After complaining that peer review is rife with politics, McCutchen recommended that peer-reviewed project grants be replaced with institutional block grants. "Universities would go to the federal government for support. Let them bring citation scores, rumors of Nobel Prizes almost awarded, whatever they want. Out of this free-for-all, a formula would emerge, no doubt with loopholes and exceptions. . . . The schools would decide who to support however they wished, using any system they wished, from despotism to democracy. . . . Still, researchers would continue to compete within the school, so to dull the teeth of university politics, perhaps 10 percent of federal support should remain at grants to individuals."[6] Absent from McCutchen's promotion of block grants was any consideration of the biases of the political system – that certainly some universities would be greatly favored with block grants simply as a result of influential representation in Congress, aided by the ever-present contract lobbyist. More important, McCutchen made no mention of the national interest in this advocacy of a crazy-quilt, special-interest-driven pattern of institutional funding.

The federal government's support for academic science is not designed to promote the careers of scientists, so that they can publish in certain journals or add more lines to their vitae. Nor is it to further the ambitions of university presidents who seek to lead more prestigious institu-

---

6. Charles W. McCutchen, "Peer Review: Treacherous Servant, Disastrous Master," *Technology Review*, October 1991, p. 40. For an earlier discussion about the proper mix between peer-reviewed and formula funds, see Don Price, "Federal Money and University Research," in Harold Orlans (ed.), *Science Policy and the University* (Washington, D.C.: Brookings Institution, 1968), Ch. 1, especially pp. 45–6. The amount of institutional funds considered acceptable was 25 percent, though "How institutional funds should be allocated . . . was far less clear."

tions and please boards of trustees. Rather, the purpose of federal support for university science is to enhance the nation's science and technology capabilities; to achieve certain goals, such as those associated with national defense, space exploration, and public health; and to promote the nation's ability to compete in the world economy. If project grants and peer review achieve these goals most effectively, that must be the overarching consideration of Congress in determining which procedures to employ when allocating its scarce resources.

Even members who are responsible for overseeing the traditionally formula-driven field of agricultural research express concern that earmarking encroaches on grants and peer review and undermines scientific quality. Rep. Charles Stenholm (D-TX), a subcommittee chair of the House Committee on Agriculture, held hearings in 1993 on the future of DOA research. He noted that real funding for formula programs had dropped in the past decade, while earmarks had grown from 10 to 30 percent of cooperative research funding between 1985 and 1993. Whereas earmarks in the Cooperative States Research Service budget totaled $30 million in 1985, by 1993 they were over $130 million. Stenholm, furthermore, criticized the quality of formula-funded research, noting, "You have to draw the conclusion that the formula funds are not adequate, because the formula, or the peer review process that are there are not adequate. I personally come down very strongly on the side of saying that whatever we do, there ought to be a good amount of peer review. It can't be just one appropriator and one university with one good idea making these decisions."[7] Thus, said Stenholm, the fact that an institution receives its entitlement-like share of funding does not guarantee high-quality results or obviate the need for peer-reviewed research.

Academic earmarking, in any case, will continue into the foreseeable future. The institutional incentive structures and ambitions that produced these earmarks in the first place remain intact. The constrained spending that characterized the federal budget during the last two decades of high deficit spending is likely to be relaxed somewhat as deficits become surpluses, which means that more funds will be available to be earmarked. For FY 1998, the House Appropriations Committee received a spending allocation 4.3 percent higher than in FY 1997 and the highest spending total since FY 1992, when the dollar value of academic earmarks was at its peak.[8]

7. "U.S. Department of Agriculture Research and Extension Priorities," Subcommittee on Department Operations and Nutrition, Committee on Agriculture, U.S. House of Representatives, March 25, 1993; interview with Rep. Charles W. Stenholm, March 24, 1993.

8. The 602a spending allocation for the House Appropriations Committee for FY 1998 was $511.5 billion in budget authority; for a comparison with previous years, see footnote 26 in Chapter 7.

Moreover, the higher education community seems to be bereft of leadership that is active and willing to challenge earmarking presidents. AAU appears docile and tolerant of hundreds of millions of dollars in annual earmarking, much of it accrued in behalf of member institutions. The association has no plan, for example, for attempting to educate new appropriations subcommittee chairs and members of Congress in the reasons why earmarking wastes taxpayer dollars and undermines the nation's science. There is no plan for mobilizing scientists to write to their representatives in Congress to encourage them to oppose earmarking. When individual members of Congress undertake the difficult task of challenging their colleagues' earmarks, nothing is done by the higher education associations that oppose earmarking to aid these members in their reelection efforts or to make their constituents – or even other academicians – aware of the service they render in the fight against earmarking. These members receive no special ceremonial presentations or honorary degrees, unlike their counterparts who earmark. When President Clinton vetoed academic earmarks in the use of the line-item veto in 1997, the academic science community was deathly silent in its praise. In short, little or nothing is being accomplished within the academic science community to counter the incentives to earmark or to promote incentives to oppose earmarking.

The call to reject earmarking as a way to obtain federal research funds came from higher education; Congress has never passed a resolution against earmarking or adopted a moratorium. The academic and scientific communities' stand against earmarking was created by university presidents and their associations, and they have the responsibility, as leaders, of either abiding by and enforcing their own resolutions or declaring publicly that earmarking is an acceptable supplement to the peer and merit review processes. Unfortunately, the higher education community now appears insincere on this matter, as the leaders of many of its most prominent institutions say one thing and do another.

The peer and merit review system therefore will continue to be compromised by earmarking, but as a whole, the system remains the dominant process for allocating federal research funds. Even serious critics of peer review, such as John Silber, look to earmarking not to replace peer review, but rather as a means to be more competitive in obtaining peer-reviewed funding. Meanwhile, the distribution of earmarked projects will continue to reflect the hierarchy of power in Congress. The benefits of earmarking will go predominantly to a handful of states and universities, and the results will be mixed, at best, as to whether even these recipients improve their research competitiveness or the quality of American science.

Select Bibliography

Aaron, Henry J., Thomas E. Mann, and Timothy Taylor, eds. *Values and Public Policy*. Brookings Institution, 1994.

Academic Earmarks, Parts I and II. Committee on Science, Space, and Technology, U.S. House of Representatives, June 16 and September 15, 1993.

Academic Earmarks, Part III. Committee on Science, Space, and Technology, U.S. House of Representatives, September 21 and 22 and October 6, 1994.

Academic Research Facilities: Financing Strategies. National Academy Press, 1986.

Agres, Ted, "Conference Sees Cloudy Future for Federal Funding of R&D." *R&D Magazine*, July 1996, p. 10.

Alston, Chuck. "Sen. Byrd Launches Crusade against Influence Peddling." *Congressional Quarterly Weekly Report*, August 5, 1989, p. 2010.

Alston, Julian M., and Philip G. Pardey. *Making Science Pay: The Economics of Agricultural R&D Policy*. American Enterprise Institute, 1996.

Anagnoson, J. Theodore. "Politics in the Distribution of Federal Grants: The Case of the Economic Development Administration." In *Political Benefits*. Ed. Barry S. Rundquist. Lexington Books, 1980, pp. 61–92.

Anderson, Christopher. "In Space, No One Can Hear You Oink." *Nature*, October 10, 1991, p. 406.

Anderson, Jack, and Michael Binstein. "The President's Pork List." *Washington Post*, April 5, 1992.

Andres, Gary J. "Pork Barrel Spending – On the Wane?" *PS: Political Science & Politics*, January 1995, pp. 207–11.

Appendices to Brick and Mortar: A Summary and Analysis of Proposals to Meet Research Facilities Needs on College Campuses. Committee on Science, Space, and Technology, U.S. House of Representatives, 1987.

Arnold, Christian, K. "The Government and University Science: Purchase or Investment?" In *Science Policy and the University*. Ed. Harold Orlans. Brookings Institution, 1968, pp. 89–100.

Arnold, R. Douglas. *Congress and the Bureaucracy: A Theory of Influence*. Yale University Press, 1979.

"The Local Roots of Domestic Policy." In *The New Congress*. Eds. Thomas E. Mann and Norman J. Ornstein. American Enterprise Institute, 1981, pp. 250–87.

The Logic of Congressional Action. Yale University Press, 1990.

Atkinson, Richard. "Science Gets Political: Congress' Pork-Barrel Grants Threaten Our Progress." *Los Angeles Times,* March 29, 1987.

Atkinson, Richard, and William A. Blanpied. "Peer Review and the Public Interest." *Issues in Science and Technology* (Summer 1985): 101–14.

Axelrod, Robert. "The Emergence of Cooperation among Egoists." *American Political Science Review* 65 (1981): 306–18.

The Evolution of Cooperation. Basic Books, 1984.

"An Evolutionary Approach to Norms." *American Political Science Review* 80 (1986): 1095–1111.

Bailey, F. G. "The Ordered World of the University Administrator." In *Elites: Ethnographic Issues.* Ed. George E. Marcus. University of New Mexico Press, 1983, pp. 93–112.

Bailey, Stephen K. *Education Interest Groups in the Nation's Capital.* American Council on Education, 1975.

Balz, Dale. "Clinton Isn't Sweating This One Alone." *Washington Post,* August 17, 1994.

Baron, David P. "Majoritarian Incentives, Pork Barrel Programs, and Procedural Control." *American Journal of Political Science* 35 (1991): 57–90.

Barr, Stephen. "OMB Releases Budget 'Hit List.'" *Washington Post,* March 14, 1997.

Barton, Paul. "State 39th in Academic 'Pork' as U.S. Feeds Higher Education." *Arkansas Democrat,* May 13, 1990.

Beardsley, Tim. "Sausage Factor: How Congress Passes the Pork to Back-Home U." *Scientific American,* November 1993, p. 11.

Bell, Robert. *Impure Science: Fraud, Compromise and Political Influence in Scientific Research.* John Wiley & Sons, 1992.

Bendor, Jonathan, and Dilip Mookherjee. "Institutional Structure and the Logic of Ongoing Collective Action." *American Political Science Review* 81 (1987): 131–54.

Berke, Richard L. "Hatfield Failed to Tell Senate about Art Gifts Worth $9,265." *New York Times,* March 9, 1991.

Berry, Jeffrey M. *Lobbying for the People: The Political Behavior of Interest Groups.* Princeton University Press, 1977.

Bianco, William T., and Robert H. Bates. "Cooperation by Design: Leadership, Structure, and Collective Dilemmas." *American Political Science Review* 84 (1990): 133–47.

Bingaman, Jeff, John C. Danforth, and William Proxmire. "Research Funds Shouldn't Have a Pork-Barrel Fate." *Los Angeles Times,* June 2, 1986.

Birnbaum, Jeffrey H. "Overhaul of Lobbying Laws Unlikely to Succeed Thanks to Opposition of Lobbyists Themselves." *Wall Street Journal,* May 30, 1991.

The Lobbyists. Times Books, 1992.

Blum, Deborah. "UCD Scientists in Pork-Barrel Feast, Critics Declare." *Sacramento Bee,* September 3, 1990.

Blustein, Paul. "U.S. Budget Increasingly Free of Pork-Barrel Spending." *Washington Post,* March 21, 1988.

Board on Agriculture, National Research Council. *Investing in Research: A Proposal to Strengthen the Agricultural, Food, and Environment System*. National Academy Press, 1989.

Boesman, William C., and Christine Matthews Rose. *Equity, Excellence, and the Distribution of Federal Research and Development Funds*. U.S. Congressional Research Service, Report No. 88–422, April 25, 1988.

Boren, Susan H. *Appropriations Enacted for Specific Colleges and Universities by the 96th through the 100th Congress*. U.S. Congressional Research Service, Report 89–82 EPW, February 6, 1989.

Bourbeau, Heather, and Adrienne Roberts. "Line-Item Veto Put to the Test." *Financial Times*, January 9, 1998.

Brick and Mortar: A Summary and Analysis of Proposals to Meet Research Facilities Needs on College Campuses. Committee on Science, Space, and Technology, U.S. House of Representatives, 1987.

Bromley, D. Allan. *The President's Scientists*. Yale University Press, 1994.

Brown, David. "Grant-Awarding System Gets Decent Score in GAO Report." *Washington Post*, July 28, 1994.

Brown, Kenneth T. "Indirect Cost Rate Composition and Myths." *Science*, April 1981, pp. 411–18.

Browning, Graeme. "Colleges at the Trough." *National Journal*, March 7, 1992, pp. 565–9.

"Budget Chief Withdraws Special-Projects Directive." *Wall Street Journal*, July 11, 1988.

Burd, Stephen. "Challenge to Peer Review." *Chronicle of Higher Education*, April 6, 1994.

Burger, Timothy J. "Chairman Barbecues Anti-Pork Measure." *Roll Call*, June 25, 1990, p. 7.

Bush, Vannevar. *Science: The Endless Frontier*. U.S. Government Printing Office, 1945.

Butterfield, Fox, "Tufts President Helps His University Stand Tall Amid Giants of Academe." *New York Times*, April 1, 1992.

"New Prisons Cast Shadow over Higher Education." *New York Times*, April 12, 1995.

Butterworth, Robert L. "A Research Note on the Size of Winning Coalitions." *American Political Science Review* 65 (1971): 741–5.

Byron, William J., S.J. "Why Universities Employ Lobbyists." *Washington Post*, August 3, 1989.

Cain, Bruce, John Ferejohn, and Morris Fiorina. *The Personal Vote: Constituency Service and Electoral Independence*. Harvard University Press, 1987.

Carlton, Ralph, Timothy Russell, and Richard Winters, "Distributive Benefits, Congressional Support, and Agency Growth: The Case of the National Endowments for the Arts and Humanities." In *Political Benefits*. Ed. Barry S. Rundquist. Lexington Books, 1980, pp. 93–116.

Cassidy, Gerald, S.J. "Letter: On Lobbying, a New Disclosure Law Is Desireable." *New York Times*, August 25, 1989.

Chong, Dennis. *Collective Action and the Civil Rights Movement.* University of Chicago Press, 1991.

Chubin, Daryl E., and Edward J. Hackett. *Peerless Science: Peer Review and the U.S. Science Policy.* State University Press of New York, Albany, 1990.

Clifford, Frank. "Research Funds: Not So Scientific." *Los Angeles Times,* November 27, 1987.

Cloud, David S. "Georgetown Wins Friends and Funds on Hill." *Congressional Quarterly Weekly Report,* June 4, 1988, pp. 1502–5.

"For 'Mr. Rural Development,' Small Ideas Go a Long Way." *Congressional Quarterly Weekly Report,* September 30, 1989, pp. 2548–9.

Cohen, Linda R., and Roger G. Noll. *The Technology Pork Barrel.* Brookings Institution, 1991.

Cohen, Michael D., James G. March, and Johan P. Olsen. "A Garbarge Can Model of Organizational Choice." *Administrative Science Quarterly* 17 (1972): 1–25.

Cohen, Richard. "Appropriators Losing Clout." *National Journal,* January 20, 1996, p. 130.

Cohen, Susan. "Pork in the Sky." *Washington Post Magazine,* November 10, 1991, p. 14.

"Contributions from Lawyers, Lobbyists." *Washington Post,* December 15, 1997.

Cookson, Matthew B. "Congressional Earmarking to Institutions of Higher Education: A Necessary Evil or a Blatant Abuse of Power." Masters thesis, University of Connecticut, 1993.

Cordes, Colleen. "Colleges Seek Federal Aid to Repair Crumbling Buildings." *Chronicle of Higher Education,* September 11, 1985.

"Bypass Peer Review in Grants to 9 Colleges, Senate Panel Tells Defense Department." *Chronicle of Higher Education,* May 21, 1986.

"3 Government Agencies Scrutinize the System of Awarding Research Money by Peer Review." *Chronicle of Higher Education,* January 28, 1987.

"A Lengthy Debate Likely on Ways to Split Funds for Campus Facilities." *Chronicle of Higher Education,* July 15, 1987.

"Biggest Pork Barrel Ever: $225-Million for Projects that Bypassed Merit Reviews." *Chronicle of Higher Education,* January 27, 1988.

"Berry Research Center at Rutgers, Ridiculed by Reagan, Will Get Federal Funds after All." *Chronicle of Higher Education,* July 20, 1988.

"Colleges Received about $289-Million in Earmarked Funds." *Chronicle of Higher Education,* February 1, 1989.

"Congressional Practice of Earmarking Research Grants Does Not Broaden Allocation of Funds, Study Finds." *Chronicle of Higher Education,* March 1, 1989.

"Senate Committee Opens Debate on Earmarking Funds; U. of Cal., a Foe of 'Pork-Barrel' Projects, Seeks One." *Chronicle of Higher Education,* June 28, 1989.

"Critics of 'Earmarked' Funds for Specific Universities Now Seek to Weaken Law They Backed." *Chronicle of Higher Education,* September 13, 1989.

"Success at Winning Earmarked Funds May Leave Colleges with Little to Show for It." *Chronicle of Higher Education*, November 1, 1989.

"Congress Earmarks $270-Million for Specific Projects at Universities." *Chronicle of Higher Education*, May 9, 1990.

"Senate Is Not Expected to Limit Earmarking of Funds for Colleges." *Chronicle of Higher Education*, June 27, 1990.

"Congress Earmarked $493-Million for Specific Universities; Critics Deride Much of the Total as 'Pork Barrel' Spending." *Chronicle of Higher Education*, February 27, 1991.

"Washington Lobbyists Continue to Sign Up University Clients, Capitalizing on Academe's Demand for Political Expertise." *Chronicle of Higher Education*, October 9, 1991.

"Bush Seeks to Block Spending on Earmarked Projects." *Chronicle of Higher Education*, April 1, 1992.

"W. Virginia Leads the Way in Obtaining Congressional Earmarks for Research." *Chronicle of Higher Education*, June 24, 1992.

"Campuses Offer a Variety of Reasons Why the Earmarks They Received from Congress Were Justified." *Chronicle of Higher Education*, August 11, 1993.

"House Panel Grills College Officials about Congressional Earmarks." *Chronicle of Higher Education*, September 22, 1993.

"The Power of Pique." *Chronicle of Higher Education*, June 29, 1994.

"Academe's Pork Barrel." *Chronicle of Higher Education*, August 3, 1994.

"Opponent of Earmarks Threatens to Join His Foes at the Pork Barrel." *Chronicle of Higher Education*, September 28, 1994.

"King of the Earmarks." *Chronicle of Higher Education*, November 2, 1994.

"Congressional Earmarks for Higher Education in 1995." *Chronicle of Higher Education*, September 8, 1995.

"Report Predicts Cuts in Science Spending Under Clinton Budget Plan." *Chronicle of Higher Education*, April 26, 1996.

"Congress Slashes Earmarks for Academe by 50%, the Biggest Decrease Ever." *Chronicle of Higher Education*, September 13, 1996.

"Congressional Earmarks for Colleges Increase by 49% for Fiscal 1997." *Chronicle of Higher Education*, March 28, 1997.

Cordes, Colleen, and Jack Goodman. "Congress Earmarked a Record $684-Million for Non-Competitive Projects on Campuses." *Chronicle of Higher Education*, April 15, 1992.

Cordes, Colleen, and Katherine McCarron. "Academe Gets $763 Million in Year from Congressional Pork Barrel." *Chronicle of Higher Education*, June 16, 1993.

Cordes, Colleen, and Dylan Rivera. "Trimming Academic Pork." *Chronicle of Higher Education*, September 8, 1995.

Crawford, Mark. "'Earmarking' at DOE, DOD Rolls On." *Science*, January 22, 1988, pp. 344–5.

"USDA Grants Programs Threatened." *Science*, July 1, 1988, p. 21.

"NSF's Bloch Attacks Iowa State's Pork." *Science*, November 18, 1988, p. 1007.

Davis, Bob. "Federal Budget Pinch May Cut Amount of 'Pork' to Colleges Living Off of the Fat of the Land." *Wall Street Journal*, May 2, 1990.

Defense Research and Development: Mandated Reports on Noncompetitive Awards to Colleges and Universities. U.S. General Accounting Office, Report GAO/NSIAD-95-72, December 1994.

Denzau, Arthur T., and Michael C. Munger. "Legislators and Interest Groups: How Unorganized Interests Get Represented." *American Political Science Review* 80 (1986): 89–105.

DePalma, Anthony, "Short of Money, Columbia U. Weighs How Best to Change." *New York Times*, May 25, 1992.

"Department of Defense Report on Section 220 of Public Law 100-456." Office of the Under Secretary of Defense, March 1989.

Dery, David. *Problem Definition in Policy Analysis*. University Press of Kansas, 1984.

Dewar, Helen. "Retiring Senators Look Beyond the Beltway." *Washington Post*, December 29, 1996.

Dewar, Helen, and Eric Pianin. "Senate Is Power Source for 'Coal Miner's Son.'" *Washington Post*, June 24, 1992.

Dingell, John. "Rectifying How Tax Dollars Are Spent." *New York Times*, February 17, 1992.

Dupree, A. Hunter. *Science in the Federal Government*. Johns Hopkins University Press, 1986.

Ellwood, John W. "Budget Control in a Redistributive Environment." In *Making Economic Policy in Congress*. Ed. Allen Schick. American Enterprise Institute, 1983, pp. 69–99.

"Comments." In *Federal Budget Policy in the 1980s*. Eds. Gregory B. Mills and John L Palmer. Urban Institute Institute Press, 1984, pp. 368–78.

Ellwood, John W., and Eric M. Patashnik. "In Praise of Pork." *The Public Interest* (Winter 1993): 19–33.

Elster, Jon. *The Cement of Society*. Cambridge University Press, 1989.

Ember, Lois R. "Efforts to Stem Pork-Barrel Science Funding Likely to Be Unsuccessful." *Chemical & Engineering News*, July 18, 1988, pp. 7–16.

Epstein, Helen. "Crusader on the Charles." *New York Times Magazine*, April 23, 1989.

Evans, Diana. "Policy and Pork: The Use of Pork Barrel Projects to Build Policy Coalitions in the House of Representatives." *American Journal of Political Science* 38 (1994): 894–917.

"Who's Calling the Shots? Vote-Buying and the Control of Pork." American Political Science Association Convention, 1995.

"Appropriations Committee Earmarks and Vote-Buying in the U.S. Senate." American Political Science Association Convention, 1996.

Expertise and Democratic Decisionmaking: A Reader. Task Force on Science Policy, Committee of Science and Technology, U.S. House of Representatives, December 1986.

Federally Funded Research: Decisions for a Decade. U.S. Office of Technology Assessment, 1991.

Fenno, Richard F., Jr. *The Power of the Purse: Appropriations Politics in Congress.* Little, Brown, 1966.

Congressmen in Committees. Little, Brown, 1973.

Ferejohn, John A. *Pork Barrel Politics: Rivers and Harbors Legislation, 1947–1968.* Stanford University Press, 1974.

"Congress and Redistribution." In *Making Economic Policy in Congress.* Ed. Allen Schick. American Enterprise Institute, 1983, pp. 131–57.

Ferne, Georges. *Science and Technology in Scandinavia.* Longman, 1989.

Ferrin, Scott Ellis, "Logrolling for Alma Mater: An Investigation of the In-House Lobbyist in American Colleges and Universities." Doctoral dissertation, Harvard University, 1996.

Final Report: NSF Advisory Committee on Peer Review. National Science Foundation, 1986.

Finn, Robert. "Discouraged Job-Seekers Cite Crisis in Science Career Advice." *The Scientist,* May 29, 1995, p. 1.

Fiorina, Morris P. *Congress: Keystone of the Washington Establishment.* Yale University Press, 1977.

"Some Problems in Studying the Effects of Resource Allocation in Congressional Elections." *American Journal of Political Science* 25 (1981): 543–67.

Flint, Anthony. "Cornell Citing Lean Years Ahead, Opens $1.25b Fund-Raiser." *Boston Globe,* October 21, 1990.

Freedman, Allan, "Members' Pet Projects Survive Despite Tight Fiscal Limits." *Congressional Quarterly Weekly Report,* July 8, 1995, pp. 1990–2.

Frohlich, Norman, Joe A. Oppenheimer, and Oran R. Young. *Political Leadership and Collective Goods.* Princeton University Press, 1971.

Fussell, Paul. "Schools for Snobbery: Universities and the Class System." *The New Republic,* October 4, 1992.

Gailson, Peter, and Bruce Hevly, eds. *Big Science: The Growth of Large-Scale Research.* Stanford University Press, 1992.

Gais, Thomas L., Mark A. Peterson, and Jack L. Walker. "Interest Groups, Iron Triangles and Representative Institutions in American National Government." *British Journal of Political Science* 14 (1984): 161–85.

Geographic Patterns: R&D in the United States, National Science Foundation, Report 89–317, 1989.

Gleick, Elizabeth. "Playing the Numbers Game." *Time,* April 17, 1995, p. 52.

Goldman, T. R. "Cassidy's Big Adventure." *Legal Times,* October 2, 1995, p. 1.

Goldstein, Judith, and Robert O. Koehane, eds. *Ideas & Foreign Policy: Beliefs, Institutions, and Political Change.* Cornell University Press, 1993.

Goodwin, Irwin. "Universities Reach into Pork Barrel with Little Help from Friends in Congress." *Physics Today,* April 1989, pp. 43–5.

Gordon, Greg. "'Pork Barrel' Grants for Colleges Set off a Bitter Controversy." *Minneapolis Star Tribune,* October 24, 1993.

Gordon, Larry. "Berkeley Battles the Blues." *Los Angeles Times,* June 13, 1993.

Gore, Al. *Creating a Government That Works Better and Costs Less.* Plume Books, 1993.

Goss, Carol F. "Military Committee Membership and Defense-Related Benefits in the House of Representatives." *Western Political Quarterly* 225 (1972): 215–33.

Graham, Hugh Davis, and Nancy Diamond. *The Rise of American Research Universities*. Johns Hopkins University Press, 1997.

Grassmuch, Karen. "Colleges Scrabble for Money to Reduce Huge Maintenance Backlog, Estimated to Exceed $70-Billion; New Federal Help Seen Unlikely." *Chronicle of Higher Education*, October 10, 1990.

Graves, Florence. "Hog Heaven." *Common Cause Magazine*, July–August 1986, pp. 17–23.

Gray, William H., III. "Pork or Providence? A Defense of Earmarked Funds for Colleges." *Washington Post*, February 27, 1994.

Greenberg, Daniel S. *The Politics of Pure Science*. New American Library, 1967.
"How Two Lobbyists Work the Washington Scene." *Science & Government Report*, November 15, 1983.
"Working on Capitol Hill for Science and Profit." *Science & Government Report*, December 1, 1985.
"Mark It for Science." *Washington Post*, October 10, 1994.

Gugliotta, Guy. "Rooting around for the Pork in 'Plant Stress' Research." *Washington Post*, February 14, 1995.
"Earmarking Can Cap the Pork Barrel." *Washington Post*, September 5, 1995.

Guston, David H., and Kenneth Keniston, eds. *The Fragile Contract: University Science and the Federal Government*. MIT Press, 1994.

Haas, Lawrence, J. "Blame the Appropriators." *National Journal*, August 8, 1987, pp. 2025–9.
"Unauthorized Action." *National Journal*, January 2, 1988, pp. 17–21.
"Murtha, the Insider." *National Journal*, August 11, 1990, pp. 1947–51.
"Byrd's Big Stick." *National Journal*, February 9, 1991, pp. 316–20.
"Tiny Sequester Hits." *Congressional Quarterly Weekly Report*, April 27, 1991, p. 1042.
"Democrats Keep Tight Rein on Recissions Process." *Congressional Quarterly Weekly Report*, May 23, 1992, pp. 1433–5.

Hager, George. "Today's Appropriators Preside over a Shrinking Empire." *Congressional Quarterly Weekly Report*, May 20, 1995, pp. 1365–82.

Hall, Peter A., ed. *The Political Power of Economic Ideas*. Princeton University Press, 1989.

Hall, Richard L., and Frank W. Wayman. "Buying Time: Moneyed Interests and the Mobilization of Bias in Congressional Committees." *American Political Science Review* 84 (1990): 797–820.

Hamm, Keith E. "Patterns of Influence among Committees, Agencies, and Interest Groups." *Legislative Studies Quarterly* 8 (1983): 379–426.

Hancock, LynNell, and John McCormick, "What to Chop?" *Newsweek*, April 29, 1996.

Hanley, Robert. "Rutgers' Prestige Grows with Corporate Aid and Emphasis on Research." *New York Times*, December 18, 1992.

Hardin, Russell. *One for All: The Logic of Group Conflict*. Princeton University Press, 1995.

Harris, John F. "Clinton Urges More Money for Pork Research in Iowa." *Washington Post*, April 26, 1995.

Havemann, Judith. "'Academic Pork' Proliferates as Traditional Form Lags." *Washington Post*, March 22, 1988.

Hayes, Michael T. "The Semi-Sovereign Pressure Groups: A Critique of Current Theory and an Alternative Typology." *Journal of Politics* 40 (1978): 134–61.

Healy, Patrick, Kit Lively, Joye Mercer, Julie Nicklin, and Peter Schmidt. "Private Colleges Fight for Financial Health; Public Institutions Find State Support Unreliable." *Chronicle of Higher Education*, June 14, 1996.

Herrick, Rebekah, Michael K. Moore, and John R. Hibbing. "Unfastening the Electoral Connection: The Behavior of U.S. Representatives When Reelection Is No Longer a Factor." *Journal of Politics* 56 (1994): 214–27.

Honon, William H. "State Universities Reshaped in the Era of Budget Cutting." *New York Times*, February 22, 1995.

"Indefensible Spending: How America's 'Tight' Pentagon Budget Is Stuffed with Congressional Pork." Council for a Livable World Education Fund and National Taxpayers Union Foundation, June 14, 1994.

"Indirect Cost Rates at Research Universities: What Accounts for the Differences." Council of Governmental Relations, November 1987.

Infrastructure: The Capital Requirements for Academic Research. National Science Foundation, May 1987.

Jackson, Brooks. "Fund-Raiser Goes to Washington as Lobbyist, Democrats' Party Treasurer." *Wall Street Journal*, February 14, 1989.

Jaschik, Scott. "Defense Budget Approved by House Would Halve President's Request for University Research." *Chronicle of Higher Education*, July 6, 1994.

———. "Cut in Military-Research Budget for 1995 Upsets Universities, But They Are Thankful It Wasn't Larger." *Chronicle of Higher Education*, October 5, 1994.

Johannes, John R., and John C. McAdams. "The Congressional Incumbency Effect: Is It Casework, Policy Compatibility, Or Something Else? An Examination of the 1978 Election." *American Journal of Political Science* 25 (1981): 512–42.

Jones, Gordon S. "The Real Reasons to Punish Sen. Hatfield." *Washington Times*, March 7, 1995.

Jordan, Mary, "House to Expand Research-Cost Probe." *Washington Post*, January 30, 1992.

———. "For Little College, a Big Helping Hand." *Washington Post*, June 24, 1992.

"Juices Flow over Cranberry Remarks." *Milwaukee Journal*, January 27, 1988.

Kantrowitz, Barbara. "Wanted: Miracle Workers." *Newsweek*, April 8, 1991.

Kelly, Brian. *Adventures in Porkland*. Villard Books, 1992.

Kerr, Clark. "The New Race to Be Harvard or Berkeley or Stanford." *Change Magazine*, May–June 1991.

Kerr, Clark, and Marian L. Gade. *The Many Lives of Academic Presidents*. Association of Governing Boards of Universities and Colleges, 1989.

King, David C., and Jack L. Walker. "The Provision of Benefits by Interest Groups in the United States." *Journal of Politics* 54 (1992): 394–426.

King, Lauriston R. *The Washington Lobbyists for Higher Education*. Lexington Books, 1975.

Kingdon, John. *Agendas, Alternatives, and Public Policies*. HarperCollins, 1995.

Knezo, Genevieve J. *Indirect Costs at Academic Institutions: Background and Controversy*. Congressional Research Service, Report IB91095, November 20, 1991.

Academic Research Facilities: Funding Options. Congressional Research Service, Report IB92002, December 20, 1991.

Krehbiel, Keith. *Information and Legislative Organization*. University of Michigan Press, 1991.

Kuhn, Thomas S. *The Structure of Scientific Revolutions*. University of Chicago Press, 1970.

Kuntz, Phil. "House Agrees to Double Funding for National Science Foundation." *Congressional Quarterly Weekly Report*, October 1, 1988, p. 2726.

"Colleges and Universities Give Little But Advice." *Congressional Quarterly Weekly Report*, April 15, 1989, pp. 820–5.

"Just One More Project, Please . . ." *Congressional Quarterly Weekly Report*, July 22, 1989, p. 1866.

"Mikulski's 'Change.'" *Congressional Quarterly Weekly Report*, September 23, 1989, p. 2467.

Lancaster, John. "Legislators Use Earmarks to Bring Home Bacon." *Washington Post*, December 6, 1991.

"Clearing up a $10 Million Mystery." *Washington Post*, December 16, 1991.

Lederman, Douglas. "Political Action Committees Help Lawmakers Who Help Universities." *Chronicle of Higher Education*, April 18, 1997.

Lederman, Leonard, L. "Science and Technology Policies and Priorities: A Comparative Analysis." *Science*, September 4, 1987, pp. 1125–33.

"Science: The End of the Frontier?" American Association for the Advancement of Science, January 1991.

Linkins, Peter, and Albert H. Teich. "Indirect Costs and the Government–University Partnership." In *The Fragile Contract: University Science and the Federal Government*. Eds. David H. Guston and Kenneth Keniston. MIT Press, 1994, Ch. 4. "Lobbyists, Unmasked." *New York Times*, August 15, 1989.

Long, Janice. "Congress Persists in Approving Funds for Specific Universities." *Chemical and Engineering News*, January 20, 1986, pp. 14–15.

"Funding Bill Stirs Academic Research Issue." *Chemical and Engineering News*, June 16, 1986, p. 12.

MacRae, Duncan, Jr. and James A. Wilde. *Policy Analysis for Public Decisions*. University Press of America, 1985.

Mansbridge, Jane J., ed. *Beyond Self-Interest*. University of Chicago Press, 1990.

March, James G., and Johan P. Olsen. "The New Institutionalism: Organizational Factors in Political Life." *American Political Science Review* 78 (1984): 734–49.

Marcus, Ruth. "Lobbyists: Where the Money Went." *Washington Post*, May 7, 1996.

Marshall, Eliot. "George Brown Cuts into Academic Pork." *Science*, October 2, 1992, p. 22.

"Pork: Washington's Growth Industry." *Science*, November 1, 1992, pp. 640–3.

Martin, Joanne. *Cultures in Organizations*. Oxford University Press, 1992.

Martino, Joseph P. "Political Science: Pork Invades the Lab." *Reason*, March 1989, pp. 32–5.

Science Funding: Politics and Porkbarrel. Transaction Publishers, 1992.

Masters, Brooke A. "Cuts in College Budgets Send Students Scrambling." *Washington Post*, January 29, 1992.

Mathews, Jessica. "Pork-Barrel Research." *Washington Post*, November 2, 1992.

Matlack, Carol. "Cut to the Pork." *National Journal*, February 13, 1988.

"A Harder Sell for Home-State Colleges." *National Journal*, November 5, 1988, p. 2804.

Matthews, Christine M. *National Research Initiative of the U.S. Department of Agriculture*. U.S. Congressional Research Service, Report 91–435 SPR, April 25, 1991.

Mayer, Jean. "Earmarking: A Question of Fairness." *Forum for Applied Research and Public Policy*, Fall 1992, pp. 84–8.

Mayhew, David R. *Congress: The Electoral Connection*. Yale University Press, 1974.

McAdams, John C., and John R. Johannes. "Does Casework Matter? A Reply to Professor Fiorina." *American Journal of Political Science* 25 (1981): 581–604.

"Constituency Attentiveness in the House." *Journal of Politics* 47 (1985): 1108–39.

"Congressmen, Perquisites, and Elections." *Journal of Politics* 50 (1988): 412–39.

McCain, John. "Defense Pork." *Washington Post*, October 26, 1995.

McCutchen, Charles W. "Peer Review: Treacherous Servant, Disastrous Master." *Technology Review*, October 1991, pp. 28–40.

McDonald, Kim, "House Fails to Appropriate Funds for Berkeley Center." *Chronicle of Higher Education*, June 15, 1983.

"Insulate Science from Politics, Presidents Urge." *Chronicle of Higher Education*, November 2, 1983.

"NSF Seeks Ways to Prevent Universities from Bypassing 'Peer Review' System." *Chronicle of Higher Education*, November 28, 1984.

"At U. of Utah, Cold-Fusion Controversy Offers Lessons for Scientists, Managers." *Chronicle of Higher Education*, November 14, 1990.

Meiser, Stanley. "Halls of Ivy Research the Pork Barrel." *Los Angeles Times*, April 15, 1988.

Mercer, Joye. "Expensive Ambitions." *Chronicle of Higher Education*, April 16, 1996.

Merton, Robert K. *The Sociology of Science*. University of Chicago Press, 1973.

Meuller, Dennis C. *Public Choice*. Cambridge University Press, 1979.

Milbrath, Lester M. *The Washington Lobbyists*. Rand McNally, 1963.

Mitroff, Ian I. "Norms and Counter-Norms in a Select Group of the Appollo Moon Scientists." *American Sociological Review* 39 (1974): 579–95.

Modernizing Academic Research Facilities: A Comprehensive Plan. National Science Foundation, 1989.

Moe, Terry. *The Organization of Interests*. University of Chicago Press, 1980.

"A Calculus of Group Membership." *American Journal of Political Science* 224 (1980): 593–632.

"An Assessment of the Positive Theory of 'Congressional Dominance.'" *Legislative Studies Quarterly* 12 (1987): 475–520.

Moore, Michael K., and John R. Hibbing. "Length of Congressional Tenure and Federal Spending: Were the Voters of Washington State Correct?" *American Politics Quarterly* 24 (1996): 131–49.

Morgan, Dan. "Congress and a Company: An Alliance Fed by Money." *Washington Post*, June 13, 1988.

"Select Few in Congress Decide How the Money Will Be Spent: Disputes Intensify as Budget Tightens." *Washington Post*, May 30, 1989.

"As Federal Funding Tightens, Lobbyists Find a Surer Way: Millions Earmarked for University Centers." *Washington Post*, June 18, 1989.

"In College of 'Cardinals', a Summer of Frustration: Freewheeling Spending Now Has High Price." *Washington Post*, June 30, 1989.

"Byrd Drops Home-State Effort in Anger over Lobbyists' Role." *Washington Post*, July 31, 1989.

"Lobbyist-Reporting Bill Grew from Universities' End Run." *Washington Post*, September 25, 1989.

"Lobbying Reports: Few and Flawed." *Washington Post*, July 3, 1990.

"New Appropriators May Pass the Buck." *Washington Post*, January 1, 1995.

"Tobacco Subsidies under Attack." *Washington Post*, June 15, 1995.

Morgan, M. Granger. "Regularizing 'Pork.'" *Science*, August 12, 1988, p. 769.

Mukerji, Chandra. *A Fragile Power: Scientists and the State*. Princeton University Press, 1989.

Mulkay, Michael. *Sociology of Science*. Indiana University Press, 1991.

Munson, Richard. *The Cardinals of Capitol Hill*. Grove Press, 1993.

Murphy, James T. "Political Parties and the Porkbarrel: Party Conflict and Cooperation in House Public Works Committee Decision Making." *American Political Science Review* 68 (1974): 169–85.

Murphy, Thomas P. *Science, Geopolitics, and Federal Spending*. Heath Lexington Books, 1971.

Nadel, Mark V. "The Rise of *Political* Science." *The GAO Journal*, Winter 1988, pp. 47–53.

National Academy of Sciences. *Perspectives on Financing Academic Research Facilities: A Resource for Policy Formulation*. National Academy Press, 1989.

Major Award Decisionmaking at the National Science Foundation. National Academy Press, 1994.

Needell, Allan A. "From Military Research to Big Science: Lloyd Berkner and Science-Statesmanship in the Postwar Era." In *Big Science: The Growth of Large-Scale Research*. Eds. Peter Galison and Bruce Hevly. Stanford University Press, 1992, Ch. 11.

Nicholson, Richard, S. "Pork Barrel 'Science.'" *Science*, December 6, 1991, p. 1433.

Nicklin, Julie L. "Perpetual Fund Raising?" *Chronicle of Higher Education*, June 21, 1996.

Niou, Emerson M. S., and Peter C. Ordershook. "Universalism in Congress." *American Journal of Political Science*, 29 (1985): 246–58.

Norman, Colin. "How to Win Buildings and Influence Congress." *Science*, December 16, 1983, pp. 1211–13.

"Congress Approves Deals for Ten Universities." *Science*, January 17, 1986, p. 211.

"House Endorses Pork Barrel Funding." *Science*, August 8, 1986, pp. 616–17.

Norman, Colin, and Elliot Marshall. "Over a (Pork) Barrel: The Senate Rejects Peer Review." *Science*, July 11, 1986, p. 145.

Novak, Viveca. "Help Yourself." *Common Cause Magazine*, March–April 1991, pp. 30–41.

Oliver, Myrna. "Jean Mayer: Tufts Chancellor, Adviser on U.S. Nutrition." *Los Angeles Times*, January 3, 1993.

Orlans, Harold, ed. *Science Policy and the University*. Brookings Institution, 1968.

Ornstein, Norman J., and Shirley Elder. *Interest Groups, Lobbying, and Policy Making*. Congressional Quarterly Press, 1978.

"Out of the Pork Barrel into the Fire." *Science News*, November 19, 1983.

Page, Howard. "The Science Development Program." In *Science Policy and the University*. Ed. Harold Orlans. Brookings Institution, 1968, pp. 101–13.

Park, Robert L. "Congress Needs to Trim Its Academic Pork." *Newsday*, December 3, 1992.

Pear, Robert. "U.S. Judge Rules Line Item Veto Act Unconstitutional." *New York Times*, February 13, 1998.

Peer Review: Reforms Needed to Ensure Fairness in Federal Agency Grant Selection. U.S. General Accounting Office, Report GAO/PEMD-94-1, 1994.

Penick, James, Jr., Carroll Pursell, Jr., Morgan Sherwood, and Donald Swain, eds. *The Politics of American Science*. MIT Press, 1972.

Pianin, Eric. "Whitten's Limitless Longevity." *Washington Post*, November 6, 1991.

"Rep. Whitten on Verge of Seniority Record." *Washington Post*, January 4, 1992.

"Sen. Byrd's 'Pork Barrel' Revenge?" *Washington Post*, May 22, 1992.

"'Academic Pork' Fills Favored School Larders." *Washington Post*, September 23, 1992.

Pincus, Walter. "Parliamentary Fight Awaits Bush Cuts." *Washington Post*, March 22, 1992.

Polsby, Nelson W. *Political Innovation in America: The Politics of Policy Initiation.* Yale University Press, 1984.

Pressley, Sue Anne. "A Symbol of 'Academic Pork,' Lamar U. Feels Aggrieved." *Washington Post*, August 20, 1994.

Price, Don K. "Federal Money and University Research." In *Science Policy and the University*. Ed. Harold Orlans. Brookings Institution, 1968, pp. 23–38.

Proposal Pressure in the 1980s: An Indicator of Stress on the Federal Research System. U.S. Office of Technology Assessment, April 1980.

Quirk, Paul. "In Defense of the Politics of Ideas." *Journal of Politics* 50 (1988): 31–41.

Rapp, David. "Fight over 'Academic Pork Barrel' Evaporates." *Congressional Quarterly Weekly Report*, September 12, 1987, p. 2190.

How the U.S. Got into Agriculture, and Why It Can't Get out. Congressional Quarterly Press, 1988.

Ray, Bruce A. "Congressional Promotion of District Interests: Does Power on the Hill Really Make a Difference?" In *Political Benefits*. Ed. Barry S. Rundquist. Lexington Books, 1980, pp. 1–36.

Reid, J. Norman. "Politics, Program Administration, and the Distribution of Grants-in-Aid: A Theory and a Test." In *Political Benefits*. Ed. Barry S. Rundquist. Lexington Books, 1980, pp. 37–60.

Regan, Priscilla M. "Ideas or Interests: Privacy in Electronic Communications." *Policy Studies Journal* 21 (1993): 450–69.

"Recissions and Reasons." *Washington Post*, March 23, 1992.

Reich, Robert B., ed. *The Power of Public Ideas*. Harvard University Press, 1988.

Rensberger, Boyce. "More Scientists, Fewer Grants." *Washington Post*, December 25, 1994.

"Vital Skill in Lab Is Grantsmanship." *Washington Post*, December 26, 1994.

Report of the White House Science Council: Panel on the Health of U.S. Colleges and Universities. Office of Science and Technology Policy, Executive Office of the President, February 1986.

"Report on Extramural Biomedical Research Facilities Construction." Office of the Secretary, U.S. Department of Health and Human Services, June 1989.

"Research Facility Financing: Near-Term Options." Government–University–Industry Research Roundtable, February 1991.

"Research Funding Rumpus." *Washington Post*, July 10, 1994.

Rimer, Sara, "Columbia Sets a Fund Goal of $1 Billion." *New York Times*, October 26, 1990.

Rochefort, David A., and Roger W. Cobb. "Problem Definition, Agenda Access, and Policy Choice." *Policy Studies Journal* 21 (1993): 56–71.

Rogers, David. "House and Senate, Recognizing a Pork Barrel When They See One, Warm to the Environment." *Wall Street Journal*, August 16, 1989.

"Lobbying Firm Gets $1 Million in Fees from Institutions Seeking Federal Grants." *Wall Street Journal,* May 30, 1991.

Rose, M. Richard. "'Pork-Barrel Science' vs. Peer Review." *Chronicle of Higher Education,* October 8, 1986.

Ross, Jim. "Chiles Led Tax Bailout at UF." *Miami Tribune,* April 18, 1992.

Salisbury, Robert H. "An Exchange Theory of Interest Groups." *Midwest Journal of Political Science* 13 (1969): 1–32.

Salisbury, Robert H., John P. Heinz, Robert L. Nelson, and Edward O. Laumann. "Triangles, Networks, and Hollow Cores: The Complex Geometry of Washington Interest Representation," In *The Politics of Interests.* Ed. Mark P. Petracca. Westview Press, 1992, pp. 130–49.

Saltus, Richard. "Mass. Leads in Landing 'Earmarked' Funds." *Boston Globe,* February 13, 1993.

"Savage Cuts in Defense Research." *Washington Post,* July 28, 1994.

Savage, James D. "Federal R&D Budget Policy in the Reagan Administration." *Public Budgeting & Finance* (Summer 1987): 37–51.

"Saints and Cardinals in Appropriations Committees and the Fight against Distributive Politics." *Legislative Studies Quarterly* 16 (1991): 329–47.

Trends in the Distribution of Apparent Academic Earmarks in the Federal Government's FY 1980–92 Appropriations Bills. Congressional Research Service, Report 92-726 SPR, September 22, 1992.

The Distribution of Apparent Academic Earmarks in the Federal Government's FY 1992 Appropriations Bills. Congressional Research Service, Report 92–727 SPR, September 22, 1992.

"Where's the Pork? To Root It out, We Must Begin with a Strict Definition of What Is Unacceptable." *Issues in Science and Technology* (Spring 1993): 21–4.

Schein, Edgar. *Organizational Culture and Leadership.* Jossey-Bass, 1992.

Schlossberg, Ken. "Earmarking by Congress Can Help Rebuild the Country's Research Infrastructure." *Chronicle of Higher Education,* January 24, 1990.

Schmitt, Eric. "House Battle Threatens Big Research Universities with Loss of Millions." *New York Times,* August 17, 1994.

Schorr, Burt. "Breaking Tradition, More Colleges Go Directly to Congress for Funds." *Wall Street Journal,* March 5, 1984.

Schrage, Michael. "Pork Barrels and Science Funding." *Boston Globe,* October 7, 1990.

Schultze, Charles L. "Comment." In *Federal Budget Policy in the 1980s.* Eds. Gregory B. Mills and John L. Palmer. Urban Institute Press, 1984, pp. 379–84.

Schweber, S. S. "Big Science in Context: Cornell and MIT." In *Big Science: The Growth of Large-Scale Research.* Eds. Peter Galison and Bruce Hevly. Stanford University Press, 1992, pp. 149–83.

Science and Engineering Indicators, 1996. National Science Board, National Science Foundation, 1996.

Scientific and Engineering Research Facilities at Universities and Colleges, 1988. National Science Foundation, Report 88–320, 1988.

*Scientific and Engineering Research Facilities at Universities and Colleges,
1990.* National Science Foundation, Report 90–318, 1990.

*Scientific and Engineering Research Facilities at Universities and Colleges,
1994.* National Science Foundation, Report 94–315, 1994.

Searing, Donald D. "Roles, Rules, and Rationality in the New Institutionalism."
American Political Science Review 85 (1991): 1239–60.

Seelye, Katherine Q. "The Man Who Tried for Bacon." *New York Times*, August 20, 1994.

Seitz, Frederick. "The Threat of 'Pork-Barrel' Science." *The World and I*, January 1993, pp. 571–81.

Selby, Stephen E. "Indirect Costs of Federally Supported Research." *Journal of
the Society of Research Administrators* 15 (1984): 29–37.

Shackelford, Lucy. "Where Are They Now?" *Washington Post*, June 14, 1993.

Shear, Jeff. "Pain's the Game." *National Journal*, January 14, 1995, pp. 108–11.

"United They Stand." *National Journal*, October 28, 1995, pp. 2646–50.

Shepsle, Kenneth A., and Barry R. Weingast. "Political Preference for the Pork
Barrel: A Generalization." *American Journal of Political Science* 25 (1981):
96–111.

"Legislative Politics and Budget Outcomes." In *Federal Budget Policy in the
1980s.* Eds. Gregory B. Mills and John L. Palmer. Urban Institute Press,
1984, pp. 343–67.

"The Institutional Foundations of Committee Power." *American Political Science Review* 81 (1987): 85–104.

Sinclair, Ward. "Hill Clout Reaps Research Programs, from Catfish to Chernobyl." *Washington Post*, November 20, 1987.

Smith, Bruce L. R. *American Science since World War II.* Brookings Institution,
1990.

Snowbeck, Chris. "Lobbyists Help Push UVA Bill." *Daily Progress*, March 3,
1996.

Soherr-Hadwiger, David. "Military Construction Policy: A Test of Competing
Explanations of Universalism in Congress." *Legislative Studies Quarterly*
23 (1998): 57–78.

Spangenburg, Ray, and Diane Moser. "Rising Indirect Costs Threaten Research." *The Scientist*, May 30, 1988, pp. 4–6.

Stansbury, Dale L. "An Inventory and Analysis of Congressional Earmarking of
Agricultural Research: Trends and Inflections between Fiscal Year 1978
and Fiscal Year 1989." Prepared for Science and Education, United States
Department of Agriculture, December 1988.

Stein, Robert M., and Kenneth E. Bickers. "Congressional Elections and the
Pork Barrel." *Journal of Politics* 56 (1994): 377–99.

"Universalism and the Electoral Connection: A Test and Some Doubts." *Political Research Quarterly* 47 (1994): 295–317.

Perpetuating the Pork Barrel. Cambridge University Press, 1995.

Sternberg, Ernest. *Photonic Technology and Industrial Policy.* State University
of New York Press, 1992.

Stone, Peter H. "From the K Street Corridor." *National Journal*, February 4, 1995.

Stronsnider, Kim. "Lifting of Cap on Tax-Exempt Bonds Gives Private Colleges New Options." *Chronicle of Higher Education*, September 19, 1997.

Sun, Marjorie. "Peer Review Comes under Peer Review." *Science*, May 26, 1989, pp. 910–12.

Suplee, Curt. "The Science Chairman's Unpredictable Approach." *Washington Post*, October 15, 1991.

Taylor, Anderw. "GOP Pet Projects Give Boost to Shaky Incumbents." *Congressional Quarterly Weekly Report*," August 3, 1996, p. 2169.

Thomas, Clive S., and Ronald J. Hrenbenar. "Changing Patterns of Interest Group Activity: A Regional Perspective," In *The Politics of Interests*. Ed. Mark Petracca. Westview Press, 1992, pp. 150–74.

Thomas, Rich. "Is the Pork Barrel a Must?" *Time*, January 18, 1988, p. 24.

Tierney, John T. "Organized Interests and the Nation's Capitol." In *The Politics of Interests*. Ed. Mark P. Petracca. Westview Press, 1992, pp. 201–20.

Toch, Thomas, and Ted Slafsky. "The Scientific Pork Barrel." *U.S. News & World Report*, March 1, 1993, pp. 58–9.

Tolchin, Martin. "Lawmaker's Aid to School May Skew Federal Budget." *New York Times*, April 3, 1991.

"Traxler's Legacy: Small Print Spelled Big Bucks." *Washington Post*, April 16, 1993.

Tsuang, Grace. "'Pork Barrel Science': Implications for University Research Efforts and Interest Group Theory." Yale University Law School, May 18, 1989.

University Funding: Patterns of Distribution of Federal Research Funds. U.S. General Accounting Office, Report GAO/RCED-878-67BR, February 1987.

University Research: Effect of Indirect Cost Revisions and Options for Future Changes. U.S. General Accounting Office, Report GAO/RCED-95-74, March 1985.

U.S. Department of Agriculture Research and Extension Priorities. Subcommittee on Department Operations and Nutrition, Committee on Agriculture, U.S. House of Representatives, March 25, 1993.

Vobejda, Barbara. "'Academic Pork Barrel' Divides Universities." *Washington Post*, June 8, 1987.

   "Renewing the College 'Infrastructure.'" *Washington Post*, July 7, 1987.

   "Competition for College Feeds Elitism: Well-off Applicants Flood Prestigious Schools as Tuitions Rise." *Washington Post*, May 4, 1989.

Wagner, Richard E. "Pressure Groups and Political Entrepreneurs: A Review Article." *Papers on Non-Market Decision Making* 1 (1986): 161–70.

Walker, Jack L. "The Origins and Maintenance of Interest Groups in America." *American Political Science Review* 77 (1983): 390–406.

Walsh, John. "Adapting to Pork-Barrel Science." *Science*, December 18, 1987, pp. 1639–40.

Watanabe, June. "UH Hires D.C. Lobbyist; Some Regents Upset." *Hawaii Star-Bulletin*, September 11, 1986.

Weingast, Barry R. "A Rational Choice Perspective on Congressional Norms." *American Journal of Political Science* 23 (1979): 245–62.

Weingast, Barry R., Kenneth A. Shepsle, and Christopher Johnsen. "The Political Economy of Benefits and Costs: A Neoclassical Approach to Distributive Politics." *Journal of Political Economy* 89 (1981): 642–64.

Werner, Leslile Maitland. "40 Universities Agree to Reject Disputed Grants." *New York Times*, May 22, 1987.

"White House Seeks Overturn of Line-Item Veto Decision." *Washington Post*, February 21, 1998.

White, Joseph. "The Functions and Power of the House Appropriations Committee." Doctoral dissertation, University of California, Berkeley, 1989.

Wildavsky, Aaron. *The Politics of the Budgetary Process*. Little, Brown, 1964.

Wilson, George C. "Funneling Funds by Formula." *Washington Post*, May 15, 1986.

Wolpe, Bruce C. *Lobbying Congress: How the System Works*. Congressional Quarterly, 1990.

Wycliff, Don. "The Short, Unhappy Life of Academic Presidents." *New York Times*, July 25, 1990.

Yiannakis, Diana Evans. "The Grateful Electorate: Casework and Congressional Elections." *American Journal of Political Science* 25 (1981): 568–80.

Index